Blue Blood
by Edward Conlon

"The New York Police Department has, of course, inspired a huge variety of popular entertainments over the years, from genre novels to films to long-running TV shows. But *Blue Blood*, in terms of its ambition, its authenticity, and the power of its writing, is in a class by itself. Conlon is uniquely qualified to write about this giant yet famously insular tribe. . . . *Blue Blood* runs from the episodes of a cop's life to meditations on that life, from gun-in-hand assignments to mundane calls about vicious cats. Layered with Conlon's family history; allusions to St. Augustine and early police books; and his own views on department dysfunction, the war on drugs, and urban race relations, the book becomes a kind of rich ethnographic document. . . . The title is just right: Conlon bleeds policeman blue; 'the Job' to him is a Catholic-style calling, a vocation. . . . And the fact he's still on the job gives *Blue Blood* a charge and immediacy unlike any other police book I know."

—*The New York Times Book Review*

"Conlon stays alive to the humor and the sadness and the ironies of life even in the teeth of the city's everyday assault—bricks (and, once, a canned ham) thrown from rooftops, the festering bitterness of precinct-house feuds, the bizarro underworld of the midnight shift, the agony, both Dantean and Sisyphean, of sifting through the rubble of the World Trade Center. . . . Conlon has no ambitions as a whistle-blower or a hero—he's neither a Serpico nor a Supercop—and that keeps *Blue Blood* free of distortion and full of perspective."

—*Time*

"Conlon's look inside the NYPD is more chilling than even the most realistic cop dramas on TV. Short of getting recruited or mugged, you won't find a more up-close look at the NYPD than this gritty memoir. Harvard graduate and veteran cop Edward Conlon keeps the reader at his elbow from the time he takes his first steps in uniform to the day he earns his detective's shield. We hear the scratch and cackle of the police radio . . . We climb with him down reeking housing-project stairways, stepping over syringes and shell casings. This book is not for the fainthearted. . . . Conlon's account of the processing of a cop's corpse at a Ground Zero morgue is among the most graphic, heartbreaking images yet excavated from the 9/11 tragedy. . . . But there is also insight and humor. . . . His respect for cop life is palpable."

—*People*

continued . . .

"There are too many lame books about being a police officer written by people who haven't spent a single day in uniform or on the streets. *Blue Blood* is real, authentic, true. Beautiful and inspiring, terrifying and heartbreaking. It is a great book."   —James Frey

"There's stuff that will make your blood boil, juries and grand juries that let off defendants who've done everything but left a signed confession. And there's stuff that will make you sad, including Conlon's account of the days after 9/11. . . . *Blue Blood* is more than just a cop book. It's more than a provincial book about New York City. It's an intelligent examination of a swath of life most of us prefer to sweep under the carpet. If it were up to me, it would be mandatory pre-graduation reading for every college student who needs to learn that the real world isn't just an MTV show."

—*Milwaukee Journal-Sentinel*

"Conlon, Jesuit-educated and a Harvard graduate, examines his family's police background and the intense fraternity of cops. The fact that this book is written by a cop still on the job gives it much more urgency and immediacy than cop tales recollected in tranquility. And Conlon is a wonderful writer, street smart and poetic, arresting you with his deft turn of phrase. . . . Rapid-fire war stories capture the mania of Conlon's life as a cop, from his rookie days in public housing in 1995 to his current post as a detective in the South Bronx. Conlon characterizes being a cop as gaining entry into 'a drama as rich as Shakespeare.' Readers are lucky Conlon gives them a pass into his world."   —*Booklist* (starred review)

"A street-smart and hilarious memoir from Conlon who takes readers behind the squad-room door to reveal the inner life of New York's Finest. . . . Conlon's prose, buffed to a high sheen, mixes the rich and rowdy dialogue of police and 'perps' with department lore about legends like Eddie Egan and Frank Serpico, literary allusions, and overviews of daily routine that bristle with sharp observation. . . . It's all here: wayward crackhead informants, the roughhouse camaraderie of police units, precinct pettifogging . . . the haunting fear that a lying complaint by a civilian might derail a career, and, above all, the gravitational, 24/7 pull of 'the Job' with its 'wreckage and wonders.'"

—*Kirkus Reviews* (starred review)

continued . . .

BLUE BLOOD

EDWARD CONLON

EBURY
PRESS

3 5 7 9 10 8 6 4

Published in 2010 by Ebury Press, an imprint of Ebury Publishing
A Random House Group Company
First Published in the USA by Riverhead Books in 2004
This edition published 2010

Copyright © Edward Conlon 2004

The Random House Group Limited Reg. No. 954009

Addresses for companies within the Random House Group can be found at
www.randomhouse.co.uk

A CIP catalogue record for this book is available from the British Library

The Random House Group Limited supports The Forest Stewardship Council (FSC),
the leading international forest certification organisation. All our titles that are
printed on Greenpeace approved FSC certified paper carry the FSC logo. Our paper
procurement policy can be found at www.rbooks.co.uk/environment

Mixed Sources
Product group from well-managed
forests and other controlled sources
www.fsc.org Cert no. TT-COC-2139
© 1996 Forest Stewardship Council

Printed in the UK by CPI Mackays, Chatham, ME5 8TD

ISBN 9780091938413

To buy books by your favourite authors and register for offers visit
www.rbooks.co.uk

For my mother, Elizabeth Trust Conlon

And in memory of Marc Deiter
1964–1993

All of this book is true, to the best of my memory, with these exceptions: certain names have been changed, as well as identifying characteristics of informants. The only conscious liberties taken are chronological, in the last two chapters, in that several of the cases took place after promotion rather than before.

For love of your love, let me tell of my wicked ways . . .

—ST. AUGUSTINE, *Confessions*

Enough. All right. This one time, this one time,
I'll let you ask about my affairs . . .

—MICHAEL CORLEONE, *The Godfather*

Unless asked, don't give opinions or volunteer information.

—from NYPD GUIDELINES FOR COURTROOM
TESTIMONY FOR THE POLICE OFFICER

ONE

As I took my first steps on patrol as a New York City police officer, heading out from the precinct onto East 156 Street toward the projects on Courtlandt Avenue in the South Bronx, a deep voice called out, "There's a new sheriff in town!" We had been told that people would know we were rookies by the shine on our leather gear and the dim, soft expressions on our faces—people can smell new cop like they smell new paint. When I grinned bashfully and turned toward the voice, I saw it was speaking to us, but not of us. It belonged to a tipsy derelict in an enormous Styrofoam cowboy hat, half-swaggering and half-staggering down the street. I thought of the NYPD Department Values, which begins, "In partnership with the community, we pledge to protect the lives and property . . ." During our time at the Academy, we would recite it every day in Gym, just as my high school track team would say a Hail Mary before a meet. The partnership with the community had not begun as expected, but it might be said that education is an adjustment of expectations, and although I was done at the Academy, my education had barely begun.

I was assigned to Police Service Area 7, which covered the public housing in five South Bronx precincts: the 40th, 41st, 42nd, 44th, and the 46th, with the heaviest concentration in the Four-O and Four-Two. Like the word "precinct," we used "PSA" to mean both our building and the area it served. On the first day, the PSA was hung with purple and black crepe bunting, for a cop from the command who had died of AIDS. We knew nothing beyond that fact, but as we waited in the muster room, a cop stormed in and began to yell at us: "I don't give a fuck what these assholes say, Mike was a good guy and a great cop, so if you hear different you can tell them to fuck themselves from me!" He left as abruptly as he arrived. We were bussed up to his wake, where we barely knew what to say, even to each other. Such was our introduction to the inner life of the precinct—good-hearted if sometimes misguided, bound by duty and tradition and semi-private heartbreak—into which most of us did not rush to insinuate ourselves, knowing it would find a place for us in time.

We were met with amusement or abuse, equally unexpected and unprovoked: a lieutenant might hold roll call and scream at us as if we were late with the rent, or a sergeant would begin by saying, "Thanks for stopping by." Some of the older cops watched over us and others looked down at us, and all of them told us how we'd missed out: on the greatest cops and the worst crime, and especially the Housing Police, "the best kept secret in the city." Three months before, New York City had three separate police departments—Housing, for the projects; Transit, for the subways; and the NYPD—which were then combined by Mayor Giuliani in April 1995, into one department of nearly forty thousand police. Even our new station house—a state-of-the-art cinder-block cube, with plenty of lockers and a gym in the basement—was seen as a kind of rebuke; it was as if the old PSA, which had comprised a few rooms in the basement of a project, and was prone to rat infestations and floods, told an awful truth that we were too late to learn. We'd never know anything but the NYPD, and it was a bigger, stiffer, colder job, as we'd find out when we called to take a day off, or were on patrol and needed to knock down a door. We were little players, late for the game.

They told us things we didn't need to hear, but often had no answer to what we asked:

Why do we call it the "four-to-twelve" shift, if it starts at three?

Why do we wear clip-on ties?

Where do we eat?

In fairness, the responses to these questions—"I don't know"; "To avoid strangulation"; and "Good luck!"—may not have been any different from what I'd answer now.

We were like the equipment we carried: dangerously new. I'd put on my blue polyester slacks and shirt; black boots; an equipment belt for holster and gun; two magazines, each holding fifteen rounds of 9-millimeter ammunition; radio, mace, handcuffs, flashlight. The equipment belt was snapped to the uniform belt with four "keepers." The bulletproof vest—"bullet resistant," technically—is made of two double panels of a synthetic material called Kevlar, inside a cloth carrier that holds it around your torso like a lead X-ray smock. One cop wrote phrases from the Bible on his, "Yea, though I walk in the valley of the Shadow of Death . . ." Other cops wrote their blood type. The vest showed in the neck of the summer shirt, which has short sleeves and an open collar, but if your T-shirt showed above that, some bosses would yell at you, or write you up, or make you change. The shield was pinned to the shirt with a kilt pin, over a black cardboard backing that held the nameplate on the bottom and medals on the top. Some cops' medals stacked up so high that the backing rose above their shoulders. The clips for the nameplates didn't hold, and someone found that the stoppers of crack vials worked better. They were not hard to find. I kept a prayer card to the Archangel Michael, patron saint of police, in my hat. The uniforms made us look alike, as intended, and since I said little, I didn't so much fit in as fade in.

We had a few weeks of field training, during which a cop named Vinnie Vargas led six of us around Melrose and Jackson Houses, adjoining projects a block away from the precinct. We worked as a group, at first—Paul Tannura, Matthew Goodman, Angel Suazo, Kim McLauren, Jose Velez, and myself—and then in threes, where McLauren, Velez, and I split off, and then with Velez alone. We wandered around, checking the parking lots and rooftops. Once a day, a sergeant or a lieutenant would raise us on the radio for the "scratch," to sign our memo books and tell us we were doing great or awful work, arbitrarily it seemed. A three-car collision occurred before my eyes, and the job took me five hours to complete, listing the license, registration, and insurance information, taking statements and diagramming the positions of each car and everyone in it. When I finally got it down, I felt like I could have learned calculus and French. There were three or four radio runs a day, mostly for domestic disputes and stuck elevators, though in the evenings we would hear gunshots. We would run toward them, holding on to our radios and nightsticks so they wouldn't fly out of our belts, and miss them so completely we were like kittens hunting a flashlight beam on the floor. In the precinct lunchroom one night, I heard shots and looked out the window to see two young men walking down the block toward me. We stared at each other and then, in unison, they pointed their thumbs back toward the projects.

I nodded and went back to eating. The gunshots came from the drug dealers, at war or at play, but to wean a team of rookies on drug collars is a tricky business, and Vinnie decided against it. While this decision was prudent, it allowed the rampant crack and heroin trade to take place unobserved all around us; the dealers could have had snowball fights with the stuff for all we'd have noticed. The beat cop in Melrose-Jackson was named Scott Mackay, and I liked the way he handled himself, friendly or forceful as the circumstances demanded. I told him I thought the post was a little on the slow side and he laughed at me.

When field training was over, we crowded around the board in the muster room to find out our assignments. Any of us could be a Project Community Officer (PCO), a beat cop assigned to a particular project, or on a Target Team, one of five or six cops assigned to a sergeant, moving from project to project every few months, or in a squad car. Squad was the most sought-after, in that you rode instead of walking, and it fit our expectations of a grown-up, cop-like, lights-and-sirens deal. But I had a city kid's indifference to cars—my driver's license was only a few months old—and most PCOs and Target Teams had either Friday and Saturday or Sunday and Monday off, while the three squads—day tours, four-to-twelves, and midnights—worked a rotating chart of five days on, two days off, five days on, three days off, five days on, two days off, and so on, so that your weekends fell on the weekend only a few times a year. I wanted PCO and I got it: Post 151, Morris Houses in Claremont Village, in the Four-Two. A few cops said, "You're in for it now. Watch yourself."

Claremont Village was one of the largest projects we covered, and it combined Morris, Butler, Webster, and Morrisania Houses. There were thirty buildings, each between sixteen and twenty-one stories tall, set around courtyards and playgrounds. Like most public housing in New York City, its design was inspired by the chilly optimism of the forward-thinkers of the mid-century. For them, the tall towers and wide plazas were "cities of the future" that would supplant the stacked rows of stuffed tenements where the poor had lived for the past century. From a certain distance, or at a certain angle, you could see what they were getting at: you could walk through the grounds beneath shady aisles of sycamore and maple, past tidy lawns and playgrounds teeming with children. There would be families having cookouts, old ladies reading Bibles on the benches, pensive pairs of men playing chess. Armies of groundskeepers and janitors, as well as plumbers, carpenters, painters, and elevator repairmen, were employed to keep up the physical plant. Inside, many people kept immaculate and well-appointed apartments, and even some hallways were clean and cared for, decorated for holidays as festively as a window at Macy's. But the semi-public spaces—the lobbies, halls, stairwells—were, more often than not, literal toilets. The debris of recreational annihilation was everywhere: condoms, crack vials, syringes, and shell casings; graffiti was cleaned constantly only to return at once, while bullet holes and scorch marks lasted longer. Multiple bodily functions took place in the elevators and rooftops, where you saw beer cans and smashed rum bottles amid pools of piss, piles of chicken bones beside heaps of shit. You learned not to lean against walls so roaches wouldn't nest in your clothes. More than ten thousand people lived there, by my estimate, and maybe three thousand of them made it a ghetto.

There were many bad neighborhoods in New York, but the South Bronx was a byword for "slum." There was no renaissance in its past, like Harlem, nor any signs of gentrification or renewal, as there were in parts of Brooklyn. "Fort Apache" was the nickname for the Four-One, just east of where I worked, though the Four-Two was used as the station house in the movie *Fort Apache, The Bronx*. Though the plotlines of interracial romance and police corruption were invented, the landscape of urban wasteland was not; "Fort Apache" was later known as "Little House on the Prairie," because so much of the area had burnt down. My uncle Gerry had been a firefighter in the South Bronx in the 1970s, and he told me that they were busier than the London fire department during the Blitz. In *Report from Engine Company 82,* the firefighter Dennis Smith wrote that they responded to as many false alarms as fires, and a man from his company was thrown from the truck and killed while responding to a false alarm pulled by a nine-year-old boy. A sign was put up on the call box, telling of the death and the danger of false alarms, but a false alarm was called in later the same day, from the same box, so they took the sign down.

I was born in the Bronx, but my family moved just north, to Yonkers, when I was little. I'd taken my father's old apartment in the Bronx seven years before, the "four rooms of gloom over an airshaft" where he'd grown up. It seemed like we owned the neighborhood: Uncle Eddie, a cop for thirty-three years, never left it, and Uncle Gerry's last fire house was three blocks away, across the street from Uncle Nick's office. Nick was a doctor who had married my father's sister, Theresa, a nurse. When I was a kid, when we drove through Kingsbridge, my father would point out where Joe Louis and Mike Quill had lived, but what I remember most about the Bronx then was the windows of the abandoned buildings a mile to the south. The City had covered them with decals, of curtains and shades with flower pots, to suggest that happy families dwelt within instead of junkies and ghosts. Though the official motto of the Bronx was ominous enough, *Ne cede malis*—"Do not give way to evil"—one writer suggested that it should be, "Get out, schmuck, get out!" Our official flower was the corpse flower, a massive jungle plant so named because its bloom smells like rotting flesh. It was cultivated for the first time in North America in the Bronx, in 1937, and the borough president decided the eight-foot-tall prick-shaped flowers (*Amorphophallus titanum*) would prove an apt symbol for our future growth. However, the corpse flower might go for thirty years between blooms, which stink and die within days. I still can't figure out what they were thinking.

For a long time, I kept to myself at work. I said hello to other cops but not much else. I always carried a book with me, slipping it under my vest or in a jacket pocket. When someone asked why, I'd say gravely, "You never know when nothing's gonna happen." Two other cops were assigned to Morris Houses, and six more to the other three projects that made up "the Village." Most of them tended to stick together on patrol. Though I took to walking by myself early on, when I didn't, I was with Angel Suazo and Osvaldo Rivera. We were all brand-new, and an odd threesome. Angel was Honduran, dark-skinned, and bald, an immigrant who had come here at the age of eighteen. His English was heavily accented and he was prone to saying things like "Cut me in half!" when he meant "Cut me a break!" He had been in the Army, and when I asked him what his assignment had been, he told me, "Communications." Angel was unflinchingly cheerful, and nothing could dent his good humor: he laughed as hard as the jokers did at the jokes about his driving a gypsy cab or the INS coming to take him away. He also had a nose like a bloodhound—he could smell someone smoking a joint a block away—and he had a surprising nimbleness to him: once, a sparrow flew into a bodega and he caught it with his hands, then let it fly out unharmed. Osvaldo was Puerto Rican, and from the South Bronx. He never took his hat off, and smoked twice as much as I did, which is to say like two chimneys. When we walked, he sometimes liked to sing and to do voices from kung-fu movies. He wouldn't say how old he was, called his wife constantly, and talked a lot about dogs. Though dogs weren't allowed in the projects, half the people seemed to have pit bulls, and half the pit bulls seemed to be named Tyson, so there were plenty who needed his advice. Though Osvaldo lived in a building where dogs weren't allowed, he owned an enormous German shepherd, which he would pack up into a duffel bag to take outside for walks. I asked him how the dog liked getting stuffed into a bag every day and he said he loved it—that he reacted like other dogs do when they see you pick up their leash. Both Angel and Osvaldo were serious family men and lived in the South Bronx. Whether from college liberalism or Irish sentiment, I had some measure of softness for the derelicts and delinquents of the neighborhood, but they had none, and their belief that these people should know better was good to hear.

In time, we took to each other, becoming a familiar sight around the projects: the black one, the brown one, the white one. Angel was quick to write tickets, I was quick to make arrests, and Osvaldo was quick to let us. I had started to learn Spanish the year before, but it fell to my partners to handle the rapid-fire and highly inflected dialects we heard—I would guess that our projects were slightly more black than Hispanic, with three white people that I knew of—and so my pidgin Spanish fell away. I did most of the paperwork, eagerly, as I wanted to master the Aided Cards, Complaints, Police Accident Reports, and Domestic Incident Reports that are the basic grammar of the NYPD. We did countless "vertical patrols," taking the elevator up to the top, then splitting up to check the roof, radios down, guns drawn, hats backward at night so there would be no reflection, creeping out to see whatever we might find. And then we would walk it down, taking separate stairwells but meeting on each floor. We ran into dogfights, blow jobs, and enough sleeping bums to fill a warehouse. At first, I was inclined to leave them unmolested, but I began to think if I had to step over someone every morning when I left my house, I might feel differently, and the working people in the projects deserved the same consideration. I would leave them alone when the weather was terrible, or if they were fastidiously clean or had a plausible story, like a fight with the wife, that argued for a temporary stay. In truth, the ones who stank to high heaven also got a pass, arrest-wise, though I'd throw them out of the building. We took a lot of people in for trespass, which prevented a lot of robberies, I'm sure, and maybe a few rapes and murders as well. The trespass collar is the Swiss Army knife of the beat cop, especially in the projects, where the City is the landlord. Anyone who doesn't have a good reason to be in a building probably has a bad one, and if you run into someone hanging out on a stairwell, the burden of proof falls on the mope.

We walked around and listened to the radio, with its scratchy hum of white noise and its string of coded calls and responses for lettered sectors and numbered posts, developing an ear for our own jobs, which a seasoned cop can hear, truly, in his sleep. "One-five-one, respond to a thirty-four on a female at one-four-five-eight Webster, four-Nora on the fourth, unknown weapons, advise when eighty-four . . ." And as we got to know the turf, the code might as well have been a telegram: "Ah, the Petersons again." Because the woman assaulted at 1458 Webster, #4N, calls every payday, because her boyfriend hits the rum and then he hits her. Or the woman's already called twice, today, and she perceives the assault in the minds of her upstairs neighbors, and no matter how much voodoo she sends at them, she can't block out their mental beams. The radio is constant and chaotic, a montage of stray details, awful and comic facts:

"Respond to a woman in a room cornered by a large rodent . . ."

"Supposed to be a one-year-old baby with its head split open . . ."

"The perp is a male Hispanic, white T-shirt, blue jeans, possible moustache, repeat, possible moustache, K . . ."

"K" meant a radio transmission is over, the way the military and just about everyone else says "over," and I don't know if the NYPD has any argument for the difference beside difference's sake.

"You okay, K?"

"A-OK, K."

"Okey-doke, K."

It is a code, after all, intended to mean nothing to most people. Codes, like good children, don't talk to strangers. The official terminology has a forced flatness, a clipped neutrality that keeps a lifted-pinky distance from lurid circumstance. I heard a dispatcher revise a job for the patrol car assigned: "Be advised, unit, that domestic dispute is now coming over as a severed limb." It was part of the general oddity of cop talk, its shotgun marriage of street slang and legalese. The raw talk of New Yorkers, criminals, victims, and cops themselves, was jury-rigged with the particularity of statutory phrases: "C/V states at T/P/O above perp called him a 'bitch-ass punk' and mooshed him, causing annoyance and alarm." The abbreviations are for "complainant/victim" and "time and place of occurrence"; to moosh is to shove in the face, and is almost more insulting than a slap (here, the form would be bitch-slap or pimp-slap) because of the suggestion that there is no need to inflict injury. Naturally, cops pick up a lot of criminal vocabulary, especially in the drug trade, where the criminal words for things are the only words there are; you can call it a deck, or you can call it a "glassine envelope of a white powdery substance . . . alleged and believed to be heroin." When crack was starting to be packaged in miniature heat-sealed plastic baggies the dealers called "slabs," the official and legal term which arose to characterize them was "slabs." It's what happens in language naturally, as common speech becomes acceptable usage, but to make a rule of this kind of exception would lead to indictments that read, ". . . to wit, defendant did possess one mad fat rock of *yayo.*"

Most often, though, the babel of the city just mixed with police jargon in striking ways, as we struggled to express ourselves with bits of hand-me-down language that didn't always fit. One would-be street lawyer protested what he took to be an "illegal search and seizure" of his cocaine by declaring it an "illegal circumcision." (Now that's a civil-rights nightmare for you, rogue mohels with guns.) A rookie cop I know had her own gift of phrase, once notifying the sergeant that a shooting victim had been "glazed by a bullet," though fortunately, he only suffered from "harasserations." And I overheard a cop recall, brightly, "Oh, sure, I was the first nonfatal shooting of 1994! In the keester!" The tone is intended to impress as exacting and detached, though the prefabricated phrases can sound cold-blooded and bombastic. When I hear cops refer to their "personal vehicle," I want to grab them and shout, "Say, 'my car,' dammit!"

If the NYPD is less and less a fraternity, it will remain a kind of ethnicity, because ethnicity is defined by language. An arrest is a collar, but also a pinch; a perp can be a skell or a mope, depending on whether he's a lowlife or a thug. A DOA is someone who's gone EOT, end of tour. One under, two under, ten under, is an accounting of collars, but in Transit, a "man under" is not under arrest but under a train. After a stabbing or a traffic accident, you'd hear over the air, "Is he likely?" It was short for "likely to die," and required the cop to make a crude wager of Likely or Not to summon Accident Investigations or a detective from the Squad to the scene. It gave many reports an unwarranted note of sarcasm: "Complainant states he was sleeping when his wife struck him with a two-by-four. Not likely." Perhaps because of its paramilitary nature, the department has a fondness for acronyms, which vary from the flatfootedly functional to the downright cool: TNT, for the Tactical Narcotics Teams of the mid-1980s, is still the street name for any kind of drug cop, though the units were disbanded years ago. The Robbery Apprehension Module took the place of the Robbery Identification Program, which broadened the range of the Senior Citizens Robbery Unit. And thus SCRU begat RIP, and RIP begat RAM, with a certain loss of panache. We were learning to talk the talk.

We were also learning to walk the walk. We'd walk out the front of the precinct, beneath the green lights that have marked police stations since Wall Street was a wall, and head out to post. We would stop by the management as soon as we got up there, either if a sector car rode us up, or more often, if we took the bus from 156th Street and Melrose up to Webster and 170th. Morris Houses had a manager who was almost as new there as its cops, but Ms. Brockington was a formidable lady who enjoined everyone around her to work as hard as she did, to help tenants or to hound them, according to need. Her secretary, Sarah DeBoissiere, had been at Morris Houses for over twenty years, and she was as hard and elegant as a malacca cane. She smoked long, thin cigarettes and wouldn't empty her ashtray so she could keep track of how many she'd had. She had assembled her own rogues' gallery of problem tenants, and she had the benefit of counsel of her fiancé, the legendary Detective Irwin "Silky" Silverman, who had caught killers for almost four decades before he lost his lawsuit to overturn the mandatory retirement age of sixty-three. The problem families at Morris Houses were well known and well established, sometimes for generations, and though they wrought spectacular havoc, they had been, until recently, virtually impossible to evict. One family of brothers, the sons of a South Carolina minister, were estimated to have committed more than fifteen hundred violent felonies, and their eventual removal was through the criminal-justice system rather than Housing Court. The Housing Authority had begun to press for evictions of tenants who committed crimes, or to negotiate the exclusion of individual family members—for example, if an old woman had a nephew dealing crack from her apartment, she would have to sign a stipulation saying he was not permitted to return—and it had begun to have an effect. After catching up with Ms. Brockington and Sarah, we'd sit down for a cup of coffee and the newspapers, and then head out for patrol.

The tenants themselves were organized, at least to a degree, at least on paper. I don't know how Morris Houses compared to other projects, but I would imagine that they were not the only ones where a few people were heroically dedicated to their communities, and where a few more helped when they could. Every building had a captain, though I didn't know most of them, and the honorific may as well have been kept on the shelf like an old Little League trophy. Others, like Curtis Johnson, swept and mopped their lobbies themselves, even though they were cleaned every day. About a third of our buildings had tenant patrols of some sort: a few people would sit in the lobbies around a bridge table, with a pad for visitors to sign in, and we had to stop by to sign in and check the building. A few buildings were watched over by old women who did not look up from their Bibles and wouldn't unless the Holy Spirit entered the lobby. But others had real organizations, with a dozen or more tenants working tightly scheduled hours, and it had a definite effect, at least during the time of the watch, and if there was drug activity during their off-hours, they were at least able to let us know about it—quietly, always. Though the neighborhood had been improving, there was no guarantee that this would continue, and most members of the Resistance were wisely unwilling to declare themselves.

The neighborhood was one where children had to walk through three different brands of crack vials in the lobbies, and most people, young and old, could tell the sound of gunshots from fireworks or a car backfiring: the hard, sharp crack, like a broomstick snapped cleanly in half. But because the shocks were somehow anticipated—you knew there would be bodies—the genuine surprise was how wholesome and ordinary many lives were there: the daily round of getting the kids ready for school and going to work, wondering if they'll get another year's wear out of their car or winter coat. Life in the projects can be just like it is in suburbia, except it takes place on busier streets and in smaller rooms. Sometimes it's better, in the way that city life, when it's good, is better than anywhere else. Once, I went to the roof of a project and saw a hawk perched on the rail; always, you see the city in the near distance, its towers and spires studded with lights, both stately and slapdash, like the crazy geometry of rock crystal. There were many days when you felt sorry for people who worked inside.

And it was a revelation to see how many people in the South Bronx liked cops. In safe neighborhoods, a cop is part of the scenery, and mostly you don't have time to pay attention. Before I became one, I noticed cops like I noticed mailboxes, which is to say barely, unless I needed one. But on my beat, I noticed how people noticed me, and especially among certain classes of people—older people, young kids, single women, people dressed for work or church—they looked at me with positive appreciation and relief. I was proof that tonight, on this walk home, no one was going to start with them. Sometimes, they expressed it, which was nice. The classic antagonism was with guys on the street, in groups, from the age of thirteen or fourteen on up to around twenty, or older if they were unemployed. Sometimes they were only going to make noise, sometimes they threatened to make more than noise, and I meant the opposite to them; I was a suggestion, a sign, that this wild night's not going to be, not as they hoped, not here. Sometimes they expressed themselves, too. There were those who saw us as their protectors, and those who saw us as their keepers, and both were right. Each group taught me how to be a cop.

Early on, I wanted to tell these pure strangers who would meet me with such strong feelings, whether grateful admiration or vein-bulging rage, "Hey, I just showed up here—relax! Maybe in a minute, or a year, you'll have a reason to love me or hate me, but as of now, you don't know me!" And I did remind people, with partial success, when they verged on losing control. But I began to understand the variety and potency of the guises in which I appeared to them—rookie cop, Irish cop, white cop, housing cop, ghetto cop, good cop or bad, stone-hearted or sympathetic or scared. It was like being a kind of celebrity, and it was hard to convince people that I was not like what was portrayed on TV, because I played still another role even as I explained it that I wasn't. I was not myself, but the latest cop, loaded with symbolism, and a loaded gun. For them, for now, I was the system.

· · ·

WHEN I JOINED THE NYPD IN 1995, IT WAS NEARLY FOUR times larger than the FBI and four-fifths the size of the total staff of the United Nations. There are more cops in New York than there are people in Beverly Hills. Most people think of a cop as a uniformed officer from a precinct, or a detective in a squad, but Patrol Services and the Detective Bureau are only two of nine in the NYPD. In addition to the seventy-six precincts, Patrol also includes School Safety, the volunteer Auxiliary Police, and the Special Operations Division, for Aviation, Harbor, Emergency Services, and Homeless Outreach. Detectives are assigned to two additional investigative bodies, Internal Affairs and the Organized Crime Control Bureau, the latter of which encompasses Narcotics, Auto Crime, and Vice. The Housing Police became the Housing Bureau, whereas the Transit Police was folded into the Transportation Bureau, which also includes Traffic Control, Highway Patrol, and the Mounted Unit. Personnel covers Applicant Investigation, the Police Academy, Medical Division, and Employee Management; Support Services has the Property Clerk, Fleet Services, Central Records, and Printing; and Criminal Justice runs Central Booking for each borough and serves as a liaison to the district attorneys, the courts, and the Mayor's Office. I doubt if one cop in ten could name each bureau at the beginning of his career, and even fewer could at the end.

In terms of hierarchy, the Job was only slightly less complex: the ranks from police officer to sergeant, to lieutenant and then captain, were determined through civil-service tests, and beyond that—deputy inspector, inspector, and four grades of chief, each gaining a star up to the four-star chief of department—the positions were appointed. Detectives were semi-appointed, in that the gold shield was generally given after eighteen months in what was classified as an investigative assignment, most often in Narcotics or a precinct detective squad. Though detectives did not outrank anyone, they alone took responsibility for a case or a crime scene, and this special autonomy led them to be seen as apart from the general chain of command.

As in most American cities, crime in New York had risen in the postwar decades, steadily or in great waves, and there was a deepening belief that no police department could do more than slow the tide. But the Giuliani Administration, then in its second year, had brought a new vigor to the NYPD, under Commissioner William Bratton and his three chief lieutenants, Jack Maple, John Timoney, and Louis Anemone. Previously, it was felt that the expense of police resources on people who hopped turnstiles or pissed in public when the mayhem had risen to such levels was foolish, to say the least. But the new approach held that killers and robbers are no more respectful of the little laws than the big ones, and stopping someone for smoking a joint allowed you to search them for weapons and run them for warrants. Many a cross-country career of rape and murder ended with a casual drink in New York. The frequency of these "stop-and-frisk" encounters also changed the culture of how criminals carried their weapons: in the 1980s and early '90s, many dealers would carry guns in their waistbands, and the decision to shoot someone—because he crossed into their territory, or he said something about their mother, or he looked at them funny, or just because—was a three-second decision. After Bratton, the dealers still had guns, but they were hidden under their beds or on rooftops, and the delay from impulse to act took five minutes or ten, allowing people to move and tempers to cool.

Just as revolutionary was the "Compstat" system, devised by Jack Maple, in which commanding officers were regularly called down to police headquarters to account for crime and arrest statistics. All were gathered in an auditorium as the data was projected on a large screen and examined in a forum that was often Inquisitional in tone:

"You've had robberies for the last four Fridays on the corner of 163rd and Tinton. Why don't you have a steady post there?

"You have three burglaries at the same address. How many parolees live there?"

"Your last three homicides are drug-related. Why haven't any search warrants been executed in your precinct for six months?"

As the last and least of police officers, my class was unaware of this revolution, which struck terror in the hearts of captains and chiefs. Compstat led to a slew of resignations and transfers for those who could neither deliver on improvements nor explain why they had not. It also gave them greater freedom to address their problems, and it effected a greater degree of cooperation between bureaus, as Patrol, Narcotics, and Detectives were obliged to share burdens and pursue solutions together. For ordinary cops, old and new, it meant that what we did would be noticed, with closer attention than ever before. We were also given to understand that each arrest counted, and that, in time, we might, too.

· · ·

EARLY IN THE TOUR, THE COPS IN THE VILLAGE WOULD ASK each other, "You lookin'?"—which meant for a collar. Some cops never were; others, always. I was looking, almost all the time. In situations where an arrest was unavoidable, like a family assault where the perp was on the scene, a cop who wasn't looking usually could raise one who was, over the air, but everyone got stuck sometimes. Cops collared for overtime, or for the pure pleasure of the hunt, or in the mostly-correct belief that their efforts would eventually be rewarded. The cops who didn't like to collar thought that the day was long enough as it was, or they were uncomfortable with the combative nature of court, or because since the merger of Housing with the NYPD, we processed our collars not at the PSA but at the local precinct, where we were not always welcome. We were extra work for their desk officers, who had to inspect and sign our paperwork and were responsible for our prisoners, should they get sick or claim abuse in the cells. Our bosses were supposed to sign the paperwork, but since we might only have one sergeant to cover housing cops in five precincts, they often couldn't come. Many of the DOs were famously irritable, and one was blind in one eye and deaf in one ear, right and left or left and right—I'd forget which—so if he wanted to see you or hear you, you had to jump from side to side.

And the process itself is laborious—if, for example, you arrested a man for hitting his girlfriend with a tire iron, and then found a crack vial in his pocket, the paperwork would include a Domestic Incident Report, for follow-up visits by the domestic violence officer; a "61," or complaint, which describes the offense, perp, and victim; and an Aided Card, which contains information on the victim and what medical attention she received, which are assigned numbers from the Complaint Index and Aided and Accident Index. The Aided number goes on the 61, and the 61 and Aided numbers both go on the On-Line Booking Sheet (OLBS), which provides more detailed information on the perp, and has to be handwritten, then entered into the computer, which generates an arrest number. You would have to type two vouchers, both of which have serial numbers that have to be entered on the 61 and the OLBS, for the tire iron and the cocaine, affix a lead seal to the tire iron and put the crack vial in a narcotics envelope in the presence of the desk officer, writing your name, shield number, and the date across the seal. A Request for Lab Exam (Controlled Substance and "Marihuana," in the NYPD spelling) is also filled out and attached to the envelope. You would run a warrant check on the computer, take three sets of fingerprints (city, state, and federal), each of which has to be signed by the cop and the perp, then bring the perp up to the squad to be debriefed by detectives, who ask if he knows about and is willing to talk about other crimes.

Generally, detectives investigate specific past crimes, and the interrogation aims for a confession or other inculpatory statement. The classic interrogation, in which the detectives sweet-talk, bluff, and browbeat the perp into an admission of guilt, is seldom a part of what a patrol cop does. Patrol responds to all manner of events—drug sales, disturbances, lost children—and debriefings seek to elicit information on broader criminal activity. Some offenses—many sex crimes, most domestic violence—take place outside of any larger criminal context, due to their spontaneous or solitary nature; wife-beaters don't usually join a wife-beaters' club, and rapists don't have a union. But most robberies and all drug sales are committed by members of felony society, from suppliers to fences, and all manner of partners in crime. They know people, know things. And with every arrest, you take the time to persuade them to share that knowledge.

The prisoner is then searched again (he's been searched twice before, at the scene and at the precinct) and delivered to Bronx Central Booking, at Criminal Court, where he waits in a holding cell until he's arraigned before a judge. At CB, you photograph your prisoner, attach one picture to the OLBS and another to a Prisoner Movement slip, and have the prisoner examined by EMS, interviewed by the Criminal Justice Agency for his bail application, and searched again before he's in the system, out of your hands. You would then see an assistant district attorney to write up and swear to a document that is also called a complaint. The victim also must appear, unless he or she is hospitalized or some other extreme circumstance presents itself, or the case is dropped. The entire process usually takes six to eight hours, though it could easily be twice that, if a prisoner was sick, a computer went down, or there was a backlog at Central Booking or the Complaint Room.

The paperwork, procedure, and personnel add up to bureaucracy, which is famously wasteful or a necessary evil, sometimes both. Sometimes it reaches a nuanced complexity that is itself somehow sublime, like a martial art. Once I arrested a sixteen-year-old for burglary, whose recent birthday permitted him to be charged as an adult. Several months earlier, when he was fifteen, he'd stolen the keys to his elderly neighbor's apartment, and he helped himself to her belongings when he saw fit, sometimes with the coerced complicity of her ten-year-old grandson. The grandmother had made dozens of calls to the police, who were only able to file Lost Property or Petit Larceny reports and never had probable cause for an arrest. She had even gone to her congressman to demand an end to the reign of terror by the little boy downstairs. Finally, she caught him, held him at knifepoint until we arrived, and presented us with the perp, and her house key, recovered from his pocket. I charged him with Burglary, Criminal Possession of Stolen Property, and Possession of Burglar's Tools, to wit, the previously stolen key. The ADA reduced the charge to Attempted Burglary, and wanted me to re-arrest him as a juvenile, charge him with Petit Larceny for the theft of the key, and present him with a Juvenile Appearance Ticket at his arraignment in Criminal Court, as an adult, and release him on his own recognizance to his mother for the simultaneous Family Court case. Now, you're thinking, simple enough, but does he get the same arrest number for the adult and juvenile charges? Can he be in the system with two different arrest numbers, or since they're different jurisdictions, is the conflict irrelevant? To put it mildly, the ADA and the supervisor at Central Booking disagreed, and I was sent back and forth between them—"The District Attorney has the case now, we're the ones who decide"; "You're a police officer, and I'm a lieutenant, and you'll do what I tell you if you like getting a paycheck"—for several hours, diverted by a search in Family Court for missing forms for the juvenile arrest. When I called my sergeant to ask what to do, he laughed and said, "That's a good one! Let me know what they decide, maybe it'll be on the lieutenant's test." I know a decision was made, because I did go home at the end of that day, but God help me if I can remember what it was.

When you arrest someone, it's like a blind date. You spend a few hours with a stranger, a few feet apart, saying, "Tell me about yourself." You ask,

"How much do you weigh?" and, "Are you a gang member? Really! Which one?" So maybe I haven't been on a blind date for a while. But you do hold hands, for a few minutes, as you take prints, rolling each fingertip individually, then four fingers together, flat, and the thumb, flat, at the bottom of the card. Three cards for adults, four for juveniles. You coat a plastic plank lightly with ink, rolling it from a pad, then take each finger—"Relax!"—and roll it, on the plank and then on the card. A lot of people try to help you, rolling the fingers themselves, which usually smudges the impression; sometimes that's their intent. Crackheads often don't have usable prints, with fingers burnt smooth from gripping the red-hot glass pipe. Junkies, coming down, can go into a whole-body cramp, and have hands as stiff as lobster claws. Perps collared for robbery or assault might have bruised, swollen, and bloody fingers. You try to be gentle, and you wear latex gloves.

When you print a perp, you're close to him, and because you're close, you're vulnerable. You take off the cuffs, and you put your gun in a locker. Once, I was printing a guy as he found out he was not getting a summons, but instead going through the system. He'd been shouting abuse at the desk officer—an excellent way to prolong your imprisonment—in a routine street-guy, trash-talking way, when he was told, in effect, that he faced another twenty-odd hours in lock-up instead of less than one. And he became enraged, screaming curses and threats, and I wondered if he'd make a run at the desk, or worse, at me. But I was holding his hands and could feel them, how they were limp and loose as if he lay in a hot bath, as if his body was indifferent to the hatred in his voice. So I went on printing as he went on shouting, each of us concentrating at the task at hand.

· · ·

IN TIME, MY CLASS OF FORTY OR SO COPS BEGAN TO MAKE names for ourselves at the precinct, as workers or weirdos, or as passing casualties of circumstance. A perp flipped out on one of us, putting the cop's head through a window in the precinct; two cops made an off-duty drug collar at a bar, when a man offered them peyote; another cop fired a round when a homeless man surprised her on a roof landing. News of goof-ups or great collars were eagerly circulated, and nicknames began to stick: Smiley, Wimpy, Stix. If I had made a name for myself, no one told me. During one roll call, as names were called and duties assigned—a regular post might be changed to guard a DOA or a hospitalized prisoner, to fill a seat in the sector car, or to drive the boss—I felt bad for one poor guy, who was plainly deaf or AWOL as the lieutenant bellowed his name, without reply:

"Coyne!"

"Coyne!"

"Coyne, where the fuck are you!"

As the curses and shouts escalated, I was looking down, blithely writing in my memo book, until I felt the lieutenant's breath: "What the fuck is wrong with you, Coyne! Do you need to have your fucking head examined? Is this some kind of fucking game?"

"Um, I'm Conlon, not Coyne, sir."

The lieutenant snarled and turned away, as if I'd put one over on him. Bobby Coyne was another tall, skinny, quiet Irish guy, and our loose resemblance gave the advantage of invisibility. Osvaldo had something of a similar experience, though it was far more disturbing. One day, he received a notification from Internal Affairs, ordering him to appear downtown in six weeks, with an attorney present. When he called to ask what it was about, he was refused an answer, presumably due to the sensitivity of the investigation. He had to sweat it out, waiting sleeplessly for the date, and when he finally went down, it emerged that they had sent for the wrong man. Another cop with the same name was wanted for questioning in the "Dirty Thirty" corruption scandal that had broken not too long before.

That kind of event seasons and shapes a cop, colors his view of the Job from the inside, its bureaucracy and office politics, what it wants and how it treats its own. My outlook on the interior life of the NYPD was from a peaceful and largely positive remove, in that I thought a great deal of a lot of the bosses and very little of just a few, but I knew that the worst I could expect from the latter was a random tongue-lashing or a boring assignment for the night. For that matter, I was largely unsupervised—the forty or so PCOs ostensibly had a sergeant, but there were so many of us, working different times in different precincts, that I didn't even know who my sergeant was. When a cop makes an arrest, a sergeant is supposed to be called to the scene, but at first I didn't know that, and later I felt I knew what I was doing, and often enough, no sergeant could be found. The Job for me took place not in the precinct but on the street, and it was the public dimension of police work that held my interest and inspired my confidence. An irritable lieutenant made me more nervous than checking a rooftop alone at midnight. I preferred the outhouse to the house.

And since I tended not to work with cops who were senior in rank or experience, I learned to take the initiative and make decisions on patrol, quickly developing a rhythm and a style, a sense for when to step up or step back, as the situation required. Good cops are method actors, in that they make a controlled use of their emotions, from empathy or anger, depending on whether the scene to be played is a conflict with a crowd or persuading an Emotionally Disturbed Person (EDP) to go to the hospital. Once, a woman called to say that her son, a well-built schizophrenic, had gone off his medication, and I was able to cajole him into the ambulance, saying that I believed him when he said his medicine didn't work, but only the doctor could change it, and he didn't want his mother to worry, did he? As he walked out, his mother clutched my arm and said, "Thank you, Officer, thank you so much, this is the first time he went without fighting the cops!"

The police work of action, of confrontation and force, the roundhouse punches and high-speed chases, is what makes both the movies and the news—and, now and then, means everything in real life, our real life, too. But what you say and how you say it comes into play far more often than anything you do with your stick or gun, and can prevent the need for them. If you talk a good game, you're halfway there. A talker can do things, or undo them: I know cops who have talked would-be suicides from rooftops, and who have convinced raving gunmen to release child hostages. More often, you talk people into talking, only talking, instead of screaming and waving a knife. There are fighting words and the opposite, passwords that most people seem to have, some topic or tone that cuts them short or brings them down, reaches them through reason, decency, or shame. I once watched an eight-year-old boy silence a foul-mouthed drunk in a pizza parlor, by barking at him like a colonel: "Hey! There's ladies here!"

You also have to listen. You believe most people when they call you, because the help they need is obvious—they're hurt or sick, or they've had something stolen. And you encourage them to talk, so they can ventilate, or rant themselves through to some vital detail (my favorite witness: "He was tall! Five-ten! Maybe even five-twelve!"), or, sometimes, to give themselves enough rope. When a robbery victim told Angel, Osvaldo, and me that three white men in white suits broke into her apartment, locked her in the bathroom, and made off with her cigarettes, I felt I had to question her further before I put out an APB for the Bee Gees. Her English was poor and a great set of dentures floated in her mouth, like she was sucking on a lump of ice.

When I first suggested an ambulance come, she shook her head no. "Sometimes you don't know if you're hurt right away, the shock of it and all, it's best to be safe and check. Are you under any kind of treatment right now, do you take any medicine?"

She nodded. "For the voices."

You have to ask. The quality of information you get is only as good as you demand, vetted through repetition and playback, prodded along for further detail, probed for the soft spots in the story like dry rot in a wall. You learned to pitch your questions. You didn't ask, "Do you have a gun in the house?" because in perp-logic, an honest denial is appropriate because it's not his gun, he's only holding it. You'd ask, "Is there a gun in the house?" or better yet, "Where's the gun?" The built-in presumption saved time: if you ran a warrant check for someone with a common name like Jose Gonzalez, and there was a hit for a Jose Gonzalez of 123 Broadway, you wouldn't ask, "Did you ever live on Broadway?" but "When did you move from 123?"

For all that, you should still expect to get it wrong sometimes. Or for it to get you wrong. When I went to testify for the Grand Jury after a rape collar, I was greeted by the ADA with the eight words I least wanted to hear: "You know he has an identical twin, right?"

I wanted to shout then, but I didn't. Maybe I should have, for the practice. You have to be ready to shout, or at least show your teeth. On most jobs, I rarely came on strong at first, so I'd have something in reserve, to raise the ante, and in the daily confrontations with groups loitering in the lobbies or in front of my buildings, there was plenty of rehearsal for each manner, hard and soft. I never made an empty threat and I never let anyone make one to me: if someone said they were going to hurt me, no matter how unimpressive the speaker or the speech, they would wind up in handcuffs or I'd wind up with a profound apology. Though I never had to do much more than push someone against a wall, I gained an understanding of the old-time cops who broadcast a message of respect with a nightstick. When you walked a beat like mine, the perps got a quick sense of how much they could get away with, which was as much as you let them. Moreover, when you let things like that slide, you're "setting up the next cop," who may be less capable of handling a perp who's now willing to take it to the next level. You couldn't let a perp "hook" you, taking the bait and blowing up over his remarks about your race, your mother, or your putative boyfriend, because when you lose control, you risk losing everything, and the law and the Job will turn on a dime from ally to enemy. And even with your allies, you had to be careful: a cop from my class arrested a perp, who then thre

ported it at our command. It was probably no

cided to be safe and at least put it on record. Once

the Job, however, an exhaustive series of counterme

meetings and debriefings and directives as the Intellig

the threat, after which the cop was moved to another hap-

pened to me, I would have seen it as a defeat—it woulc erp's post

again, and mine no longer.

And it was becoming mine. The appeal of patrol is its spontaneity and variety, reacting to the rhythms of the street, with its long lulls and sudden convulsions, of pick-up jobs and radio runs that propel you into action, or interaction; into a foot pursuit, a dispute, a birth. No other post was as busy—I might answer a dozen or more jobs a day—and I had finally begun to master the territory, learning the players and the plays. I worked with Leo, the super at Morris, in putting up floodlights in a few areas favored by nighttime dealers. One day we had to check all the elevator cars for contraband, and a maintenance guy showed us how to surf the elevators, riding atop them as they shot up hundreds of feet through the shafts. Whenever I collared up, I went upstairs to the Squad at the Four-Two, to ask the detectives if they were looking for anyone in the Village. The detectives welcomed with open arms any rookie who wanted to do their work for them—except for Howie "the Hump" Denton, a cigar-chomping First Grader, who would make a show of taking the burglary or robbery complaint I gave him, crumpling it up, and bouncing it off my head—"Thanks, kid, mark this closed"—before looking at it, and I was like a mascot for two partners, Donovan and Duarte, who'd hand me a polaroid of a perp and say, "Go get 'em, tiger!"

Sometimes I got 'em, and sometimes they got me. The first ten-year-old rape victim I interviewed, I had to camouflage what I felt, and I don't think I succeeded. When you interview the victim of a sex crime, you have to be specific. You ask, "Did he put his penis in your vagina? Did he wear a condom?" Any anxiety on your part communicates to the victim, and it can make them more ashamed, less trusting in you and hence less safe. You can't flinch, even when you ask a little girl, "Do you know if anything came out of his penis?" The second ten-year-old rape victim I interviewed, I didn't have time to feel anything: I had to get the description of the perp over the air, collect information on the victim, an adult relative, the paramedic, and the hospital, direct the sealing-off of the crime scene (one elevator, the fourth- through the eighth-floor stairs, where he led her at knifepoint), and brief the succession of perior officers as they arrived. An old family friend, Inspec- Mullen, responded that afternoon, and I was proud of the casual dence with which he asked me, "Whaddaya got, Eddie?" But when it was over, I only thought about going home.

"Whaddaya got?" That's what the boss asks when he arrives at the scene, to make a decision or review one you've made. You gotta have a story, as they say. You tell him, I got a dispute, a matched pair of bloody noses, a shaky ID on a chain snatch. I got a lady with a stopped-up toilet who thinks I'm gonna help mop the bathroom. I got an order of protection that says I have to throw the husband out of the house, but he has custody of the three kids because she's a junkie and they have nowhere to go. I have twenty-seven facts in front of me, too many and not enough, in a broken heap like they fell off the back of a truck that left yesterday. I have a mini-mob beating a man bloody. *Pardon me, mob, but why?* Because he tried to lure an eight-year-old boy down the alley, to tell him special secrets. *All right then, mob, hold off a bit, let's talk to the boy.* The boy is found, he says it wasn't him, it was his friend Jose, who left, without a last name or address. . . . The beaten man refuses to press charges, just wants to go home, less a half-pint of blood, a few teeth, and now that he notices, his watch. *All right, mob, your work is done here, now you can go chase Frankenstein into the burning windmill.* Whaddaya got? I got nothing, Sarge, and plenty of it. Good work, Officer, I knew you had it in you.

You may only have seconds to take stock, to make a nearly instantaneous appraisal of a jumble of allegations, injuries, insults, histories, and relationships between neighbors, brothers, lovers, ex-lovers, lovers again, with roots of enmity as tangled and deep as those between Balkan tribes. You say, "No, I just need to know what happened *today*. . . ." The outpouring of stories can move like a horse race, a hectic and headlong jostling for position, but all moving in the same direction, toward the same finish. Or it can end up like a four-car crash at an intersection, where all the drivers sped up to lay triumphant claim to the right of way. Brawls often conclude with such a profusion of contradictory stories that you simply take the losers to the hospital and the winners to jail. Legally, the difference between harassment, for which you cannot make an arrest unless it happens in your presence, and assault, is whether or not there is an injury or "substantial pain." Certain bodily grievances are tough calls: a bruise, a gash, a good lump is clear evidence of an assault, but I've surveyed people with a flashlight, trying to find a scratch as if it were a dirt road on a map—"There it is—no, there!"—and had to come up with kind words to inform the victim that she hasn't suffered enough.

When a woman named Tonya called, she seemed to qualify squarely on the side of assault. She was surrounded by female relatives who let out a steady stream of consolations and curses, all attesting to her assailant's history of violence. His name was George, and he was the father of her baby girl. Tonya moved stiffly and was covered with scuffs and scratches, and her earlobe was notched from where an earring had been pulled out. I asked her about it, and she said, "Oh, that's old," and looking closer, I saw that it was, as were many of the marks on her. But then she lifted up her pant leg and showed a fresh red scrape that covered most of the kneecap, and the course was clear. I asked for a detailed description, and got one: "He's about five-eight and two hundred pounds, a lotta muscles and a bald head. Gonna take a lot of you cops to lock him up, 'cause he on parole for armed robbery and he say he ain't goin' back for nothin'!"

"Does he have a weapon now?"

"Wouldn't be surprised."

We set out to canvass the neighborhood. When Angel spotted him on the street, I called him over. He was as described, not an enormous man but a substantial one.

"You George?" I asked, and he said that he was, in a clear, precise diction that was unusual for the street. He'd spent his time well upstate. I asked if he'd fought with Tonya and he laughed, with mild embarrassment, as if he'd found out they'd awakened the neighbor's baby.

"Yeah, we did argue, over some stupid little thing."

"Tell you what, take a walk with us up there, let's straighten it out."

The only thing to be straightened out was the "confirmatory identification," a procedural nicety for which I was glad to have his innocent cooperation. His complete lack of concern was puzzling, and suggested that either her story or his mind was plenty shaky. Upstairs, Tonya made the ID, I discreetly put my location and condition—"Holding one"—over the air and asked George for a lengthy, time-killing version of events, as if there was more to be discussed. But even when plentiful reinforcements arrived, and his alarm became demonstrable as he caught on to what was happening, we wanted to talk. We wanted him in handcuffs, but we would talk. Given his strength and the dimensions of the cinder-block hallway where we were gathered, no one wanted a brawl. And he didn't fight, but he didn't give up, pulling back as someone tried, gently, to take his arm, and he began to shake, and to bellow, "I did not hit her!" and "I am not going back to prison!" We were tempted to believe both statements, but managed to coax him into restraints, though he continued to shout, calling for neighbors to find other friends, his sisters, to let us know what was really going on.

As we put him in the car, George told us that Tonya was a crackhead, that he had custody of their infant daughter, that he was angry at her because she left the baby alone, that her marks were from a fight she had yesterday, that many people saw her attack him earlier that day, and saw how he never raised a hand. One woman, who looked like a crackhead, said she'd fought Tonya last night; a man, who didn't, said he'd seen George endure Tonya's beating without protest. Denise, another baby-mother—George had two daughters, each a few months old—whom he referred to as his fiancée, stood by him, shaking her head in disapproval of Tonya. But I still had a complainant, an ID, a fresh injury, and no choice. And when George admitted he "might have knocked her down," I didn't feel bad about taking him in.

At the precinct, he was still convinced he could convince me: "She's *wrong,* man, I'm telling you, you know she's *wrong!*" I told him, "Look, she's the mother of your kid, you roughed her up, and you know that's wrong. If she's a crackhead, you shouldn't leave the baby with her. I hear what you're saying, but she's hurt and says you did it, so there's nothing I can do. You got a story—tell your lawyer, tell the judge, you'll probably be all right." He nodded. George underwent profound changes in manner as his thoughts strayed wildly from dark reveries of injustice, where his voice would drop an octave ("She's *wrong!*") to civil, smart, and likable reason, to soft-voiced and agile menace, where you couldn't tell if he was putting on a mask or dropping one: "I did *time,* man, time. I know people who rob every day, I know people sell guns, sell machine guns. I know people, sell you a grenade, man, I could help you out. . . ."

I was interested. I told him so. But I didn't want to get greedy, let the balance tip from buyer to seller. I knew if he meant it, he'd say it more than once, and for it to work, he'd have to be willing to keep talking when he wasn't wearing my handcuffs. So I treated him with consideration—"You got change? I'll get you a soda"—told him what to expect (seeing a judge within twenty-four hours; time served, probably, on the assault), and continued to process the arrest. As he predicted, Tonya dropped the charges, and she even came down to Central Booking to take George home. ("It isn't right what he did, but he takes care of the baby, we'll work it out. . . .") He was elated as he left, telling me, "I'm gonna get you a gun collar!" I laughed as he turned away, and said, "Give me your number," watching to see his reaction.

He hesitated, then turned and gave me his beeper number. "I'm telling you," he said.

· · ·

THERE ARE ARRESTS THAT COPS HOPE AND TRAIN FOR LIKE athletes, and in this felony Olympics, collars for homicides, pattern crimes, and drugs by the kilo are considered gold medals. They used to call it "the Door," and if your name was on the bottom of an On-Line Booking Sheet for the Son of Sam or the French Connection dealers, it would open for you. Sometimes you can almost hear the lock click open: on a routine car stop or hallway patdown, you can feel that this perp will take you more places than the Commissioner would, even if you married his daughter. But the likelihood that things will go wrong with arrests seems to escalate with their importance: a baroque legal system, combined with the whims of chance, provides an inexhaustible source of misadventure. You feel like a diver on the platform who has just noticed that all the judges are Russian.

There had been a number of sexual assaults on elderly women who had been followed into their buildings and taken at knifepoint into the stairwells. A sketch was circulated, of a Hispanic man in his mid-twenties, with short dark hair and a slight moustache. Ten percent of the neighborhood might have matched the description, except for the fact that the rapist was supposed to have striking green eyes. There had been numerous panicked sightings, most of them entirely without value, but when a number of calls came over about a suspicious person lurking on the 12th, 15th, then 16th floor of the building where the last rape had occurred, Osvaldo and I ran there. In the lobby, two people claimed to have seen him, but when we began to speak to a third, the first two disappeared. The last witness said the man was banging on an apartment door on the 16th floor. We called for backup, and Osvaldo stayed to freeze the lobby while I went upstairs.

The elevator was crowded as we started up, thinning out as it stopped on each floor. After two young guys got out, the older man next to me said, "Those are the ones who robbed me last month." I felt like I'd been slapped: how many empty stairwells I'd walked, how many hours on rooftops I'd waited, watching for the bad guys, to have this sudden embarrassment of riches thrust upon me. But the older man insisted that he hadn't reported it then and didn't want to now, and I didn't push him like I might have, as the elevator reached the 16th floor.

At the apartment, a young woman told me, "My mom's not here, but this guy was just banging on the door, asking for her. I don't know him, I said she wasn't here, and he tried to get in, he turned the knob and pushed." She thought she had seen him before, in passing; her mother, whose name was Barbara, was similar in type to the other victims. Another neighbor, who had followed me to the door—she had called 911—was horrified to hear the story: she knew that the man used to go out with another woman on the floor, but she had called only because she'd seen him standing in a stairwell with a strange look on his face. We had a male Hispanic in his twenties with a moustache, who was familiar with the building, wandering around, acting bizarrely, and attempting to enter the apartment of an older woman. It looked better than good.

I went downstairs to get Osvaldo, and when a sector arrived I asked those cops to freeze the lobby. We went up for a vertical patrol, and when we reached the 16th floor, we came upon a man in the hallway. We walked toward him and he walked away, a little faster, though there was nowhere to go—"Hold on, boss, slow down"—and he broke into a run, and as we tackled him, he began to scream, "Barbara! Barbara! I love you! Help me! Someone get a video! They didn't identify themselves as a police officer! Help!" He got something into his mouth and chewed it, and we got him down but for a long time we couldn't get any further. We wrestled with him for what seemed like ages, he was limber and strong and sweat-soaked, slippery as a live fish; we tried to get him to spit out what he had in his mouth—it turned out to be cocaine wrapped in a dollar bill—and at one point, Osvaldo and I actually took a break, sitting on him, looking at each other and catching our breath. When we finally cuffed him up, his hands and mouth were bloody. He looked just like the police sketch, with the distinctive green eyes. We later found out that his ex-girlfriend, who lived on that floor, had thrown him out on the day of the last attack. When Sgt. O'Hagan arrived, he looked at him, and then he looked at us, and smiled. "It's him. Definitely. You got 'im." Visions of medals and promotions danced in my imagination, sustaining me through the long night ahead.

At the precinct, he collapsed, and he told the paramedics he'd ingested three grams of cocaine, half while he lurked in the stairs, half in the dollar bill while we wrestled him. At the hospital, his heart rate was 220 beats per minute, and they made him drink an electrolyte solution and eat activated charcoal, which made him drool black. He was handcuffed to the cot in the ER, while the midnight pageant of medical catastrophes were brought in: one Emotionally Disturbed Person, who bit clean through his tongue, clipping it into a precise impression of his upper teeth. Another EDP, an enormous drunk picked up from the streets, floating in and out of consciousness, writhed and thrashed as a little Filipino nurse tried to draw blood: "Now I prick you! Now I just prick you!" An old man threw up and another prisoner-patient, hand-cuffed to the cot next to him, kindly handed him the closest receptacle he could find—a plastic pitcher half-filled with urine, which splashed back as he vomited and made him vomit more. And a beautiful teenage Spanish girl, who had choked on cotton candy hours before at a carnival. Her problem was long gone, as were her once-worried friends, but she had been told to re-main for examination. She was more than a little embarrassed.

"Well, I hope we all learned an important lesson about chewing our food."

"Shut up."

But she soon went home, and I was left with the wretched strangers. We'd made the arrest eight hours into the tour, and I waited with him at the hospi-tal for another nine, and only then did I begin the arrest processing. I'd worked almost around the clock before Special Victims called to say that my perp had already been taken in for a line-up and had not been identified. In my mind, I began to rehearse the arguments: they were elderly victims, trau-matized, maybe with bad eyesight . . . but it was pointless. In this kind of case, without an ID, there was often nothing to go on. And then, suddenly, I hated him. Throughout our ordeal, I'd felt nothing toward him, no contempt or anger, even when I fought with him, even though I believed he had done hideous, brutal things. Suddenly, I hated him, because he had changed; he was no longer a trophy, a magnificent and malignant catch, but some random asshole who had stolen an entire day of my life. He asked me mildly what he was being charged with and I told him. His tone was pouty when he re-sponded, "Criminal trespass, isn't that a little harsh, Officer?"

I just looked at him, but it must have been expressive. "Sorry," he said, turning away. You can't cry for every crime victim you come across; you can't even cry for the awful ones, not if you want to work for twenty years, and often the way to catch someone is to want to, very much. A few days later, I saw him on the street, and he said hello. I didn't. A few days after that, he beat up his girlfriend again, then disappeared. There weren't any more rapes.

· · ·

WHAT CAN YOU SAY? MOST OF THE TIME, IN THE END, YOU say 90-X, 90-Y, or 90-Z. These radio codes give dispositions, meaning unfounded, unnecessary, or gone on arrival. The terse dispatch of them—"You can X that, Central"—can reduce an epic to a letter, scraping it clean of context, all the drama and the decisions. My uncle Eddie had been a cop for over three decades, and when I first looked at his memo books, I was surprised at how little they said, given the zany color of his stories. The jumpy, crabbed notations of "all normal" and "nothing to report" were barely less vivid than the occasional mention of a parking ticket issued or "three under arrest—burglary." But in time, I came to appreciate the telegraphic brevity of the codes, which allowed me to finish stories I barely knew how to start.

Angel and I once went to a 10-10, a possible crime, in this case a "dangerous animal condition." The complainant was a woman on the 19th floor of one of my buildings, and a familiar caller. A stout, opinionated lady in her early fifties, she claimed to be the frequent victim of espionage on the part of her cable company, the Housing Authority, and several less terrestrial bodies, against which she protected herself by covering the walls and ceilings of her entire apartment with tinfoil. I sometimes wondered if it was a cop who had recommended it, to buy a few weeks' peace while she busied herself with the defenses. I know it wasn't a fireman, because the foil, which was tattooed all over with pentagrams, covered a thick layer of crisp and dry newspaper, mostly department-store circulars for men's underwear.

"I need you to get rid of my cat, it attacked me, it's crazy, it changed. I can't have it here, it used to be so wonderful, it's a mystical cat, you know, a Jewish cat. I tried everything, petting it, feeding it, throwing boiling water at it—nothing works, nothing!"

It was five in the afternoon, and our options were limited. Her son was with her, a large, shambling man in his early thirties who kept a weary and sheepish distance, meeting my eyes briefly when I looked to him, then shrugging and shifting aside. It was too late in the day to call the ASPCA for a pick-up. I doubted the cat was dangerous as much as I doubted the cat was Jewish, but the last thing I was going to do was call Emergency Services. When you call out the SWAT team for a kitten, other cops tend to bring it up now and then—one guy couldn't talk on the radio for months without hearing meows in the background. She rambled on, "I would have called Augie to take it out, you know, Augie's in the Mafia, he'd kill anyone for me, but he can't do it now, he can't, and the cat's in my bedroom and I can't go in. . . ."

I began to tell her that the best thing to do was to confine the cat in another room and leave it alone, while I would make an appointment with the ASPCA to take it off her hands the next day. She would have none of it, and with one hand on a hip and the other slicing the air she let me know she had dealt with my type before: "You will take care of this now or I will call the Housing Authority! I will call your captain! I will call Jim Jensen at Channel Seven News! I will call Eyewitness News! Yes, I'm calling now, give me Eyewitness News!"

As she marched to the phone to punch random numbers, I sidled over to the son and said, "Listen, why don't you shut it in another room?" He looked at me weakly, and his mother hung up the phone. "My son," she hissed with dry distaste, "is mentally ill." Silly me. Silly all of us.

Though I had decided our course by then, I thought I'd check the cat, to make sure it was in fact safe enough to remain in the apartment overnight. When I opened the door to the woman's bedroom, I saw a small white cat lying on the bed. A brown patch of fur on its head did look something like a yarmulke, but otherwise neither its religious affiliation nor its menace was obvious. When I took a step toward it, however, the transformation was profound: the back arched, the ears flattened, the eyes narrowed, and it seethed and spat like a cobra on crack. This lady didn't need a cop, she needed an exorcist. I withdrew and closed the door.

"Okay," I said. "The cat has to go."

From there, mother and son became my loyal aides-de-camp in the campaign that followed. A large piece of plywood was set up in the hallway to block access to the living room, and all doors were shut except for those to the mother's room and a smaller, spare room beside it. The first phase would be to isolate and contain the cat in a secure area, and the second phase . . . the second phase would certainly commence when the first phase was brought to a successful conclusion. Angel kept mother and son stationed behind the barrier as I put on my gloves, picked up a broom, and reentered the bedroom. Again, the cat bared its teeth and swiped with its paws, coiling up on the bed to prepare for a leap, but as I came closer it bolted for the radiator, and the merry chase began: the cat dashed to the top of the cabinet and then to the radiator, and then under it, and then under the bed, paused to turn and fight, meeting the broom and tearing at it as I tried to herd it out to the door. Again and again, it would bolt and then turn and fight, and hiss and spit, its lithe swiftness as amazing as its hatred. Once more it fled between cabinet and bed before it charged me and I fell back, swinging the broom, before it dodged and sped into the hall. But before the cries of acclaim could erupt from behind the barrier, the mother and son fell back, too, as the cat raced to them, leaping up and over the plywood as they dropped it, and pursuing them into the living room, where the field of battle was greatly enlarged.

"Get back! Get back! I've got it!"

I picked up the barrier again and sent them behind it, and once more engaged the cat: its rage, speed, claws, and teeth against my broom, my paramilitary training, and a chorus of meows on the radio echoing in my head. Here, it had the couch, chairs, cabinets, and shelves, a windowsill with heavy drapes, and an entire kitchen for its guerrilla maneuvers, and it made use of all of them in its rounds of flight and fight. As I fought on without success, my supporters were galvanized, and the woman cheered me on and brainstormed: "I know! Fire! We'll burn him out! All animals are afraid of fire!"

"Don't you dare! Angel! Stop her!" I shouted, but as I swept the cat from beneath the drapes, he darted for the kitchen, and after reconnoitering atop the refrigerator, he dove to the floor and under the stove. I paused to think and to breathe. As far as I saw it, we were still in Phase One.

"Still out on that ten-ten, unit?" came the call over the radio.

"Still out, Central."

Clearly, there was need for further revision of our strategy. The barriers were changed again, so that they led to the open door of the apartment. Once out, I figured, all of us—cat, crazies, Angel, and myself—would return to our better natures, and resume our lives on some kind of normal footing. Also, I didn't care anymore. So I returned to the kitchen and lifted up the stove, where the cat, writhing beneath, had become coated with the grease of a decade of breakfast bacon and Easter hams. The broom seemed to hold no more terrors for the cat, and I wielded it less adeptly as I also had to hold up the stove. I had to escalate, and I gave it a few blasts of mace—the old kind, which was a kind of weak cousin to tear gas—and though it had no apparent effect on the cat, it drove me, choking, outside into the hall. As I gasped for breath, I saw with my reddened eyes the woman leap across the living room with a great cooking pot stuffed with blazing newspapers, the flames reflecting off the foil walls.

"All animals are afraid of fire!" she shrieked, and I bellowed "No!" and raced back inside. Angel ran in to take her outside, and though I stamped the pot out before the fire engulfed the apartment, I was now doubly choked by the acrid bite of tear gas and the unfurling plumes of smoke, which set off the fire alarms throughout the floor. Neighbors began to step out of their apartments to investigate. I sent them back inside.

"It's all right, folks—the police are here, everything's in hand, nothing to worry about."

I was humbled and a little worried—if help arrived, I would have much to explain—but the woman was delighted. She called the police twice a week, and usually got a couple of guys who walked away a minute later, muttering about straitjackets; here, a hero had arisen who brought down forces of destruction that might well be commensurate with her perception of the threat. I had turned the place into Beirut, and she couldn't be more grateful. I opened the windows until the air cleared, and I almost toppled the stove to sweep the cat out from its refuge. Ignoring the open door, it bolted over the barrier and fled back into the bedroom. There, it darted between bed and radiator again, as if to show that the learning curve for both cat and cop remained flat, before it took off for the window, and slipped outside to the ledge. And then, I had a revelation: a vicious cat could not be put up for adoption. No matter the provocation, the cat would have no day in court; my nemesis had no future beyond being drugged, bagged, and caged before being put down. I moved forward without thought, but as if guided by some mysterious force. As I put my hands on the window, the cat scrambled to turn and come at me, but lost its footing and dropped from sight. The woman called the precinct for weeks afterward, demanding to talk to the captain to tell him what great work I had done. But when the desk officer asked me what had happened, I just shrugged and repeated what I'd told the dispatcher when she asked about the job:

"Still out, on that ten-ten, unit?"

"Make that a ninety-Z, Central."

The technical term for that kind of event is "clusterfuck," and whenever I began to feel I had a handle on the Job, some cluster would break out, reminding me of how much I was unready for. The novelty of knocking on a door and calling out "Police! Open up!" had passed—*Yeah, I mean me!*—and I was comfortable on post, answering jobs, learning more faces and names. And in time, as I ran into cluster after cluster, I began to see them not as testimonials to how much I had to learn, but as proof that I never would get it all. And that was the better wisdom, because when a cop thinks there is nothing left to see, he may not take the trouble to keep his eyes open.

· · ·

FOR THE MOST PART, THE TIME YOU SPEND WITH PEOPLE you tend to like and respect occurs when they're at a very low point in their lives: they've just been robbed, or are having severe chest pains, or their husband is dead in the back bedroom. You are less the bearer of bad news than the proof of it. More often, you become bound up in lives that are dismal and messy: junkies who take too much, EDPs who won't take anything for their pains. As you make the acquaintance of their broken minds and ruined bodies, you reluctantly invade their privacy, and you must vigilantly protect your own.

It can be troubling to be so intimate with these random strangers. And not just with criminals, though you see more of a person searching drug dealers ("Lift 'em. Arright, turn around and spread 'em.") than you ever wished. There are matter-of-factly named "lift jobs," for the elderly or ailing who have fallen down. I did one for a man who weighed more than 300 pounds, with two-thirds of it on the hips and legs, which were massively swollen and corrugated like Godzilla's. He wore a short nightshirt with no underwear, and his bladder control was chancy at best. His condition was the result of having been told he had cirrhosis of the liver years before and saying, "Hell, I'm still gonna have a drink now and then." Do you help him? Of course, you lift him up. Do you feel for him? *All right then, move along now, nothing to see here, move along.*

It was near the end of tour, and I was headed back to the precinct when an Aided case came over the air. Aideds are among the most frequent jobs, usually entailing an escort of EMS to the scene of an illness or injury. When Osvaldo, Angel, and I arrived in the apartment, I could tell from the smell why someone had called. Walking down the hall, past numerous, spacious rooms, the rank, ripe odor of a body grew stronger, and when an expressionless sixteen-year-old girl directed me to the last bedroom, I was thrown less by the sight of the still, frail old Puerto Rican woman in bed than by that of the four EMTs working around her. Two were crying.

The old woman was naked, lying face-down, stuck to plastic sheets, and her body made a crackling sound when she was unpeeled from them. She had once been a hefty woman, but she looked now less slimmed-down than deflated: her breasts were empty, pressed against her chest, and the bones of her hips and thighs were plainly visible, draped by loose, lifeless skin. Maggots crawled on her, inch-worming along, popping off like broken watch springs. There was rodent excrement in the bed with her, and examining her legs, one EMT said, after a horrified intake of breath, "Those are rat bites! Whoever did this to her should go to jail!"

The old woman let out a breathy moan as she was rolled over, feeling pain wherever her body was alive. And that's why the EMTs, who see dead children and bodies in pieces as a matter of course, were brought to tears. This woman was dying, was in fact dead in lesser percentages, as maggots do not eat live tissue. And she didn't live alone. I turned away and went to talk to the teenage girl: "Who takes care of this lady?"

"Well," she huffed, in a long-suffering tone, "I'm the one who does most of the work."

"Who lives here? How old are they?"

"Me and my sister and my grandmother. My sister's twenty-three but she's out now. I'm the one who does most of the work."

"Can you tell me why you didn't feed her?"

"She said she wasn't hungry."

"Why didn't you call a doctor?"

"I'm the one that did."

"Before now, why didn't you call?"

"My mom said not to."

Her mother lived in another part of the city. I told her to call her mother and tell her to go to the hospital. I asked how they lived, and she said her grandmother got checks, and her sister cashed them to run the household. I called a sergeant over and explained the situation in a rapid, dazed manner that made him look at me, carefully, before we all went downstairs. Ordinarily, EMS prefers to have a relative ride with the Aided, but when the teenager approached the ambulance, the no-longer-crying EMT told her, curtly, "You want to visit Grandma? Take the bus."

Back at the precinct, it took a while to figure out how to write the complaint, aside from descriptions of rat bites and maggots. The girl was too young to be charged. And the offense was not clear; while there are many laws regarding the care of children, the elderly are less explicitly protected. I found a misdemeanor called "endangering the welfare of an incompetent adult," and named the adult sister and the mother as perpetrators. The sergeant pointed out that there were checks coming in, so "investigate larceny" was added. And that, I realized without satisfaction, explained the family's nearly homicidal neglect. The old woman was the keystone of a tidy edifice of subsidies: a large apartment, Social Security, welfare for the teenage girl. If she went to a hospital or nursing home, all these benefits would vanish from their pockets. People talk about living from paycheck to paycheck; this family almost let a woman die that way.

I found out later that detectives made arrests at the hospital. I was also told that the two sisters sometimes visited their grandmother in the nursing home where she was later sent, and were trying, without success, to bring her back home. Another cop's mother worked there, and he told me, "And the old lady, she's kind of nasty herself."

Sometimes, the victims are less sympathetic than the offenders. When a woman called to say that her thirteen-year-old son had locked her out of her house for hours, Osvaldo and I responded, and we told her we couldn't knock down the door unless there was an emergency. She would have to pay for it, and we would have to wait until it was fixed. For more than an hour, we knocked, reasoned and threatened, fiddled with the locks. She had obtained a Family Court warrant that allowed her to call the police whenever she couldn't control her son, and we would bring both parties to court, or the child to an overnight facility if court was not in session. It was a responsible act, on her part, but one of few, it seemed. We had ample time to find out about the family.

"Is there someone he isn't mad at, who could talk to him, get him to open the door?"

"Oh, he's not mad at me," she said. I let it go.

"Maybe a friend from school?"

"I been tellin' him to go to school since last year," she said, adding that he stopped because the other kids beat him up. Asked why, she said that he wore makeup and women's clothes. Osvaldo went to get a coat hanger, to see if he could work the chain off. The woman went on about her troubles, how the boy's father had left her, how she worked, how the boy stayed out till dawn, how all kinds of adult men called him. She paused a moment, as if she'd just remembered, and said, "I had a three-year-old, she died. She was pretty." She paused again, and said, "I wish that faggot never was born."

Osvaldo got the door open. The thirteen-year-old, a light-skinned black boy with hair dyed a sunny yellow, was asleep. He seemed genuinely asleep, and I hesitated, unwilling to take him to kiddie jail for being a sound sleeper. But he admitted that he heard us, pounding and shouting through the afternoon, and I told him to get some things together, that he was going to court in the morning. I saw by his bedside a list of about twenty names, all male, and all but a few with beeper rather than phone numbers. His mother showed us the warrant, then picked up a skimpy pair of gold satin shorts, held them up to her substantial waist, and said, "Who wears these? Not me!"

What friendly or fatherly advice was there to offer? *I didn't peddle my ass when I was thirteen years old, young man, and now I have a cushy civil-service job. . . .* We drove downtown without saying much, and I haven't seen him since.

Another time, as I stood outside the management office, I saw that a middle-aged woman was staring at me, in the throes of indecision about whether to approach. I went over to her and asked if I could help. "My husband, he beats me, he beats me very bad." I pressed her for details, telling her how even if I couldn't make an arrest, she could get an order of protection, but she brushed me aside: "No, no, that's all no good. My daughter, she says she's just gonna get somebody to take care of him."

I told her that if he was beaten, he'd probably take it out on her anyway, and again, she saw I didn't get it: "I don't mean beat him up, I mean, *take care* of him. You know!" She raised her eyebrows, like she was letting me in on a sweet deal. "What do you think?"

"Lady, you noticed I'm wearing a blue hat, badge, the rest? That I'm a cop? And you want to know what I think about having your husband killed?"

We parted before she could ask me to quote a price, each convinced that the other had only a flimsy grasp of reality. A few hours later, I responded to a call of a "violent domestic dispute," and a cop named Anna Ramirez backed me up. A middle-aged man answered the door and allowed us in. He was in his underwear and seemed at ease, showing us around with a cavalier smirk. He was large and strong, and had a corrupt and military air, as if he were some tropical Presidente for Life. I didn't like him, and Anna hated him. There was no one else in the apartment, but as we left, I noticed the woman's picture on the wall. She was trying to win our argument, I think, saying, "Look at him. Look. If this one ended up dead, would you really come after me?"

The dead are commonplace for cops, and the sight of bodies never troubled me much, even from the beginning. My first murder was an awful one—an old man, on the floor in a hiked-up flannel nightshirt, who had been strangled, stabbed, and beaten, his arms bent into unnatural angles like chicken wings, and though I felt sorry for him, I wasn't unduly troubled. Sometimes homicide victims have a peaceful expression, while deaths from natural causes can appear as horrific as the worst crime scenes: one elderly diabetic fell down, and apparently tried to crawl to the phone as he died of cardiac arrest. It looked like he had been picked up and smashed around the room: his face was contorted and his body was bruised all over; there were bloody handprints on the wall and long, slashing smears of blood and shit on the floor. The stillness of the dead transfixes me, reminding me that nothing living doesn't move, not the deepest sleeper or a cat on the prowl, poised to leap. There is always some rhythm, some tremble or shift, that betrays animation. Only when that goes do they become motionless as photographs, as stones, and their meaning, like their movement, is only in what they inspire in those around them.

One old man lived alone, and died crumpled on the floor in the little alley between the bed and the wall, wearing a dirty shirt and no pants. His room was small and cluttered, and all his clothes were in old suitcases, or stacked beside them, as if he were packing for a long trip. There were two televisions, one old, one brand-new. A manic kitten darted amid the piles of clothes and rubbish around the body. Because he lived alone, we had to search for valuables, in the presence of a sergeant, and voucher them at the precinct. We found his discharge papers, false teeth, and stacks of pornography. The other cops left and I stayed. It was my turn to sit on the DOA, waiting for the ME to have a look, then the morgue crew to take him away. A man knocked at the door and said, "I took care of him, I'm his stepson. He wanted me to have the TV."

I told him to get some proof, and until then he should take the kitten. He left and I turned on the television. Less than an hour later, he returned, with a lady friend. Both were roaring drunk, and demanded in unison, "We loved him! *We* was his *family!* Let's have that TV!"

I closed the door on them and sat back down. There was a phone call. I waited, then picked it up, hoping that whatever friends or family he had, whoever cared for him, would not learn of his death by accident, from a stranger.

"Is Mr. Jones at home?"

"No, he isn't."

"Is this . . . Mrs. Jones?"

"No." But thanks for asking.

"When will he be available?"

"No time soon."

"When should I call back?"

"Can I ask who this is?"

"Mr. Jones had recently expressed an interest in our low-cost insurance policies, and . . ."

"He's not interested."

"And who, may I ask, is this?"

"The police. Mr. Jones is dead, that's why I'm here."

"Well, do you think—?"

"Dead."

"There may be some—"

"Dead, dead, dead. He's stuck to the floor six feet away from me, guy, no sale."

"Have you considered whether you have all the coverage you need, Officer?"

I hung up and went back to watching television.

TWO

One night on patrol, I went to an Aided case, a medical call for help. A woman's ankles had begun to bleed and would not stop, because of collapsed veins, she told me. She was in her early thirties and had nine children. Her feet bled like stigmata, as if there were no cause but grief. Her children ranged in age from newborn to young teens, in color from dark to pale, and together they looked more like a United Nations assembly than one little country. The ambulance took a long time to come, so my partner that day—an older cop whose steady partner was out—and I passed the time by talking with the kids, who gathered around us. A boy of eight or nine was mesmerized by us, by the sight of our blue uniforms, our cuffs and guns.

"Lemme see the handcuffs, lemme try," he said. I handcuffed him—rear-cuffed, as per *Patrol Guide,* Section 114-08—and gave him the key. He tensed up for a moment, planning his strategy, then twisted himself around mightily before collapsing in a spasm on the floor, where he flopped about like a fish on a dock. The key went flying. I picked it up and handed it back.

"I bet you twenty dollars you can't get out in one minute."

"Three minutes," came back the immediate counteroffer. I checked my wallet: I had a twenty-dollar bill, plus a couple of singles. I planned to give him a buck for the effort.

"Go ahead, three minutes."

He sat down on the ground, drew his legs through his cuffed hands, bent his wrists perpendicular, and unlocked the cuffs. He had two minutes and forty seconds to spare.

"Want me to do it again?"

"No, I want you to shut up."

The ambulance had come, and I handed him the money, suddenly realizing that I could now afford exactly one slice of pizza for dinner. He careened around the apartment, holding the prize aloft like a pennant, followed by his pack of siblings. We left, but he ran out into the hall after us, telling me his mother wanted him to give it back. He offered the money far more matter-of-factly than I would have managed at his age, rounding out a two-minute circuit of rags to riches to rags. And though I've never been much of a gambler, I wasn't about to welsh on whatever his name was, the plucky little waif who'd taken me for a ride.

"No, a bet's a bet. Tell your mother the police said you had to," I said, and he was content that there would be no more argument. The reality of the win now seemed to set something off in him, and he attached himself to me, determined to unburden himself of all his knowledge before I got to the elevator. Random pronouncements left him with such a rising and urgent rhythm that they took on the fervor of prophecy:

"I'm gonna ride in a limousine . . .

"You better watch your back out there!

"Do you read the Bible? It says the world is gonna end pretty soon. Do you believe it's gonna end? I do!

"The guy who sells crack in the lobby, his name is Roscoe, I can watch him and you can lock him up—and then you can come over for dinner!"

For days after, the older cop could not look at me without laughing. "You're gone," he said. "You're done." He was right, though he had no idea how right. Like my great-grandfather Paddy the Cop, I was gambling on job time. Taking after my uncle Eddie the Cop, I helped a poor kid out with a little cash, no matter if it was the last thing I'd intended. And as for a resemblance to my father, I may have to reach a bit—though I did gain an informant—but I put on my hat, and walked out into the evening, and was swept up in quiet awe at how this Job and this City can pull you in with its wreckage and wonders, unsatisfied with only one lifetime.

. . .

WHEN I WAS A TEENAGER, I STAYED OVER AT A FRIEND'S house in Brooklyn. His grandfather, who had briefly served as police commissioner, lived with the family. The Commissioner was a massive and shadowed form in the corner, still as a statue, like a stone Buddha in an ancient temple lost to the jungle. He seemed old enough to know anything, and so I asked him if he knew my great-grandfather Sgt. Patrick Brown, who joined the NYPD a few years after Brooklyn joined the City, and who retired at the onset of the Second World War.

"Sure I knew Pat Brown," he said, stirring. "He used to carry the bag on Atlantic Avenue."

As my mother said when I dutifully reported this to her, "They were different times, back then." The whiff of Capone-era rascality delighted me, in fact, much more than had I been told that he was straight and upright as a flagpole. I knew good cops all too well, and to have the other kind—at a safe distance—offered novelty and contrast, the glamour and danger of bootleg whiskey. When I became a cop and began to think about it again, I wasn't proud—though it would be an exaggeration to say it kept me awake at night. Now, the memory is a curiosity, so remote from my own life that it has the discreteness of an object, like the "come-alongs" my father once showed me. They were wrist restraints, also called "nippers," and cops carried them through the 1950s. Made of a short length of chain between two T-bars, they worked like handcuffs, except you had to hold on to them, and their coiled weight, dull steel gleam, and imagined history made them satisfying to look at and feel and wonder about. You wrapped them around one wrist and twisted, and though it left a perp one free hand, you could snap the bone in a second. Come-alongs depended on a cop's control. They could do what good or harm you wanted, as long as you kept your grip.

I'd bet that many cops now wouldn't even know that a bagman collects money, as an intermediary between the underworld and the upper—it is becoming a fragment of obsolete criminal slang, like "yegg" for safecracker or "betty" for picklock. For us, "the bag" is the uniform. Almost all I know about my great-grandfather is summed up in that simple, double-edged phrase, "the bag." He spent thirty-three years on the job, mostly in uniform. The six years he lived afterward were occupied in the operation of a horse room in New Jersey. The transition from law enforcement to the sporting world, I am told, was not abrupt. Pictures of him show a handsome man, well-fed and well-tailored, a figure of overripe charm with a note of elegant menace. He looked like the kind of character played in movies by Brian Dennehy or Charles Durning, winningly fleshy, light on his feet, and quick with his hands. He seemed determined that his appearance reflect his place in the world, and if his attire was a little flashy but of good quality, bespeaking both gentleman and gangster, then it may have described him more truthfully than he intended. In fact, after he retired to the horse room, where bets were collected and paid as the teletype hammered out news from the track, the progression from crooked cop to upstanding criminal could be viewed as a step in the right direction, at least in terms of appearances.

When Patrick Augustine Brown was appointed to the New York City Police Department on June 8, 1907, he was obliged to purchase two bags, for summer and winter. The summer uniform consisted of a gray helmet, white gloves, a dark single-breasted tunic with a white leather belt, and trousers with a white stripe on the side. For winter, there were a blue helmet and greatcoat, with a double row of brass buttons. In better neighborhoods, the uniform was a thing of splendor, a fit garment for a figure of respect, and in poor neighborhoods it could make cops stand out like redcoats in a forest of angry Indians. At the time, hoodlums would wait on top of buildings and push the chimneys down on passing cops (although generally the noise gave the patrolman a chance to run), or overwhelm them and stuff them into coal boxes. These assaults were directed at the bag itself; at the dignity of office—though it could be argued that the other kind of bag represented just as pernicious a threat.

In his book *Low Life,* Luc Sante says the patrolman's lot at the turn of the century was "a choice between starvation and extortion," and Pat Brown did not go hungry. At his retirement dinner in 1940, the menu told of roast spring chicken with chestnut stuffing, rissole potatoes and "bisquit tortoni." Though Brown retired as a sergeant, his dinner was attended by a number of inspectors and the Honorable William O'Dwyer, district attorney of Kings County, former cop and mayor-to-be. O'Dwyer had worked with Brown years before, and both careers testified to the fact that New York was a place where you could go as far as you liked, and maybe farther than you should. Or maybe it suggested that, at its worst, America offered a choice between evils.

O'Dwyer, a thoughtful, large-hearted man, was an Irish immigrant with the common touch. His goodwill and good fortune, his rise from Ellis Island to Gracie Mansion, made him an epitome of New World promise, and his canny but easygoing pragmatism made him a New York natural. "Lots of people would have us believe this town is loaded with thugs, racketeers, gamblers," he said. "I said it's a friendly city. It's been friendly to me." O'Dwyer's friendliness extended to a pre-election meeting with gangster Frank Costello, and his decidedly incomplete success in the prosecution of Murder, Incorporated, nearly led to his own indictment. When a police-corruption scandal erupted involving a Brooklyn gambler named Harry Gross, Mayor O'Dwyer was hastily appointed Ambassador O'Dwyer and he finished his government service in Mexico City. O'Dwyer had an indisputable personal decency and a record of genuine achievement, but in his later years, in his retirement in the Southwest, he felt obliged to inform acquaintances that he was not, in fact, a fugitive.

Because Pat Brown left his wife and three children in near-poverty, he does not share in the amber glow of nostalgia in family memory. He married Catherine Moran on June 10, 1908, within a year of joining the NYPD. His former occupation is listed as "clerk." I don't know whether he delayed marriage until he secured his new job, or she fell for the young patrolman in his gray helmet and wing collar. They moved to 42 Butler Street, in Carroll Gardens, on the day of their marriage, and every few years they shifted to some other pleasantly middle-class row house in sedately striving neighborhoods like Bensonhurst and Borough Park. They had my grandmother Anne, then Jack, and then Eleanor, and then there is a change of address, in 1926, to 1 Prospect Park West, a massive and stately apartment building beside Grand Army Plaza that would suggest a dramatic upswing of fortune—an inheritance, or a stock windfall—but if there was, Pat Brown did not share it. It was rumored that his sister Nellie, with whom they shared a house in Borough Park, inspired the breakup of the marriage. In the family legend, Nellie was a horrible woman—she buried three husbands and two children, because "God didn't want her and the Devil wouldn't take her"—who whispered to Pat that his wife "had visitors" while he was at work. There had been much more money than there should have been, and then suddenly, for his wife and children, there was very little indeed. My grandmother was finishing grade school when her parents separated, and plans to send her to an expensive Catholic boarding school on Long Island were put aside. Catherine found such work as she was able to, and when her children were grown—or considered themselves grown, as Eleanor married at sixteen—she would "tour the family," staying with relatives when a child was born, making herself quietly useful, and then moving on, so as not to be too much of a burden.

After Anne married, her mother lived with her. Neither Jack nor Eleanor had anything to do with their father again, and they lived strange and saddening half-lives, one leaving her husband and children forever, the other dwindling and drifting and dying young.

Pat Brown paid occasional visits to my grandmother, which she bore out of duty rather than love. My mother's older sister, Ann Daly, recalls that when she was a little girl, he would "haunt us, two or three times a year. My mother would be cold to him but polite. He'd visit for maybe fifteen minutes. My grandmother would go to another room. I hid under the table." She remembers him from below, the perspective of an anxious child: a diamond pinky ring on a manicured hand ("He had polished nails, but my grandmother didn't"), stout legs in a chalk-striped suit, black shoes with white spats—ominous, glamorous, and incomplete. He would never be completed for his descendants, never known in full.

"Everyone loved him but his family," Ann told me. "Even my father loved him—he knew he was a lot of baloney, a b.s. artist, everything was 'big time' and 'big money.' But he thought he was a wonderful guy, funny, generous, everything—and he'd ask my mother what the matter was. But she didn't want anything to do with him. Pat Brown bent over backwards for your grandmother—he didn't care about Jack and Eleanor—but she would have closed the door on him. He wasn't invited to my mother's wedding, September 22, 1929. Her brother Jack gave her away.

"He always had big, flashy cars—Cadillacs, I think—and his clothes, well, I wonder who his tailor was, because he wore nothing off the rack. He had to pay something like twelve dollars a month in support, which he did without question. That was about it, though. I remember in the thirties, he took my sister Dolores and me to a precinct Christmas party, it was for the poor children in the neighborhood."

My mother's recollection of Pat Brown is more vague and less critical. She barely knew her grandmother Catherine, who died in February 1941, after catching a cold when she went to see her son Jack off to the Army. A few months later, Pat Brown married a woman named Margaret Cramer—he never divorced Catherine, and had to wait to remarry if he intended to remain a Catholic—and there seems to have been a mild thaw in his relations with what was left of his family. In any case, he did make some effort to see more of them, and it was not prevented. Margaret grew especially fond of my mother. Where Ann Daly viewed Pat Brown through her mother and grandmother, as a man who wronged them by leaving, and wronged them again by coming back, my mother had Margaret to frame and filter the view. And since Margaret was so kind and decent, my mother believed that Pat Brown must have had those qualities too in some measure, at least in theory. Even so, when my mother spoke of him, her tone was restrained and avoiding rather than affectionate. He seems to have struck her as a man who showed the wear of a lifetime spent not going home after work, with the broad, brisk gestures of affability that appeal more to bartenders and waitresses than to young children. He died when she was eight, and she remembers him, without much certainty, as being partial to scotch and steak—my grandmother died when I was seven, and while I don't remember what she would have ordered in a restaurant, my memories of her are vivid and warm.

My mother remained close to Margaret, and I remember visiting her as a child—she was a sweet old lady in Bay Ridge, who was related in some way that I didn't understand. Her apartment was spacious and immaculate and looked like nothing had moved in thirty years. There was a dish of peppermint candy on a coffee table that stuck together into one big glom of sweets, so you had to wrestle it to break off a piece. That was fun, but there was nothing else for children there. After Pat died in 1946, Margaret married a retired inspector named John Sullivan, who also was recently widowed. Both couples had been good friends and childless. Sullivan lived only a few years longer, and so Margaret, who must have feared becoming an old maid, ended up a widow twice over, in a fairly short time. Margaret once told my mother that my father reminded her of Pat Brown; that he was a big man, handsome, and good company. When my mother told me, she made the kind of face she'd make if she had to eat the grubby, sticky candy, adding with some emphasis that she never saw any resemblance. She even said that Inspector Sullivan was a little more like him. Sullivan, of all people, her step-grandmother's second husband. She put the compliment aside, like an unwanted gift.

This private antipathy colored their view of Pat Brown as a public servant: the distance allowed the family to look at his life as a cop from a cold distance, an aerial view without detail or context. Sonny Grosso, one of the heroes of the French Connection case, once told me that even a lousy cop does more good than an ordinary person, in spite of himself—even if he stands there like a scarecrow, he can stop fights and robberies and make old ladies feel safe. Pat Brown received no such benefit of the doubt: unaware of any of his accomplishments, indifferent to whatever explanations he might have offered for his choices, his family knew little of him and liked less. Had he stuck around, his days at work would have been the talk of the dinner table, and his troubles and jokes, his feats and foibles, would have been cherished threads woven into the family lore. And his gambling life, taking money from bookmakers and then becoming one himself, would likely have been glossed over, or else recast as a kind of quaint and rather comic, olden-time malarkey, as if he made moonshine in the bathtub. The world of corner bookies survived the era of the speakeasy, but both have an air of nostalgia; when you imagine them, it is in sepia tones, with a jazz soundtrack, more redolent of period charm than positive menace. Like most New Yorkers, my family did not believe that a glass of beer or a game of cards imperiled their souls, and there was something ugly and silly about those who insisted that they did. The prevalence of betting and drinking when both were banned—Ann Daly said that it seemed that "every empty garage had a teletype," and "you got knocked over by the runners going down the street" as they delivered their slips—led to an increase in cynicism about law enforcement, but since that was the kind of enforcement the public seemed to want, the arrangement struck many as pragmatic rather than hypocritical. The fact of the matter was that Pat Brown was not respected at home, and so his career in the station house and the street was viewed with derision. His personal life shaped his public appearance, and those who were inclined to condemn him were amply accommodated.

The divide between his work and his life, or rather the way he broke apart the pieces of his life, was an arrangement that allowed most memories of him to fall through the gaps. He was said to frequent a bar called McLaughlin's on Flatbush Avenue, and to be friends with the undertaker Austin Moran. How many years have passed since Moran was a name to drop, or "the crowd at McLaughlin's" was rich in meaning? McLaughlin's may have been a favorite of cops, judges, gamblers, or Brooklyn Dodgers, or some combination of all of these—my aunt said it was "supposed to be a classy place, full of politicians." Moran, I would guess, was a figure of middle-class respectability, as successful funeral directors tend to be, friendly with professionals and priests. Ann Daly recalls Pat Brown as prominent in Catholic laymen's groups, and as she is devout herself—her daughter Patty is a nun—she held his own devotion against him: his practice and his profession were glaringly distinct. Maybe most people loved Pat Brown unless he gave them reason not to, but those who thought better of him have little to say now. You gotta have a story, and he never told us his.

On the single index card that constitutes Pat Brown's entire surviving NYPD record, it states that he was punished three times and praised once, all in his early years. On February 29, 1908, he "failed to make report of ambulance case," and one week later, he was cited for being "absent from post and in restaurant," for which he lost five days' pay. The next year, in September, he "did not properly patrol," and lost another day. (Ninety years later, my command discipline for "improper patrol" cost me three days, so maybe the Job's toughened up since then.) All three reprimands are in the same handwriting, which suggests that he was not a favorite of a particular sergeant or lieutenant. In October 1912, he stopped a runaway horse, for which he received a medal for Excellent Police Duty. The next three decades of service were unremarked upon.

If Pat Brown was troubled by anything in his life, there is no evidence of it. Though he did not see his children Jack and Eleanor, apparently by mutual agreement, his visits to his daughter Anne bespoke some confidence in a fuller restoration of relations. He lived at the St. George Hotel, the most fashionable in Brooklyn at the time, the seasonal residence of many of the Dodgers. Park Slope was nearby, as was McLaughlin's, on Flatbush and Atlantic—*He used to carry the bag on Atlantic Avenue. . . .* His horse room may have been up and running before he retired, perhaps in Jersey, perhaps closer. He took to frequenting the Copacabana, where he was known as "Paddy the Cop," and he was friends with the comedian Joe E. Brown. He would die in January 1946, a few days after his old friend O'Dwyer was inaugurated as mayor.

When *The Brooklyn Eagle* broke the Harry Gross story in 1949, "Thank God your grandfather isn't alive" became the household refrain. His partner in the horse room was sent to prison. The details of Pat Brown that survive in family memory are few and fragmentary, like the debris in a hit-and-run accident. I know that his parents survived the potato famine, which emptied Ireland of a quarter of its population; when he went to work in 1907, more than two million people a day went to nickelodeons, and when he retired in 1940, the Manhattan Project was under way. Because corruption was pervasive in certain eras, it can seem odd to observe that the prisons were filled and refilled, by and large, with people who belonged there. And year after year, cops died fighting the same gangsters who made their peace with the politicians. I know a little about how Pat Brown was a bad cop, but I don't know how he was a good one; if he saved lives or took them, delivered babies or calmed angry crowds. There is that one decorated act of bravery, but I don't know much more about him than the horse. Did he sleep well at night, dreaming of showgirls on his mattress full of money? Or did he sweat like O'Dwyer, and try to do good with one hand while the other strained against the come-alongs held by the gangsters in Brooklyn? I don't think people change, too often or too deeply, but many are quick to adapt. Like his old friend O'Dwyer, Pat Brown escaped judgment but paid with his reputation, escaping fond and common remembrance as well.

. . .

I THINK MY PARENTS WERE MEANT FOR EACH OTHER NOT because theirs was an especially happy marriage—though it was—but because they met through an undertaker called Charlie Le Chance. The name of the man had a peculiar music, vaudevillian but haunting, and he lived up to its billing. Le Chance, a friend of my father's, worked as a freelancer for several funeral homes, and he either owned or had easy access to a hearse. There must have been a shortage of cars in my father's circle in the Bronx during the fifties and early sixties, because the hearse saw a lot of social mileage. I heard a lot of Charlie Le Chance stories, and they all featured a corpse in the back seat. Either Charlie's passenger would casually examine the back to find a post-mortem chaperone, or a friend would be given a lift somewhere, and told not to mind the cargo. After the friend's protests were dismissed— "You're the one who asked for the ride, pal"—Charlie would announce that he had a quick errand to run, and when he hopped out of the car, his return would be mysteriously delayed. The passenger would wait uncomfortably as the minutes passed, perhaps glancing back, and wonder if it was his imagination when he heard the body bag slowly unzip. The punch line can be imagined. In any case, Charlie was my parents' matchmaker, and since he could bring together the living and the dead, I think of their marriage as almost an arranged one.

My mother's name was Elizabeth Trust, and she was known as Betty. Betty Trust is not a musical name but it has an evocative flair, as sweet and warm and homey as a cake. Le Chance met her at a wedding, through another undertaker she was dating at the time. I don't know if it was an all-undertaker affair, though more than one guest probably wondered where the flowers came from. When my mother broke up with her undertaker, she later told me, Charlie saw an opportunity for himself, having formed a wishful impression from the few facts he knew of her. "I was studying psychology, and had spent the summer in Europe," she explained. "He assumed that 'Free Love' was next." When it became clear that she was not the girl for him, he thought immediately of my father. He told each of them what he had in mind, and both seemed amenable to a meeting. It was not an obvious pairing, at least not for my mother, but then again, Le Chance was my father's friend.

My father was fifteen years older than my mother, approaching forty as she had just passed twenty. They were old-fashioned and good-hearted people, both the most intellectually ambitious of their families, but at ease with those who were not. As an FBI agent and a doctoral student in psychology, probing the underworld and the unconscious, they must have had a touch of the exotic about them, though exoticism in the working-class Irish world—or half-Irish, in my mother's case—was a large enough category, and could have included missing Mass or liking opera or living alone in Manhattan. Each had been engaged before: my father for several years, to a woman who kept postponing the date—in part, I was told, because my Uncle Gerry, a somewhat feral teenager, would join them in the new household. My mother broke off an engagement to a man who expected a more traditional wife than she was willing to become. My mother's undertaker followed, and my father must have begun to wonder if he'd meet his own undertaker before he met his wife.

My father dropped by to see her at Columbia University, where she was studying, and they went out for coffee. It was the late fall of 1960, an era that is harder to picture than those that preceded and followed: hair was still short, but the more current men had stopped wearing hats, as President Kennedy would, at his inauguration a few months ahead. My father kept his hat—always—and it covered gray hair. He wore a trench coat, stood six-foot-two, and weighed just over two hundred pounds (I have his FBI files, and these facts were noted). When he met my mother on campus, the other students probably would have guessed she was meeting an uncle before they suspected a date. The political temper of Columbia was earnest and liberal, with pro- and anti-Communist factions, and though I am sure the campus supported Kennedy over Nixon in great numbers, many would have preferred Adlai Stevenson to either. My father admired Kennedy, on the strength of his war record and as an epochal advance for Irish Americans, though he disapproved of his playboy lifestyle, which even then was something of an open secret. He voted for Nixon, perhaps following the inclination of Cardinal Spellman, who was said to be furious at the prospect of losing his position as First Catholic. My mother voted for Kennedy. As a subject for contention, I don't think presidential politics would have divided them any more than the fact that one was from the Bronx, the other from Brooklyn.

They weren't the kind of people who argued over these things any more than they were the kind who settled arguments by arm wrestling. It certainly wouldn't come up on a first date.

Their first, proper dinner date was on the evening of December 15, at the Commuter's Cafe, on Church Street in downtown Manhattan. The restaurant was owned by a close friend of my father's, an Austrian immigrant named Joe Tretter, and two of his brothers. The choice was shrewd: the food was good, the price was right, and they would be treated with extreme consideration. My father would be comfortable and confident there, unlike anywhere else respectable enough to bring a date. To walk into a good restaurant, exchange pleasantries with the maitre d', look at the menu, and order food—forget about wine—would have been an unnatural act, as alien to my father as flamenco or the Japanese tea ceremony. For many working-class New Yorkers, the most commonplace aspects of city life—restaurants, taxis, nightclubs—were as familiarly unreal as movies, and while you saw them every day, to find yourself in one could be traumatic. It may seem odd that headwaiters inspired more fear in my father than hijackers, but it doesn't now, to me—you're afraid of what you don't know. The date went well enough, until the plane crash.

There were two plane crashes, in fact, or two planes that collided in midair, over Brooklyn, killing one hundred and twenty-nine people in the air and six more on the ground. One little boy lived for a day, after falling from the sky into a snow bank. At the Bureau, they call this kind of event a "special," and the term can cover anything from a kidnapping to a jailbreak. Agents are pulled from their normal assignments to work on the incident. My father was working on railroad thefts and on my mother, though not necessarily in that order, but both had to be left alone for the moment. One special preempted another. He dropped her off at home and went to the crash site.

For the next several months, they went out once a week and regularly spoke on the phone. My mother thought he was a good man and enjoyed his company, but the relationship just seemed to amble along. When he picked her up for their next Saturday-night date, she told him that they had something important to talk about. As they drove, she told him that they should break it off—he was a nice guy, but things didn't seem to be going anywhere.

"Oh," he said. "I was going to ask you to marry me."

My mother reconsidered her assessment of their progress, and told him she'd have to think it over. After she decided in the affirmative, she told her mother, Anne, who in turn told her husband, Bill, "We're going to have a wedding in the family." Bill assumed that it was his son, and said, "That dumb kid, he doesn't have a nickel to his name, what is he getting married for?" Anne corrected him: "No, it's Betty who's getting married." And Bill said, "To who?" My mother said it was the most impulsive thing she'd ever done, and it was all the more telling in that her life was not exactly lived on a whim. And so what Le Chance began, choice finished.

. . .

THEY WERE DIFFERENT TIMES, BACK THEN. IN 1961, THERE WAS more time—so it seems now—for everything. There was less variety in how things turned out: more people got married sooner and stayed married longer. As my mother explains it, to be engaged meant something less than it does today: it meant you might get married, and you'd decide as you went along, and wouldn't date other people in the meantime. In that sense, it was a faster and less formal arrangement, which is not how I think of life then, when marriage was the substance and purpose of most women's lives. It was a given, as the draft was for men, and if it scared you during the haircut and physical, you were proud of yourself when all the fuss was over. To worry about it too much, or to try to escape, was either a weakness or a luxury, and my parents' backgrounds discouraged both.

My father met my mother's parents, and they got on well—he was as much their contemporary as hers. That he had a fine mind, a good heart, and a sense of humor would have been quickly apparent, and the fact that he was a gentleman—and a large, armed one at that—would have made them feel sure that their daughter would be safe with him. They liked him a great deal as a man, but his job and his background gave him no natural advantage in their sympathies.

The term "Irish cop" didn't have the same sentimental pull for the Trusts, in sum or in its parts, as it did for the Conlons. The Trusts were more Catholic than Irish, beyond even the obvious ethnic math of a match between Bill Trust and the former Anne Brown. St. Patrick's Day was not a landmark on the calendar, and bagpipes did not stir any deep feelings of ancestral glory and strife. Union jobs and the civil service did not earn the nearly cultish devotion they did on the Conlon side. The Browns came over after the Famine of the late 1840s; it had been three generations since anyone had spoken with a brogue. As for the police, they were to be respected, always, but the Irish cop they knew best was no hero to them, as Pat Brown had a long career in the NYPD but a short one as a husband. Despite the fact that my father was a very different man, I wonder if to my mother, or to her mother, he felt like a throwback sometimes. They were past that, and things got better all the time.

The Trusts were more American than the Conlons, in that sense, more comfortable and more optimistic. My mother was the third of four children—Ann, Dolores, Betty, Bill. Her two sisters married businessmen, and her brother became one. The roll call of the five Conlons read down from the FBI, the NYPD, the Transit Authority, nursing, and the New York City Fire Department. It surprised me when my mother told me that her family didn't have any more money than my father's—her father was a bookkeeper for an oil company, his was a laborer for the phone company—though both had remained employed through the Depression. Both my parents loved their families, but my father's childhood seemed one of confinement and loss, whereas my mother's was of warmth and safety. Their lives were differently lit: the six Trusts had a bright apartment in Flatbush, Brooklyn, where I can picture the family in the parlor, listening to Fred Allen on the radio. The seven Conlons lived in four small rooms at the back of a building on Kingsbridge Avenue in the Bronx, on the first floor over the alley. Sometimes an extra uncle took the kitchen floor. In the summer, the kids slept on the fire escape. They ate greasy legs of mutton and drank milk from jelly jars. My mother's family fussed over birthdays and took vacations every summer; my father's did neither. Later on, when we did celebrate his birthday, he accepted the custom with a dutiful confusion, as if he'd landed in Hawaii and we'd garlanded his neck with flowers. He'd raise his glass and say, "Happy Birthday, everybody." When I picture each childhood, my mother's has the genial formality of a sitcom from the 1950s, with amusing dilemmas resolved in twenty-six minutes; my father's is like a newsreel from the 1930s, set against a backdrop of breadlines and war.

My father's young life, which seems as remote to me as the war in which he fought, was related as a succession of sad facts and funny stories. He was the oldest in his family, and his parents had been dead for decades; all I knew of him was from his tales. But I knew my mother's parents, and her sisters' memories reached further back than hers. Her life was more lifelike to me, less a series of allegories than transparent memories without a moral, even, but also without a beginning or an end.

"Joe Daly would take us to see the Dodgers at Ebbets Field, and he'd always look so sharp in his porkpie hat . . ."

"When I was a little girl, you could ride the subway alone, even when you were eight years old, and they had wicker seats and windows that opened . . ."

"When we had a party, we'd gather around the piano and my mother would play . . ."

As I remember her, my grandmother Anne wore short-sleeved dresses and had large, freckled arms that shuddered rhythmically when she laughed and erratically when she didn't. She wore a gold charm bracelet, which also shook, and narrow glasses on a chain. At our house, she played a dinky electric organ, coaxing out "East Side, West Side" and "Give My Regards to Broadway" in a sweet, nostalgic wheeze. She and my grandfather joked and played cards and drank red-white-and-gold cans of Rheingold beer, which was made in Brooklyn, and which you had to open with a "church key." Their accents were old Brooklyn, and they sometimes said "terlet" and "erl" for "toilet" and "oil." I can't remember Anne being unhappy with us, or even ever being unhappy.

The blessedly ordinary life my mother led was her mother's doing, for the most part. Anne Brown had come from a broken home, and so she made hers rigorously whole. At one time, Anne thought about becoming a lawyer, but she decided to stay in with her children. And though she was a talented musician as well, she only played at church and home. Her mother Catherine lived with her after Anne married, though she died when my mother was two. Anne's brother, Jack, moved in after the war. Her younger sister, Eleanor, had a husband, who was also in the service, and three children. Eleanor patiently awaited victory and homecoming and then packed up and left, asking for nothing and offering less; more than half a century passed without a word from her. I'd heard of fathers who "went out for a pack of cigarettes and never came back," but I'd never heard of mothers doing that. "The war was hard on families," my mother said, tactfully.

My great-uncle Jack was in show business for a while. He was a crooner in the thirties, singing sentimental ballads in the low, smooth style suitable for radio broadcast at the time. He was as handsome as a leading man, athletic and elegant, with fine, strong features. In one photograph, he shares a studio microphone with a brunette wearing white flowers in her hair. The brunette is as white as the flowers, with wide, dark lips, and she looks at the camera. Jack is tan, darker than the Cuban-style shirt he wears, his hair is slicked back to show a widow's peak, and he looks down at the sheet of music. Her mouth is open, as if to sing "Ahh!" and his is half-closed, as if to sing

"Ooh!" The sheet he holds is folded in thirds, and the only part of the title you can read is ER KNOW. Maybe it was "You'll Never Know." In the late thirties, Jack was married to a piano player named Marie, and they played the big nightclubs in Manhattan. When Marie became pregnant, Jack went into a fugue state and disappeared for six weeks, until he was found, emaciated, wandering in a bus station. Marie stood by him for years, until she discovered him with company in their hotel room; when she told my mother about it, more than fifty years later, the shock was so fresh and the telling so elliptical that my mother suspected it was something beyond ordinary adultery. I felt the same way, when Marie told me, because when she reached the climax, she halted and said she couldn't, wouldn't *ever* say what she had seen. But Marie was a professional entertainer, after all, and perhaps it was better to leave it at that: *You'll never know . . .* After Marie left him, Jack took to drinking and declined from singer to singing waiter to waiter, and that's when he moved in with his sister Anne. He died a few years later.

My mother's young life strikes me as rich in every way except anecdote, which seems to need a degree of misadventure to thrive. As a teenager, she was bitten by a dog and had to suffer through the course of rabies vaccination, sixteen shots in the stomach. Aside from that, her life varied between things she liked and things she loved, and the majority fell into the latter category. She liked her neighborhood and she loved school; she loved her friends, she loved her family, and she loved her Church. Religion made her good, and it made her happy as well; it was a like a walled garden, where you were sheltered as you grew.

The Trust family had its share of calamity, to be sure, but even when it struck them, it seemed that they were shielded by some hidden and benevolent hand. From the 1950s on, at the end of every summer they went to the Pocono mountains for two weeks, first to a little bungalow colony in a town called Matamoros, and then to a hotel called Locust Grove. The other guests were like them, mostly Irish and Catholic and from Brooklyn, working-class and white-collar, for whom vacations were as new and American as highways. They sat, they swam, they played cards, then went for walks and began again. Every few minutes, someone would say, "Ah, what a delightful breeze," or, "Smell that country air!" My grandparents put plastic shields on their noses, or zinc oxide, or both; my mother avoided the sun as much as she could. She could get sunburn from a flashbulb. She liked the country better than the beach—the sun was less severe, and you didn't get sand in everything. When they swam, they went to the Delaware River, which by August is gentle, slow, and brown as tea, and you can walk across it in many places. Trees lean in over the banks, and you can put blankets down on the grass.

In the summer of 1955, the Delaware flooded. Heavy rains brought flash floods, and the river rose and swept its banks, taking from them houses, couches, horses, coffins. From the ridge in Matamoros where the Trusts were, they saw the flotilla pass by, a waterborne catalog of what people once had, like in the tornado scene in *The Wizard of Oz*. The ridge itself had been cut off from the land, and the river gained wildly in its new course. Trees and tons of earth were torn up, and the water was half-mud and trash-ridden, running fast and hungry. The Trusts were atop their diminishing sliver of land, waiting with a rowboat to see if they would be forced to flee. Within hours, they'd gone from vacationers to refugees. I wonder if they thought that if they reached the sea, they might row back to Brooklyn.

The water rose, and with it came the decision to leave. The family boarded the boat, a hectic chorus of afterthought and advice: "You sit there!"

"Not there—there!"

"Is everyone here?"

"Gently! Gently!"

The boat was filled with canned food, jars of water, blankets wrapped in plastic bags, wallets, purses, money, and jewelry—all they could not bear to part with that would not kill them on their trip. As they put in, my mother was looking into their bag of provisions, when she leapt out and ran back to the house—

"Betty! Wait!"

"Betty! What is it!"

"Betty! Come back, you little—!"

"Bill!"

Moments later, she emerged from the house, and ran back to the boat. She took her place again and set the bag down as the boat eased into the water. I try to imagine that moment when the force of nature and the force of family met, and which promised the greater violence. She was asked to explain her actions.

"It's Friday," she said.

Asked again for clarification, she reminded them of the ban of meat on Fridays.

"We took the wrong soup. We had chicken noodle, so I had to go back in the house to get the tomato."

If there had been a priest in the boat, he might have thrown her overboard, but as it was, her response was the only one that could not be gainsaid. I'm sure there was some comment, but what was even the risk of death next to the commandment of God? Circumstance did not permit further discussion. They set out upon the waters, then, and were spared the wrath of the flood, finding instead sanctuary on the far shores of the land, where they prospered and multiplied.

· · ·

MY FATHER HAD A RIVER IN HIS CHILDHOOD, TOO, AND A mother. His mother's name was Delia Laffey, though on some documents it was Della, and her age was a mystery as well. Delia was from County Mayo, twenty-odd miles away from the village where William O'Dwyer was born. Mayo, in the northwest of Ireland, is craggy and windswept, and the people were especially poor and Gaelic-speaking, which, in certain quarters, meant they were especially Irish. My grandmother came over as an indentured servant, just after the First World War, and on postcards she wrote home, the name is spelled Laife and Laffe before becoming Laffey, the Irish spelling suffering the same Anglo alchemy as that of her fellow immigrants from Naples or Kiev. No numbered address is given, only the family name in a village— more of a crossroads, really—that is alternately spelled Mohollogy and Mocollogan, a point on a map modified by place names almost as obscure: Tuam, Shrule, Ballinrobe, Mayo. Whatever shape the words took, Delia never had a problem making herself understood.

The river was the Hudson, dirty but still beautiful, gray as a battleship and as massive, flanked on its western shore by the tawny cliffs of the Palisades. Fifty Delawares could flow through its course. The sea washes up into it from the harbor with the tide, and over from the Harlem River, which is a tidal channel, flowing back and forth between the Hudson and the Long Island Sound. The Harlem River changes directions every six hours, running between Hell Gate and Spuyten Duyvil, Dutch for "Spit on the Devil" or "In Spite of the Devil," each a tribute to the treachery of its currents. When my father was eleven or twelve, he and his friends had a little rowboat they played with, below Spuyten Duyvil, in the stretch between the rock face with a huge "C" painted on it, for Columbia University, and the railroad bridge that marked the edge of the Hudson. Inwood Hill Park is on one side, and wild land along the railroad tracks on the other, and the boys could imagine they were the pirates who had worked the river through their grandfathers' days, or the Indians whose arrowheads still littered the hills of Inwood.

I don't know how my grandmother Delia found out about the boat; whether my father mentioned it innocently, or his brother Eddie did out of revenge for not being taken along. I don't know how well the boys could swim, if at all. Delia was from a part of Ireland where the fishermen could not, and their sweaters were knit in patterns to show which village they were from, so that their drowned bodies could be claimed if they ever washed ashore. She could have knit a "231st Street and Kingsbridge Avenue" sweater for my father, or she could have forbidden him to go boating. On the day the boys had planned the next river outing, she confined him to the house, leaving him to brood heavily on the injustice of it all. His mood did not lighten that evening, when he learned that the boat had capsized and two of his friends had drowned. My father was swept away, too, in wonder and dread, at the luck that mixed like the waters where the rivers met, pulling some under until their breath left them, sparing others to walk home to their mothers in the summer night. Delia must have seemed to have some power of fate in her, awesome in its love, awful in its cost.

My father also had a summer vacation, once. It was around the time that Delia sent him upstate with the Colored Orphans League, as I remember him calling the organization. The Boy Scouts were known as a Protestant group, and in her reckoning, he was better off as a white rarity than a Catholic one. Regardless, he had gone away grudgingly, and wanted only to go home. He was sent there with two vast cardboard suitcases of clothing that weighed more than he did; his mother anticipated that he would not spend much time doing laundry. She was right, my father told me: one suitcase remained unopened and the other was barely unpacked. I don't suppose he sweated much: he spent most of his time as the scorekeeper when the other kids played basketball or baseball. On the bus trip back to the Bronx, he watched the alien greenery of the countryside give way to asphalt and brick, the heat and crowds of the city, the thrill of home. When he arrived back at his apartment, he dragged his suitcases up the stairs and eagerly banged on the door.

But instead of the familiar, foreign voice of his mother, the consoling brogue to which he was more accustomed than to his own accent, the people inside spoke a different language entirely. A Sicilian family lived there, and the exotic sounds and smells made the shock of his displacement all the more acute. *"Little boy, those people, they move . . ."*

Down the stairs he went, weak in the knees from his luggage and loss, and he sat down on the sidewalk, crying. For all I know—and all he knew—he would have stayed there until he died of hunger among his clean clothes. But another Italian passed by, a vegetable and fruit vendor in his horse-drawn cart, and asked him what was the matter.

"Little boy, don't cry. You come with me, maybe we find them. . . ."

And so my father got up beside the vendor and wiped his nose, and put his belongings with the lettuce and potatoes and strange things he'd never seen before, like eggplant and artichokes, and watched the streets anxiously as the horse shambled along. Their progress was painfully slow as they moved through the route, but the novelty of the horse ride and the revival of hope distracted him from his plight. And they had ridden less than half a mile before he saw his brother Eddie in the street, playing handball with a group of kids, new to him but clearly friends.

"Hey, Eddie! Where do we live?"

Eddie was in the middle of the game, and pointed to a five-story apartment house of tan brick, with the name "Vanity Court" painted on the transom. My father blurted out his thanks, grabbed his bags, and ran inside to pound on the door. When Delia answered, his rage and relief took over him, and he complained senselessly through his tears. She laughed and kissed him, and said, "Ahh, Johnny, we knew ye'd find us."

Today, she would have been arrested. We might be doubly stunned, as my father was, by her apparent lack of feeling and her cold confidence in her son. But Delia had sailed to America in her teens; she knew no one, and she would never see her parents again. I don't know if she expected to. Sacrifice was ordinary, and survival was its sometime reward. In Mayo, the famine was especially harsh, and memories of it were recent and fierce. When my parents visited her village, in the 1970s, they looked up the family records in the church and found that after Delia's grandparents lost two children named Thomas and Bridget, they named their next two children Thomas and Bridget. You could see it as a commemoration and a forgetting at once. You moved on. Ireland then was both the Old World and the Third World, an economy in which sentimentality had little place. For my father, who was American-born, the divide between generations was compounded by culture, and he learned in time not to quarrel with it. Then again, she might have left a note.

A woman like my grandmother takes a war in stride. When Delia suspected it was coming, in the late thirties, she went to see Edward Flynn. Known as Boss Flynn, he had run the Bronx Democratic Party since the early twenties, as no one before or since. He represented machine politics not only at its most effective but its most progressive; he was one of the three or four men responsible, more than anyone else, for the election of Franklin Delano Roosevelt as President, and he remained an influential advisor and back-room champion of the New Deal. Delia went to see him to pursue an appointment to West Point for my father, reckoning shrewdly that his education would amount to a kind of deferment, and that the Army would be more thrifty with the lives of its new elites than with those of ordinary enlisted men. I don't know how she got in; Boss Flynn was atypical of those in his position in both his reputation for honesty and his inaccessibility—he was a lawyer, a cool-headed strategist rather than the smiling *padrone* handing out holiday turkeys. In any case, she did not secure the appointment, though I am impressed by the presumption of an immigrant woman demanding the best for her son, and by a politics that took immigrant women into account.

When she made decisions about her children, Delia was as hard and canny as Flynn, deploying her resources where they were needed most and could best succeed. I don't wonder why she never asked, "Well, if you can't take my Johnny at West Point, what about my Eddie?" Eddie had attended a series of high schools, and was asked to leave one because he rode a motor-cycle down the halls. His education was exclusively in Catholic institutions, in the apt belief that he needed the discipline, and the rest of the kids followed suit. My father, she felt, could go it alone among the pagans. As he recalled his grammar-school graduation from St. John's, when the Monsi-gnor read the list of graduates and which high school they would attend— Cardinal Hayes, Fordham Prep, All Hallows for the boys; Sacred Heart, St. Catherine's, Mount St. Ursula for the girls—the announcement of "Conlon" and "De Witt Clinton" was intoned like an obituary. The Monsignor did not shake his hand. My father did well at Clinton, and he graduated early; Delia had been right, no matter if it was little comfort at the time.

She was right about the war, too. When the Japanese attacked Pearl Har-bor, my father was enrolled at Manhattan College. In October 1943, he en-listed in the Marines. He went through boot camp at Camp Lejeune and Officer Candidates School, and was duly appointed second lieutenant. He continued his training and his education for the next year while stationed in Pennsylvania, before being moved to Los Angeles, in preparation for ship-ping out to the Pacific theater. Then Delia fell ill, with what was eventually diagnosed as liver cancer. She found this news extremely irritating, as she didn't drink, and thought the neighbors would whisper that she was a secret tippler. Around Christmas of 1944, my father received word that she had days to live. His superiors were sympathetic, but unmoved: no leaves were to be granted. Despondent, he found himself in the Officers' Club one night, where he met a Catholic chaplain. He confided in him, and as the details came out, the priest stopped him—he had been assigned to St. John's in Kingsbridge, he said, and he knew Delia. He told my father not to lose hope, and that he would be in touch. Within days, my father's leave was arranged, and he was home when his mother died, on New Year's Day, 1945. His unit shipped out without him, to what would become the battle of Tarawa. His OCS class suffered the highest casualty rate in the history of the Marine Corps. Delia had saved him, again. And then she moved on, again, beyond where he could find her on a horse-drawn cart, much farther than she had gone in her first emigration.

· · ·

MY FATHER MARRIED MY MOTHER BECAUSE HE LIKED HER life, I think, and hoped to have a family that fate would treat more like hers than his own. Often enough, when he got a call from a relative, it was because there was trouble to be sorted out: someone needed a job or was in jail. When she got a call, it was because someone wanted to know if she could bring a casserole to a christening. For her, marriage would be a great continuation of life, remaking for herself what she had known in childhood. For him, it would be a change: if they moved while a son was away at summer camp, she would let the child know. When the river rose, it would bear them to safety, and take neither them nor their friends down to the bottom. They would pack the right soup. As for war, they would have to trust in God, as everyone would, but He seemed to show special favor to Betty Trust.

My father's hopes were rewarded: they had nearly thirty years together, and five children, and even through the end of their years, they would take walks in the evening, holding hands. All the while, history happened: the *Daily News* headlines for each of our births tells of a million-dollar jewel heist at the Hotel Pierre (for Marianne); the ejection of a Cuban spy (for Stephen); a strike on the Long Island Rail Road (for Regina); a two-million-dollar drug raid (for me); and for Johnny, the oldest, on November 23, 1963, PRESIDENT IS SLAIN. My father spent his spare time reading about history, and he knew it well enough to keep it out of the house.

My parents didn't always agree, but I can remember only one argument between them, when he wanted us to get in the car before she was finished cleaning up the kitchen. It might have lasted two minutes, and their voices were barely raised. My father could aggravate her with his devotion to garage-sale bargains, and with his near-fanatic habit of book-buying, which at one point inflicted structural damage on the house. My mother had enough trouble keeping order with five kids, but she said, "I'd like him to lose some weight, and to try going to the library instead of the bookstore for a while. But he doesn't drink, smoke, gamble, or cheat, so how can I give him a hard time?" When you don't make many mistakes—or when whole worlds of mishap are closed to you—you begin life better than if you were rich.

I can say they were meant for each other, regardless of fate or Le Chance, because they matched. Not only in that they were loving and loyal to each other, a true union in what they worked for and believed in, but because she was tireless and giving, running the house and pushing him to do things he wouldn't have done on his own—which is to say, anything beyond sitting in his easy chair and reading. He brought the strange gift of his history, the sad facts and funny stories, the talent for wonder at the wild, wide life outside what little we thought we knew. Every marriage is a mixed marriage, joining two pasts for a new possibility. And one superstition was observed at their wedding, no matter if they were unaware of it. He was old, and she was new. The borrowed part was time, as all time is. The blue was in the blood.

THREE

Whenever I ran into George on the street, he told me things. The information was always good, but never quite useful. He confirmed things I knew, told me about witnesses to assaults and robberies who wouldn't come forward. He had an eye out for my gun collar: "There's a guy, he's in the park sometimes? He carries a nine. When he's with his girl, she's got the piece, in a knapsack." All right, that's some guy, known associate of some girl. Got it, ten-four. I paged him once or twice, and the call was never returned. Still, I knew there was more to come.

A month after I arrested him for his fight with Tonya, George slapped another teenage girl around, leaving her with a swollen cheek. She had argued with him, telling him some bad news about one of his baby-mothers, and he was furious because he believed her, or didn't, I forget which. "I don't know his last name," she said, and I told her not to worry, as I filled out the complaint, writing his vital statistics from memory. George lay low for a while, knowing I was looking for him. When the girl told me she had decided against pressing charges, I went to the record store where he worked—his brother, who was on parole for murder, owned the store—and left word that he wasn't wanted anymore. The next day, after roll call, a cop at the desk called me over and said, "There's some perp on the line, he wants to talk to you." George wanted to know for certain that he was in the clear, and after I reassured him that he was, he thanked me profusely. On the street, he was even more friendly and eager to provide. George played both sides, comfortably and well.

And then something happened at the record store. It was a successful business and a legitimate one, in that they made a lot of money selling a lot of records. But I'd bet that drug money started the place and moved through it, and that it served as a kind of information clearinghouse for serious gangsters, who planned and bragged of robberies, looked for crew and targets for new jobs. One evening, near closing time, when the staff and the last few customers were readying to leave, a man walked up to the glass door and fired five or six shots inside. No one was hit, no one was even cut by the rain of broken glass. The sloppy botch of it left it unclear who the intended victim was, and there was the usual chaos of conflicting statements—a dark-skinned man with dreadlocks, or short hair, was seen walking away, and running, into a black Lexus, a white Mercedes—and a tenor of cordial noncooperation. A dozen cops responded, a large crowd gathered, and I quietly took George aside. He told me, "We don't know what's up, but we're gonna find out. People gotta take care of business, but this was not right. There was women here, coulda been hurt. There's things I gotta check, I'll let you know."

That was the real pleasure of being a beat cop, the local authority and the free agency, to find things out and follow them where they led. I knew the seventeen red-brick towers of Morris Houses as well as anyone on my side of the fence, and when other cops were looking for someone from there, they were put in touch with me. A fire marshall asked me to help him collect an arsonist. Manhattan detectives showed me blurry video stills from a jewelry store stickup and I could tell them the guy wasn't around, I'd been to the apartment the other week for an Aided case. A detective in Staten Island was looking for a guy known as "Man" who had stabbed his girlfriend and thrown her puppy out the window; I'd locked him up for beating up a deaf kid, and was hunting him for assaulting another girl in his building. Child Welfare called me because one of their workers had been harassed by a man named Larry during the investigation of a case of child neglect, and I was quick to interrupt, "That would be Crazy Larry." He sometimes dated an enormous drunk woman who had loose custody of her niece's children, and when they were on the outs, he would leave threatening notes under her door. He had somehow obtained stationery from Bronx Lebanon Hospital, but the woman was able to discern that the crude scrawls of "You got the AIDS, Bitch! Fuck you, You got the Clapp!" were not the diagnosis of a qualified physician. In fact, I was there for the removal of the children, early one Sunday afternoon, when the woman's brother tried to wake her, pinching her nose and covering her mouth till she came to, pitching and bucking like a Brahma bull—she'd risen and fallen early that day, on fortified wine—and the caseworker walked past the three smiling children in playpens to examine the refrigerator and its solitary container of sour milk, when there was a furious pounding on the door. I inquired, "Who is it?"

The reply came: "This is the police! Who are you?"

I said, "This is the police! Who are you? Crazy Larry?"

"No, I'm the police, you're Crazy Larry!"

"No, you're Crazy Larry, I'm the police!"

"Police!"

"Crazy Larry!"

"Police!"

"Larry!"

In the end, I think I won the point, because he left first. Moreover, although we both get checks from the City, I still wear a blue uniform while he yells at fire hydrants on 169th Street and Washington Avenue. But I became known as the go-to guy of the Village, and because I didn't talk much except to mumble a number-heavy answer to a question—"Thirty-six-oh-three Third, Five Boy, yeah, I know, kid's wanted for a shooting, twelve-sixty Webster"—one cop took to calling me "Rain Man." Was it any wonder that I looked forward to work every day?

On Sunday mornings at my girlfriend's, I barely spoke, knowing the new week began in hours, and I felt the gleeful fear you get in the belly as the roller coaster idles at the crest before the first big drop. Once, I had a dream about work that drifted into a scene where someone was pounding furiously on my apartment door, and as I woke, I realized that the pounding was my own heartbeat. The crash course unexpectedly accelerated, after a year, when Osvaldo was transferred to another project and then Angel began coaching the NYPD soccer team, which meant that he mostly worked days. I was by myself most of the time afterward, and though a car would back me on heavy jobs, the routine pick-ups and run-ins had to be handled alone. I could make of them what I would, mountain or molehill.

One evening, I was called to an unbelievably petty domestic dispute. The woman was smug and derisive, the man looked like he was about to cry. They had argued, and then he'd taken a bunch of her videotapes and destroyed them. There was an irritating consensus to their positions: she demanded that I arrest him, and he demanded it, too, saying yes, he took the tapes, and yes, he destroyed them, because he hated her, and yes, most definitely, I should arrest him. While I usually didn't hesitate to make an arrest—I once locked up a woman who was eight months pregnant for robbery—she was such a bitch and he was such a baby that it became clear that I was not brought in to solve a problem but to join one. At the same time, I had two misdemeanors—Petit Larceny and Criminal Mischief—arising from a Domestic Incident, which, in the aftermath of the O. J. Simpson case, was treated by the Job with an inflexible severity. I took him in, not incorrectly but not without embarrassment, and I was glad that the DO didn't grill me on the details of the collar.

When the perp provided me with the details, I felt even worse. They had fought, and then she'd told him that she'd had an abortion, in the way she might have said she'd thrown away a box of candy he gave her. She'd been six months pregnant. When I called her later for additional information, she confirmed his account, telling the story in a rushed, victorious tone which might as well have ended with her saying, *Gotcha last!* I felt terrible for him, and I bought him soda and candy as we finished up, acting as much like his butler as his captor. He had a bench warrant in Manhattan for fare-beating, it turned out, and so I had to take him downtown from the Bronx. Hours had passed since the arrest, and when I dropped him off, he reached out with his cuffs for a kind of handshake and said, "You been good to me. I know a guy with a lot of guns in his house, I want to tell you about it . . ." I shook his hand and took his number.

I was clueless about how to obtain a search warrant, still less how to execute one. Suffice it to say at this point that it requires many hours of investigative and procedural labor, and the application itself must be approved by a captain even before you take it to a DA, and then to a judge. I met my guy a few days later, walked him in, and got it done. When I returned to the precinct, warrant in hand, and found the Special Operations lieutenant and the sergeant from the PSA's gun squad—it was acronymmed "FIST," for Firearms Interception . . . Something . . . Team—they were equally amazed by the wrongness of method and rightness of result, as if I'd gone to the Supreme Court and gotten a parking ticket dismissed. My guy—he wasn't even registered as an informant yet, which was one of many missed steps—was brought back in and grilled by both bosses. His story was as detailed and plausible as it had been before: he met a man he knew as "Bird," a street acquaintance of many years, who'd told him he had guns to sell. Bird had brought my guy to his apartment, which was the second building down from the southeast corner of College Avenue and East 170th Street, and taken him up to the third floor, into the second apartment to the left of the stairs, and in which there were a dozen semiautomatic and two automatic weapons, in the bedroom closet, inside a Pampers box. He said the reason he was doing all this was to thank me, and because he didn't like guns—his brother had been shot and killed. We put him in a van with tinted windows and he pointed out the building as we drove by; a Hispanic cop in plainclothes checked the inside and found everything to be as described. The cop also said the building was a cesspool, a hive of crime. They wanted to send them both back, together, but my guy began to stammer and shake; he thought Bird would know it was him. When they asked him to go back on his own, the fear spread through him like a fever, and he sweated and quaked, nearly in tears, telling me that he had no idea he was in for all of this. Other cops told me to watch it, that he was a perp at heart, and perps live to hurt cops. He did have a decades-old rap sheet, mostly for little things like stealing hubcaps, although Bird must have shared the cops' opinion to some degree, as he showed him the guns for a reason. But I didn't believe the other cops: I thought some perps lived to get high, and others lived to steal money, and others lived to show women why they ought to be afraid of them. And while I believed that most would prefer to see me get hurt if it meant I wouldn't catch them, I didn't think this guy, especially, would take such elaborate pains to just make me look like a jackass. But time would tell, wouldn't it?

When we readied to hit the door, we kept my guy in the precinct, so that if he was playing us, he wouldn't be able to call Bird to warn him. He seemed to shrink into the couch in the lunchroom, nearly catatonic. Twenty-odd cops were deployed in their various roles, and I drove the gun sergeant, a somber man with arms that were bigger than my legs, and who had never spoken to me before—all rookies and even most cops were invisible to him, aside from those who worked with him on his hunt. As we rode toward our destination, it was as if we were old friends; when we drew close, forming a line with the other cars, he quieted down, breathing deeply, and his intensity of focus had the torque of a diving fighter plane and the stillness of prayer. "There is nothing like this," he said. "Nothing." I believed him. We drove to the front and leapt from the cars, raced inside the building and up the stairs, and someone handed him a battering ram and with one swing he sent the door flying from the hinges, and he charged in, shouting, "Police! Get down! Don't move!" And

I was right beside him, gun in hand, bellowing as the rooms of the apartment opened up to us like conquered cities.

"Down! Down! Down!"

"Cuffs! Cuffs!"

"Hands! Lemme see your hands!"

"Clear!"

"Get down!"

We were inside for seconds before the dismay set in. There were women and children, and a few heavyset men in their underwear whose bellies shook as they raised their hands so high it looked like they were grabbing for God. There was supposed to be one young man and his girlfriend; the kitchen was supposed to be to the left, and there was supposed to be one bedroom, not three. Everyone was handcuffed and brought outside, and from the outset, the lieutenant took a pacifying tone, explaining that we had a warrant and what we had to look for. There were no protests, and a few tears. I searched the back bedroom, starting with the closet, which was packed from top to bottom. I found a Christmas tree, the good china, a dildo. I had never seen as many roaches in my life. I sweated through my T-shirt, vest, and even my blue nylon raid jacket, soaking it as if I'd been swimming. As a matter of course, we checked the entire apartment, and found nothing. The head of the household was one of the heavyset men; he was an EMT, recently retired, with a heart condition. He told us, "You could have hit any other apartment in this building and got a drug dealer." With abject apologies, we withdrew. My guy had been released from the precinct as soon as we hit the door, and apparently he fled at a gallop. I never saw him again, and never learned what kind of mistake I'd made. A few other cops patted me on the back and said, "They can't knock you for trying," but for the gun sergeant, I receded back into invisibility. I stripped off my wet clothing and returned to the paperwork, registering the informant. When the Special Ops lieutenant told me I had to pick a code name for the informant, I chose "Hindenburg." He didn't object.

As General Custer might have said, it was quite a learning experience. Afterward, I had mixed feelings about moving on to the next step. When I first came on the Job, I was hell-bent on getting my detective shield as soon as possible: complex and far-ranging investigations were what I was made for, I felt, not to mention the most exciting and rewarding part of the Job. But the best detectives were just that because they had years of street experience behind them, and the more I saw on patrol, with its daily wonders and horrors, the more I knew how far I had to go. I had a "hook"—once known as a "rabbi," a high-ranking officer I could call on for a favor—in my parents' friend Inspector Mullen, but I thought I'd better stay put for a while, and grow in the Job. The gun sergeant was right, there was nothing like it, that feeling when you're about to hit a door, but the feeling afterward, when I knew we were wrong, was distinctive as well. And there was a family on College Avenue who had their own feelings on the matter.

You can do it right and get it wrong, I knew, and I had no expectations that I'd leave that experience behind me, as a cop, no matter how long I was on the Job. One afternoon, a call came in for the sexual assault of a mentally retarded woman, who said she had been gang-raped by staff and residents at the group home where she lived. There was a sluggish chaos to the scene, as if the weight of the allegation made the littleness and lateness of what we could do all the more trivial. A plump young black woman with a heart-shaped face sat on the couch in her boyfriend's apartment, neatly dressed, surrounded by EMTs. She was in her late twenties, with the nervous smile of a schoolgirl at a piano recital. Her boyfriend, a wiry Puerto Rican man, had a rigid grin, and spoke in the roundabout affirmations of a drunk at a reunion: "I will always take care of her, she can stay with me, she wants to stay with me." I had asked him what happened. I asked him when she got there, and he began, "I will always take care of her. . . ." I took her aside and asked if she was raped, and she said yes. She said that she had since bathed and changed her clothes. The actions were typical of rape victims, but destructive of evidence. We left for the hospital.

We sat in the crowded emergency room, amid its flea market of trauma and disease. For a few minutes at a time, I was able to bring her into an examining room. When asked what happened, she shook her head, and said nothing. "But you were raped?" I asked again, and she nodded. I began the dismal catechism: "Did he put his penis in your vagina?" She nodded.

"Did he put his penis in your mouth?" She shook her head, no.

"Did he do anything else? Did he hit you or take anything from you?" Again, no.

"And you didn't want to have sex?" She nodded.

"Did you tell him you didn't want to?" She nodded again.

"Did you try to stop him? Did you try to run, or fight him, or yell for help?"

She said she did none of these things. How did she tell him she didn't want to have sex with him? "I told him I didn't want to."

"How many times? Once, more than once?"

"One time."

"And did anyone else do anything to you, was anyone else there when this happened to you?" They were alone, in her room.

"And do you know the man who did this?" She did. She gave his name, Roberto. I asked her how she knew him, and she said they both lived in the same group home.

The entire landscape of the facts had changed, like a beach swept away by a storm. The new contours of events left the old maps useless. I didn't know how the first allegations of gang rape, which the EMT had relayed to me, had been made. If the young woman was revising a gang rape to a date rape, the case might be lost. For most people, there is no easy transit between the territories of lies and truthfulness. If you're coming from one place, it's hard to believe you've been anywhere else. I had trouble asking her if she was retarded. Though I have managed to find the detachment to interview children about the vilest details of sexual assault without squeamishness—it gets easier with practice—to ask this young woman her IQ seemed like an insult: *Exactly how dumb are you?*

"Why do you live there, in the home?"

"Because my mother died."

"How long have you lived there?"

"Not too long."

"How long? A week, a month, a year, more?"

"A month."

"Your mother died a month ago?" She assented, and I said, "I'm sorry. Where did you live before? Here, in New York?"

She nodded, but when I asked where in the city she lived, she made the same face, mute with pain, as when I asked her to tell me about the rape, as if her old address was not just forgotten but successfully repressed. "Manhattan, the Bronx, Brooklyn, Queens?"

"Brooklyn."

"All right. Maybe it was Flatbush, Bed-Stuy, Canarsie . . ."

She confirmed that it was Flatbush, and I marshaled these particulars for the report. We waited a few hours, but there was no gynecologist available, so we were sent to another hospital. It was against the law to turn away rape victims, but the preferable course; the nurse apologized but said that we were expected, and the young woman would be seen immediately. I called for a car, and the victim seemed excited by the ride, looking around at the instruments and lights. At the next hospital, I stayed with her until they began the physical exam. She yipped like a puppy when blood was drawn.

Outside, I met a staff member from the group home. I didn't much like him. Though the initial allegations had been set aside, the home itself seemed tainted, still, in its failure to protect her even if its employees had committed no offense. He was a delegate of the crime scene. And he readily accepted her claims except for one: "The only thing that bothers me is her saying it happened at the home. Supervision is very good. I think it's highly probable that something did happen, but that it took place somewhere else." His version, unsolicited and abridged, was free of institutional liability.

I asked about the perpetrator, Roberto, and was met with a confused look. After some discussion, we concluded that it was an Alberto we were after: he had been her boyfriend, and he had recently been pressuring her for sex, even though she had broken up with him.

"She was sexually active?"

"Yes, she is. She uses birth control. Retarded people have rights, too. Our residents, they're adults, and can do whatever adults enjoy doing."

Something in the way he said it left me with the impression that there was lots of adult enjoyment going on there, and an image of the group home as Playboy Mansion idled uncomfortably in my mind. When the woman came out from the exam, she reacted with alarm at the sight of the staff member. "I don't want to go back there," she said. I assured her that it would not happen, and when two detectives from Special Victims arrived, they took her aside for a private interview. The administrator of the group home then entered the hospital, along with two more employees. My first impression was that she was organizing a counterattack. That was my second impression, too, when she announced, "I think all this is about her wanting to move in with her new boyfriend."

The flat-out dismissal of her story was startling. I didn't argue, partly because I was surprised, but mostly because her certainty, however ugly, cut through all the muddy misinformation. I wanted to be sure of things, too. I remarked that the woman might still need time to get used to the place, so soon after her mother's death. "Soon after what?" the administrator asked.

"Her mother's death."

"Her mother died when she was a child."

"How long has she been with you?"

"For years, since she was a young teenager."

"She didn't live in Brooklyn with her mother till recently?" Her mother and Brooklyn were inventions. My questions to her were leading, I knew—she'd picked Brooklyn from a menu of choices—but if she hadn't been drawn out to tell me what happened, she wouldn't have spoken at all. Without her story, we had nothing, and I was certain there was something there.

But when the doctor and the detectives had all concluded their interviews, there were still more revisions. The rape allegations were dropped entirely, and she now said only that Alberto had molested her. The medical findings were inconclusive. One detective reminded me that whatever sympathy I might feel for this woman, the perpetrator was also retarded, and if we were to move forward on her allegations, we would appear for him like a bad dream as he ate dinner or watched TV, hauling him off in handcuffs for a night—at least—in a cell. "We can't go forward with this," he said. "It's an unstable story. You can't put a retarded boy through all that with a story that isn't stable."

I went to talk with the young woman again, asking her the same questions she'd been asked all day, which somehow meant something different to her each time they were put to her. She had the same flighty, schoolgirl manner, with eager smiles alternating with pursed, apprehensive frowns. I asked her if Alberto put his penis in her, and she said no, and I asked her if Alberto put his hands in her, and she said yes. I offered to get her a drink or some candy, but she declined. "You must be getting tired of all these questions, over and over," I said. She smiled and nodded.

"You remember before, when I asked you if Alberto put his penis in you, and you said yes? And now you said no? Can you tell me why, did you not understand?"

The smile left her as she looked at me, plaintively, as I led her out. "Come on, now, it's time to go home," the administrator said. The woman began to tremble, then to cry.

"It's all right, honey, nobody's gonna make you do anything—" and I was about to say, "that you don't want to do," which I had told her before, but instead said, "that isn't right." She cried and she looked at me; she may not have told me the truth, but she knew that my promise would be broken as well.

The administrator was her legal custodian and had the right to compel her to return. I pointed out that there was a core of consistency in her claims some kind of abuse had occurred, that her bathing and washing her clothes were telling, that if the police could do little, for now, the group home had to do more, at least in keeping Alberto away from her. The administrator concurred, and the detective also agreed I would rewrite the rape complaint as "Investigate sexual abuse," for follow-up by the precinct squad. And the young woman cried now like a motherless child, sobbing with such force that she could barely catch her breath, wailing she didn't want to go, she wouldn't. The administrator and the staffer led her away, not without kindness, but with a cool finality because nothing she could say would change a thing.

· · ·

I MADE MY FIRST CONFESSION WHEN I WAS SEVEN YEARS old. Though I don't remember what I said, I suspect it wasn't even half the story. The other kids talked about making things up, so as not to disappoint the priest, but I never would have done that. The confessional was of the old, highly cinematic variety: a dark and curtained booth, walled to separate the priest from the penitent child. When you walked in to kneel on the velvet bench, a little grille slid open with a whoosh and a click, like a secret passage in a haunted mansion, prompting you to speak: *Bless me, Father, for I have sinned . . . this is my first confession.* Later on, you would say that it has been ten days or one month or twenty years since your last time, but this was the first, which is why I wanted to make an impression. The terror of the encounter was eased by the grandeur of what was promised: full pardon from God, and the assurance that the priest could not tell anyone what we did, ever, not even if he was tortured by Russians. I had a hard time coming up with things to say, knowing that, all in all, I was a good boy—I think I owned up to fighting with my brother, not cleaning my room, and the like, which were suggested examples of age-appropriate offenses—and also that I had some real grasp of true sin; of hate and greed and self-pity. My experience of these may have been more in thought than in deed—though I may have been genuinely enraged at being sent to bed when I wanted to watch TV, I didn't burn the house down—but my inability to confess was only partly because I couldn't find the words. Had I known them, I would have been just as reluctant to speak. I couldn't say that I'd wished my sister was dead when she broke my toy, even if I'd taken it back as soon as I'd thought it. And so when I confessed, I felt good and clean and new not only because I had been pardoned for the little things I had done, but also because I had escaped the ordeal with my real sins safely locked away, where they belonged.

A few pages into his *Confessions,* St. Augustine says that no one is without sin, even a newborn child. Because he is not only talking about Original Sin, he is ready to be ridiculed—"Was it a sin to cry when I wanted to feed at the breast?"—but he nonetheless holds that "if babies are innocent, it is not through the lack of will to do harm, but the lack of strength." Unlike most saints, Augustine was also a father, and the icy bite of the perception seems unsentimental rather than unloving. Babies strike out and scream not only for what they need, but for all that they want, whether food, attention, a lit candle, or a sharp knife. With children, this absence of judgment and control springs from natural limitation rather than any moral shortcoming, but it shows that sin is something missing, and that it can be seen in human nature from the beginning. And often we do not know what is missing until we look for it and find that it is not there.

At home, my first real confession came six years later, when I was thirteen. The teenage conflicts with my father were yet to come, and even within my family, I was thought of as truthful, more quick to come clean than the others when the five of us skulked around a broken cookie jar. I could be depended on to admit what I had done. I would confess, but not inform, and I don't recall ever being especially pressed to do so. But in a sense, all children are informants for their fathers—though perhaps the comparison would only occur to a cop—in that what they do and how they think tells a father things, which he would bear in mind to meet whatever trials or mysteries lay ahead. My father knew that I would make mistakes that he never would, and encounter possibilities that he could only imagine; that I would be the cause of many troubles, and that I would have to help him find their cure. I wonder if he had any ulterior motive when he told me—apropos of what, a war story, a history lesson, nothing?—that it was a rarity for anyone to hold up under a sustained interrogation. Almost no one holds out, he said, and it was not long after he told me this that he proved it.

In the winter when I was in eighth grade, there was a tremendous blizzard, and I went out with a few friends early in the evening to enjoy it. We did so by making heavy, wet snowballs, heaving them at random houses in the neighborhood, and then running like hell. One highly satisfying shot walloped a glass front door, prompting an unexpectedly rapid response from the man who lived there. We scattered: I ran with another boy named Joey Quinn, and as the man drove up on us we split again, and the man caught me. He then returned me to my house, where my father thanked him and said he would deal with it. To give some indication of how my luck was running at that point, after a brief conversation it emerged that the man was not only a police officer but that he worked in the same precinct as Uncle Eddie.

He left, satisfied that justice would be done. I offered up terrified denials of having thrown the snowball, as I had done on the ride home, but for some reason the line of questioning was exclusively directed to the identity of the boy with me. I said I couldn't tell, I wouldn't, and my father took me downstairs to the basement. He had never hit me, and he didn't then, but there was something significant and dreadful in the transit. My mother was alarmed, calling out, "John . . ." The syllable carried every meaning, as if to speak his name should remind him who he was, which was a good man who did not lose control, no matter the provocation. But he was also an interrogator by trade, and downstairs we went. It did not take long. His voice was cold and concentrated, with a force that seemed all the greater for being held in check, like the surging of a river at the head of a dam.

"*Give . . . me . . . his . . . name!*"

"Joey Quinn . . . but we didn't do it!"

The speed of my surrender astonished me as much as the defiance of my lie. There was another call from my mother—"John!"—which brought it all to an end. The glass was not broken—there were no damages to be paid, only order to be restored—and so it went no further. My punishment was sufficient, I think, when I heard my father tell the man in a tone that was modest but final, "I know Eddie. He's an honest boy, and he wouldn't lie."

And though the glass did not shatter, my friendships did. My father was disappointed to hear Mr. Quinn's testy denial that *his* son could *ever* do such a thing, though in truth, Joey was a bit of a thug. Those boys and a few others made much of it for a month or two, yelling insults and cutting me out of their circle. To my shame, I knew that this exclusion was only slightly more vehement than others I had known in the past, when I had joined in the derision of whoever was the outcast for the season. I knew also that in time, if I took my lumps, I'd be let back in. But when time did pass—not much time, but it didn't pass quickly—I didn't want back in. Had any of them been walked down to the basement, I was sure, names would have been supplied as well as Social Security numbers, not to mention a complete confession of every snowball ever thrown. We were in the eighth grade, and would go on to different high schools the next year. Most of my friends would attend Catholic schools in Westchester County, whereas I was going to Manhattan, and if I accepted the prospect of change with equanimity before the winter, afterward I positively looked forward to it. Somehow the finality with which I discarded my friends now seems colder than their playground swinishness. But as I look back, I note both that the role of the informant presents itself to those in need of escape, and that a confession, even if its candor is not complete, can take you much farther than you expected to go.

. . .

BEFORE YOU HAD A CONFESSION, YOU HAD TO HAVE A COMplaint. For cops, there was never any shortage of complaints, formal and otherwise: the crime reports we wrote were called complaints, and when the DA wrote up a charge, it was called a complaint, and when a civilian accused a cop of wrongdoing, it was also a complaint. We complained among ourselves, about bad food, hurting feet, lousy bosses, long hours, and little money. We complained about the sun and the rain. We did have a lot to complain about, within the Job and without, but some cops seemed to lose the power of speech altogether, except for complaining. And most of the others tried to stay away from "hairbags," as they were called, not so much because the complainers were wrong about anything in particular, but because you didn't want to be persuaded of the larger point of view. It was tempting sometimes, though, because if you listened to the neighborhood, the news was rarely good, at least when it was talking to you.

At the same time, I was becoming friendlier with the cops at the command. For the most part, we got along in the house, and on the street, I knew I could depend on them. I didn't hang out much, aside from the occasional Christmas party or racket, as benefits are called, but in general I became less standoffish. I was known as a collar guy, dependable on the street, and the bosses treated me well. They even finally learned to tell me apart from Coyne. I was offered a spot on one of the Target Teams, but I turned it down. I still liked my post, and it seemed that in those groups, there was always one cop who annoyed the hell out of everyone else. But I was starting to itch for something more, and I admired the plainclothes teams, Anti-Crime and SNEU, the Street Narcotics Enforcement Unit, whom I'd sometimes see sweep through the project and come up with a heavy stash or a gun. I was mostly self-taught, which you have to be, if you want to learn how to handle yourself on the street, but there were a lot of cops in the command who played at an entirely different level, with perspectives and moves that were well beyond my own. Still, while I waited for the next step, I would take things as far as I could. And when you took that approach, things could move faster than you expected.

At first glance, and occasionally even after some thought, it could appear that the worst of the neighborhood *was* the neighborhood. Though the obvious signs of the ghetto were painfully plain, the subtler attributes were equally depressing. One day it struck me, as I looked around for a newspaper, that there were only three or four places around the Village that carried them, and I doubted if they sold a hundred copies of the *Post* and the *News* a day, and half as many Spanish-language papers. The *Times* was not found at all. At a rough but generous estimate, 2 percent of the neighborhood read a daily paper. You saw what happened when people got used to not paying for things: though the hospital was a block away, people called for ambulances constantly when they had 99-degree temperatures or mild diarrhea; or worse, they claimed to have chest pains or difficulty breathing because they needed prescription refills, and didn't want to walk to the pharmacy or wait in line. The ride cost them nothing, so they'd take it every time.

Whenever there was an attempt at physical improvements to the projects, it usually reflected a Charlie Brownish determination that this time—*this time!*—things couldn't be smashed or burnt so easily or so often. Good old Charlie Brown: after a spate of fires, the Housing Authority repainted every single stairway with fireproof paint. All the talk about the fires led some people to set even more, proving that the paint was not as fireproof as advertised. Was the paint even fire-retardant? No matter—to make a difference it would have to be shit-retardant and bullet-retardant, or maybe just retard-retardant. The Housing Authority then stripped the hallways down to the bare concrete and cinder block, which became saturated with urine and graffiti, neither of which couldn't be mopped away. If you needed to get onto the elevator for an emergency on the eighteenth floor—a robbery, or a violent dispute—you often risked riot by telling people they had to wait for the next elevator. I did take some pleasure on one downward trip, with a DOA. The gurney was too long for the elevator, and it was stood up; the bagged body was on its feet, just out of sight of the doors. When we stopped on a floor, midway, a man stepped toward us and I said, "Sorry, you'll have to get the next one." He made the spit-face and the spit-sound—*Ptuh!*—because nobody was going to tell *him* what to do, and he strode inside. He met the corpse, face to face, and fell silent. His deliberately reversed footsteps had the quality of mime: *Here I am, leaving.* "Thanks for your cooperation, and have a nice day."

As a cop, I took some consolation from the fact that when people did wrong things, they did them the wrong way, too—nearly thoughtlessly, with the lazy malice of a chain snatch, or the drunken impulse of a punch. If the bad guys put much thought into what they were doing, we'd be hard pressed to catch most of them. And so when I responded to a "possible shooting," I felt it was one of the more sinister incidents I'd run across: an eighty-year-old Jamaican man heard a knock at his door, and when he opened it, he felt a slight resistance, and then he heard a pop and felt a sting in his hand. The elevator was directly in front of his apartment, and he saw the elevator door close as he opened his own. He had to think for a while, he told me, but he came to believe that he'd been shot in the hand—there was a pockmark in the flesh between forefinger and thumb, which an X-ray later proved to be a pellet. But while the crime itself resulted in relatively minor injury, the scene revealed a perpetrator of some elegance and real evil: the light bulb was unscrewed in the elevator, and a length of string dangled from the doorknob. The perp had waited in the dark, with the string attached to the pellet gun, so that when the door opened, it pulled the trigger. The old man believed it to be a boy in the building named Hassan, a hulking and I thought doltish teenager, who'd threatened him after he'd told him not to hang out in the lobby, smoking blunts and leaving garbage. The crime did show an adolescent delight in whiz-kid plots and gadgetry, but there was also a cold-blooded calculation, and several aspects—the choice of victim, the staging of the trap so that the victim would participate and the perp could watch—were so disturbing that I felt there was more to come, from Hassan or whoever it might be, and that his future efforts would be felt beyond the Village, long after I left.

Old people told me how beautiful the projects had been when the buildings were new and people were proud to live there. And while there was something forlorn about those whose ideal of civilized living was the public housing of the South Bronx, circa 1960, it was perhaps sadder still to consider the eye of the beholders, myself included, and what they now beheld. For those immigrants, whether from Kingston, the Carolinas, San Juan, or even Harlem, Morris Houses was a new world of elevators and refrigerators and mowed lawns, a cherished opportunity and a respected trust. And so when people from the neighborhood took it upon themselves to demand a restoration of dignity and decency to their surroundings, I was glad to work for them as hard as I could.

In one of my worst buildings, two women decided to set up a tenant patrol. The building had half a dozen crack spots and was the scene of a recent rape and murder; it was a place that belonged to the bad guys. Chief among them was a family named Bodie, whose apartment had seen occasional shootings, constant drug sales, and the death of a child who'd overdosed on crack, eating it from the table where it was being packaged. I knew the eldest son, Alvin, who was alleged to be the worst of the bunch, and, strangely enough, he liked me; early on, I'd walked into him buying heroin on the street, and because I could only grab the seller, he thought I'd given him a break. Also, his mother was ailing, which brought me to his house a number of times with EMS, and he appreciated how I treated her. (The mother was also the reason management was unable to evict the family.) Alvin held no menace for me: he was in his late twenties, scrawny and a little stooped; I knew he was a junkie and I'd heard he had AIDS. I felt that sooner or later I'd catch him at something, or turn him to work for me, and if he was the worst the building could offer, the odds were not so daunting.

The two women who constituted the new tenant patrol were not to be easily dissuaded, either. Both were middle-aged black ladies, though the resemblance ended there. Ms. Smith was proper and devout, and her conversational style was one of gentle persuasion. Ms. Cunningham hit you like an A train. I'd had a brief confrontation with her once before, after I'd written her son a summons, I think for Disorderly Conduct, and she'd come at me bellowing, "Why you gotta harass my son, who's minding his own business! Mm! If you cops went out to catch the rapists and killers like you go to bother my child, then this would be a lot better neighborhood!" It was a classic project-mama harangue, delivered in the timeless and full-throated black-lady gospel voice whose dug-in defiance is a beautiful thing when directed against injustice and a huge pain in the neck when it's directed against you. "It's just a ticket, lady, he deserved it and he's getting it." But somewhere along the line, Ms. Cunningham decided that I was the least of her problems, or maybe not the problem at all, and we worked well together.

Ms. Smith and Ms. Cunningham sat together, almost every night, without any help from the other tenants. I'd stop by two or three times, if I could, and do a vertical, top to bottom, or just wait with them. Anyone who didn't want to sign the visitor's log got an earful from Ms. Cunningham, and if that wasn't enough, a 911 call that brought me over. If she complained about a tenant, they'd better watch their step. While many tenant groups worked with the police, usually in a somewhat clandestine way, Ms. Cunningham and I had an openly declared alliance, which reflected her own fearlessness more than any faith in me. She told me about a girl who'd let her pit bull loose in the playground, and the next time I saw the girl, I wrote my first and only unleashed-dog summons. It was difficult to see any immediate effect on the building, but the effect on us lightened the heart. Though I knew several of the crack spots beforehand, Ms. Cunningham told me about the rest of them, and I sometimes stood guard in front of their doors. It was not what you'd call interesting work, as such, but it felt important, and it pointed out a lesson of the peculiar value of patrol: when in doubt, don't just do something, stand there.

As I stood, I watched. When I saw certain children, I wondered how much time it would take to tell if they'd grow into the next generations of Cunninghams or of Bodies. The day after I locked up a man for beating his wife, I saw his two daughters in the street. They were perhaps six and eight years old, and they clung playfully to my hands like a favorite uncle as they asked, "Where's Daddy?"

I knew that some Mafia mothers told the kids, "Daddy's away at college" when their husbands were guests of the state, but I could neither think of a fairy tale to tell them nor see the point of telling it. "He's in jail," I said.

Neither stopped hanging from me, but the older one took a peevish tone, as if I'd said there'd be no dessert until she finished her dinner: "He didn't kill nobody."

"No, he didn't. But he treated your mom bad."

The little one did an uncanny imitation of her immigrant mom: "Oh! He a no-good man, he a no-good man!" And then the older one asked, "When can we come see him, tonight?"

"No."

"Can we see him without permission?"

"No, you cannot," I said. I patted their heads and they ran off to play. Whenever I'd run into them, they'd rush over to greet me. The last thing I wanted was to trouble them, but I was struck by how untroubled they seemed to be.

My own troubles were becoming clear, at least in type. While certain incidents bothered me for a while because of the misery I'd seen, like the maggot lady, or because of the mistakes that I'd made, like Operation Hindenburg, I'd take what I could from them and move on. But certain kinds of encounters were becoming more common, and more tiresome. While it was rare that I didn't feel safe on the street—even when I've faced off against hostile crowds, I've known that help, in droves, is moments away, and I'd usually be more concerned with someone getting hurt racing to help me, if the background noise on my radio sounded like the fall of Saigon. Almost all the people I've fought with, hard, were trying to get away. It was the little things that got to me, and the little things had a knack for getting bigger.

The issue was "Quality of Life," one of the cornerstones of the crime-fighting policy of the new regime at the NYPD. The theory was that if you ignored all the other forms of low-grade disorder that formed the backdrop of inner-city life, the center-stage crimes like robberies and shootings tended to thrive. The practice meant nearly ceaseless confrontations with people hanging out, whether they were relaxing on a Friday night after a hard week of work, or did so as a way of life. The groups that loitered in the lobbies and in front of the buildings provoked perennial complaints from management and the tenant patrols. Sometimes they were just noisy and messy, leaving beer bottles and blunts all over, and often enough selling drugs was the pastime if not the purpose of the congregation. While many people called 911 to report drug sales or a gun merely to get cops to clear out some loud teenagers, others were as crankily suspicious of their neighbors as any white bigot from the sticks, and could not conceive of any innocent meeting of a few friends with a free hour. One man in Manhattan had recently been charged with manslaughter, after a cop was killed racing to the scene of the "shots fired" he routinely and falsely called in to clear his stoop of rowdies. But for every gun run that proved unfounded, there were many others that went unreported, and the irony was that, on my beat, even when the calls were false, they tended to become true, if the buildings were neglected.

In the process of working for a better quality of life for a neighborhood, the quality of life for a cop usually went downhill for a long time before its theoretical ascent. When I worked alone, the dynamic changed: I got better but the Job got bigger, and the cornerboys were more likely to step up to one cop than two. As I learned the beat and the beat learned me, the warning called out over the dice game changed from "The cops are here!" to "That cop is here!" (One kid called me "Cuco," a Puerto Rican word for "bogeyman," which I took as a compliment when I finally found out what it meant.) Often it went smoothly, but it never stopped, and I sounded like the bartender at last call, "You don't have to go home, but you can't stay here." They came back and I cleared them out; they iterated and I reiterated. I was a glorified hall monitor, and it was often hard to see the glorification. The paradox of these petty run-ins was that the power of the cop increased as the stakes grew less. As long as the offense was a violation, it was completely within my discretion, as a matter of statute, whether or not to issue a summons. In the event of an assault or a theft, the facts and the law dictated my actions; in the event of three or more persons gathered together in a public place who refused a lawful order to disperse—one of the seven subsections of Disorderly Conduct—the person decided what I'd do. I was constantly amazed by how many people talked me into arresting them.

If I saw a bunch of guys on a bench with their boom box and beers, I'd stroll over to them, taking into account how late it was and how loud they were, which would determine whether I'd say, "What's up, guys?" or "You gotta keep it down, guys," or "That's it, you guys gotta break out, we got complaints." But what I wanted most was a reaction, offering my blue uniform as a litmus test, to see how they saw me, which is to say, how they saw the rules. Would we both bend them together, showing enough respect to earn a little give? Sometimes I'd pass by and I'd get an almost friendly acknowledgment, especially when they realized the party wasn't necessarily over, and sometimes I'd get a catcall after that, as I was walking away, and sometimes I took it for a weak little joke that wasn't worth a response, but other times, the challenge was unmistakable, and then impossible to ignore.

"What the fuck are you gonna do about it?"

For as long as there has been an NYPD, every cop has had to answer that question, and always—at least at first—alone. In Pat Brown's early days, he would have beaten the cobblestones with his locust-wood nightstick to summon aid, while cops of Uncle Eddie's era might have had to find a callbox. Although I had instant access to faster backup, the moment would be as it was for them, and the answer would have to be the same, too: *Whatever I have to.*

For cops, respect is seen as the foundation of safety. While individual circumstances were always open to interpretation, rudeness or even overfamiliarity can be seen as an opening to physical threat. When people start to scream at you, their loss of control can escalate into violence. And whatever has to be said, whether in anger or in need, should be said from at least five feet away. No one is going to point a finger in my face, or step up, chest to chest, as if they're protesting a call to the umpire, thinking the technical lack of contact will keep them from being thrown out of the game. Drunks often want to shake your hand, and so do ordinary people on occasion, if you've returned their runaway daughter or decided not to write them a ticket, and though I'll return the gesture for the latter, it's never without a flicker of awareness for what could come next, now that someone has a grip on my hand. In the balance between preparedness and paranoia, the more lopsided confrontations can be the more dangerous, especially when older people, young teenagers, and women in general need to be separated or stopped. If you have to get physical with someone with whom your upbringing forbids you to be rough, your concern is with your dignity rather than your safety, and both are put at risk. In one of my buildings, a cop was slashed in the face by a woman with a razor. I knew them both, and wondered if his vigilance was less because she was a female, if only because I suspected mine would have been.

In some ways, the cop code and the ghetto code reflected each other in a fun-house mirror. Respect was everything, though on the streets, it meant so much that it meant nearly nothing. It should mean a kind of esteem or at least an equal regard—*R-E-S-P-E-C-T, find out what it means to me*—looking eye-to-eye at someone, if not up. When a drug dealer told me I was all right, that I treated him with respect, I had to laugh. What did that mean, that I didn't slap him around on sight? I would nod at people, good or bad, when I walked, but for the bad guys it was a way of saying I'm out here, watching you. Maybe they misunderstood me. In the ghetto code, respect could mean fear, as in I won't attack you because you're bigger than me, or it could suggest some small consideration, as in I'll sleep with your girlfriend but I won't feel her up in front of you. But while respect was reduced to some tiny and temporary relief from contempt, perceptions of disrespect—the infamous "dis"—could be seen all around, in the nuances of a word or gesture, even a glance, provoking violent and sometimes lethal reaction. And the ghetto could be a world of three-dimensional, three-hundred-sixty-degree insult, where no one had enough so they ruined what they had, and then came looking for yours. Here, you moved up as others fought their way to the bottom. You had to *represent*, it was said, and often people did it too well.

Rap music has its roots in the Bronx, in the 1970s, with DJ Kool Herc and Afrika Bambaataa, and though gangsta rap started as a West Coast style, it is heard—and felt—here, too. A musical style became a personal stance, for the last man standing. The civics lesson of gangsta rap is of feral individualism, where desperate claims to fame rest on girls, guns, and gold. While the music's embrace of drug dealers and pimps is widely and wearily decried, to describe gangsta rap as a new low in the culture is, at best, half true. In the lyrics and the police reports, thug life is a litany of petty slights that lead to brutal slaughter, but it is also the story of the Trojan War. Ten years of siege and suffering began with an insult to Paris and continued through an insult to Achilles, inspired by gods you wouldn't trust with your wallet or your sister. "I sing of arms and the man" might sound a loftier note than the nigga-trigger rhymes of Tupac Shakur, but the spirit is often the same. We might not like it, but it's not as if we've never seen it before.

Once, someone hit me with a brick from a rooftop. Glancingly, off the arm, and it barely left a mark. I wondered whether they considered it a hit or a miss, and then wondered if I really wanted to know. There was a hideous litany of assaults on cops, some fatal, that had gone unpunished: in the Five-O, PO Vincent Giudice responded to a violent domestic dispute, in which a man with a long arrest record was beating his girlfriend. He threw a mirror that cut Giudice's femoral artery, and he bled to death. The perp was convicted only of a misdemeanor assault on his girlfriend. There was no conviction for the attempted assassination of a captain named Joseph Plavnick, who was shot as he stood outside the Four-Six precinct; or for the shooter of Capt. Timothy Galvin, of Bronx Narcotics, who supervised a search warrant at the apartment of a black nationalist, where a cache of weapons was recovered. The subject wasn't home at the time, but when he returned, he shot Capt. Galvin in the face, and later claimed that he mistook him for a burglar. After the verdict, one juror was quoted as saying that Galvin "got what he deserved."

From twenty stories up, bottles, eggs, and blocks of ice can cause immense harm, and this kind of "airmail" has missed me by a few feet or less, more times than I'd like to count. A canned ham once, too, which would have made me one very pissed-off ghost. It's hard not to take that kind of thing personally, and I keep a piece of that brick on my desk. Sometimes I thought of mounting it on a plaque that said PRESENTED TO POLICE OFFICER EDWARD CONLON BY THE PEOPLE OF 420 EAST 169 STREET, IN APPRECIATION FOR HIS DEDICATED SERVICE. But it would have been wrong, for any number of reasons. First, because it wasn't true—I knew good people in that building, including Mr. Ferguson, a retired Housing cop who sat tenant patrol. And maybe more important, because it's a bad way to think, to imagine that it was a message from the people, that there was an "everybody" out there, unappreciative of my work or even looking to hurt me. Many people were unappreciative, and, too plainly, there was at least one person who thought it a joke or better to see me die, but there is no such thing as "everybody," anywhere. The way I worked as a cop was to know the basics, trust my instincts, and make it up as I went along. I had to be careful that it didn't make me up as I went along, too.

. . .

FROM THE EARLIEST DAYS, THE PUBLIC HAD A MIXED VIEW of the Department, a melange of derision for the loafers who hid in taverns and admiration for the stalwarts who kept peace on the street corners. The middle classes tended to hold them in more favorable regard than did the poor. Through the 1880s, most cops were Irish, as were most criminals, and it was only later that ethnicity compounded with economics to exacerbate tensions between the police and the poor. In general, popular support of the police department reflected that of the administration they served, for whom they provided a strong arm and a public face. Problems in the government were most visible in the police department, and it was often the test case for experimental medicines for the larger body politic. Municipal housecleaning often began and ended there.

As a result, the police viewed their lot with pride and resentment, with the latter predominating. In the view of one historian, the rank and file "had little faith in their leadership and little pride in their calling," and "faced with an impossible task, they responded with less than total dedication." Police stations also served as lodging houses for vagrants and transients, exposing cops to all kinds of communicable diseases. Although they were paid somewhat better than the laborers at the time, and enjoyed benefits such as paid vacations and a pension, they worked an arduous and complex schedule, and even when they were off duty, they had to be available in the event of a riot or other emergency. A schedule for Monday through Thursday for a patrolman, beginning at six a.m., would include two hours of patrol, five hours of reserve, five hours of patrol, six hours of reserve, then six hours of patrol—twenty-four hours of work, on the first day. After twelve hours at home, on Tuesday, he'd come back at six in the evening for six hours of patrol. From midnight Tuesday through eight a.m. Wednesday he could go home again, followed by five hours of patrol, eleven hours of reserve, and six hours of patrol again from the next midnight. Thursday at six a.m. brought twelve hours at home, followed by six hours of patrol, six hours in reserve, and you were then back again at 0600, to begin the four-day chart again. The insularity of police culture derives in part from this schedule, in which the police tended to socialize with one another during their free hours, few and odd as they were. Station houses were so called because the cops effectively lived there.

Alone on patrol, sometimes far from their precincts, without means of communication, the patrolman had to be able to defend himself. The 1870s saw an increase in crime, including attacks on police. Though patrolmen could carry firearms, some did not, relying instead on their nightsticks and their reputation. Violence was simply a far more common currency at the time: it was largely acceptable for husbands to hit their wives, parents to hit their children, bosses to hit their employees. The Irish hit everyone, and, for them, the fistfight had an almost conversational quality. Sholem Aleichem, the "Yiddish Mark Twain" and Bronx immigrant whose tales became the basis for *Fiddler on the Roof,* had a character in one story explain it: "They have a habit of fighting in the street. Not that they want to kill you, knock your eye out, or push a few teeth down your throat like they do here. God forbid! They fight just for fun. They roll up their sleeves and slug away to see who beats who. . . ."

The vagaries of the criminal-justice system, which allowed politically connected criminals to go free while sometimes jailing complainants, if they could not guarantee their appearance on the witness stand, encouraged a degree of street justice. When Cornelius Willems was a rookie at the turn of the century, as he recounts in his memoir, *Behind the Green Lights,* he brought in two perps and their victim from a robbery. The perps were untouched; the victim, bloody. The sergeant berated Willems, "Look at the condition of this poor fellow and not a mark on these two bums!" He ordered two patrolmen to return the perps to the street for a moment, to balance the scales. Thirty years later, Willems reflected, "In a lecture I once stated, with perfect truth, that I had beaten up hundreds of hardened criminals . . . I've forced confessions—with fist, blackjack, and hose—from men who would have continued to rob and kill if I hadn't made them talk. The hardened criminal knows only one language, and laughs at the detective who tries any other."

Confessions were obtained through beatings or other coercion, known as the "third degree," and the practice was a matter of public knowledge and, generally speaking, heartfelt approval. Even the reformers didn't object to bad guys getting beaten, but rather the careless extravagance with which certain cops used their nightsticks. One cop even clouted former President Ulysses Grant, when he was part of a crowd pressing in to watch a fire. When a reporter pointed out what he had done, the patrolman nearly fainted, but Grant lodged no complaint.

As it happened, the police were punished for everything but serious wrongdoing. Civil-service protections made prosecution for brutality or graft an elaborate and lengthy process, and the political will to achieve them was spasmodic at best. But patrolmen nonetheless saw themselves as hostage to myriad regulations, peculiarly contrived and arbitrarily enforced, as if the police department had created a make-believe world of order to compensate for the larger corruption of city government and the chaos of the streets. The cop who accepted a payoff to leave a gambling house alone would rarely face sanction, while one who took momentary shelter from a snowstorm could lose a week's pay. Patrolmen were supervised by roundsmen, so named because they walked counterclockwise from post to post, and the roundsmen were evaluated by how many complaints they issued. Patrolmen were punished if a store on their post was vandalized, or if they were observed in social conversation with a passerby. One cop lost a day's pay for failing to report a dead cat on his post. They were expected to be investigators, social workers, bouncers, and soldiers, but they were often treated like errant schoolboys.

These contradictions led many New York City police officers to develop a decidedly ironic point of view. Then as now, the distance between the loftiness of the ideals that we embodied and the smallness of so much else—the bosses, the newspapers, the politicians, the people, and, often enough, us—could make your head spin. And you needed your head, sometimes, though not for what you thought. We had a captain who would watch us race to gun runs and ask us afterward why we weren't wearing our hats. I might spend hours on a frozen rooftop, watching below, and when a sergeant raised me for the scratch, he would reach out and feel my shield, to see if it was cold to the touch. Whenever I hear denunciations of police power, in solemn editorials or in routine street static, I have to laugh a little. I think of the Transit cop's line, "You want to know what my job is like? Go to your garage, piss in the corner, and stand there for eight hours." Or I think about how when we are sick at home, we have to call in for permission to leave the house, and call again when we return. Or better yet, I don't dwell on it at all; as we like to say to bosses when we screw up, "Yeah, but Sarge, you've said so yourself—they don't pay us enough to think." More than anything else, this mind-bending knot of paradox explains the vaunted "blue wall of silence"—it's not so much that cops don't want to talk, it's that they can barely begin to explain.

· · ·

GEORGE DID TELL ME ABOUT THE RECORD STORE, HAVING gotten my attention in the usual way—by beating a woman. This time, Danielle called: the night before, George had knocked her down, shoved her against a wall, and confined her in a bedroom when she threatened to call the police. He'd slept at the door of the room, on the floor, to prevent her escape. The next morning, he'd gone out and brought back breakfast, made her a bath, and then walked her to her mother's house, where she called the cops. She cried and could barely walk, and though there was no visible injury, I could charge an assault on the basis of "substantial pain," as well as unlawful imprisonment, another misdemeanor. I left as the ambulance arrived, and I told the EMTs to stop by the record store on the way to the hospital.

"We got another problem," I said, returning George's greeting and asking him to step outside the shop. He stiffened, like he was immersed in cold water, and began his rebuttal, as edgily eloquent as the last time: Yes, they argued but no, he didn't hit her—"Did you see a mark, a single mark on her?"—and if he shoved her once, it's because she said she'd have him arrested if he ever left her. A cop witnessed that, we have to find him. And he has a letter, in which she makes that threat, we have to find it. I have to find them for him, he says, now. As I cuffed him, Tonya approached to offer him her sympathy and support, knowing that her turn to take him in had come round again.

I reminded him, "George, what I gotta do now is bring you in, I have no choice, like last time, and maybe like last time it'll work out..." He shrugged his acceptance as the ambulance pulled up. I got the nod from Danielle, and we left for the precinct.

Once there, he saw the cop who had witnessed his argument with Danielle the afternoon before. George had flagged him down for a "clothes job," an escort to their apartment for him to remove his belongings. The cop told me he'd heard Danielle say she'd get him sent back to prison if he left her, but the two then decided to try to work things out. "Looks like they didn't," said the cop. George looked to see my reaction, and I told him that whether he had good reasons to beat her or bad ones, it didn't matter to me. "I got things to tell you," he said.

For a year or so, it had been procedure to debrief every prisoner who came into the precinct. Most perps wouldn't talk, and many were as blankly ignorant of the local underworld as they were of Vatican intrigue. The Squad asks, "Do you have information about robberies, homicides, guns, arson, hate crimes, chop shops, terrorism?" I've had people say, "Chop-chop? What chop-chop?" You'd also get perps who would offer dirt on the order of "Psst! John Gotti runs the Mafia!" and expect to walk on a gun collar. When George's turn came, he said, "Yes, yes, yes, yes, no, yes, and what was the last one?"

My prisoner was the Rosetta stone to scores of violent felonies, past and planned. People approached him to do hits and robberies every week. The narcotics king of Atlanta wanted to open nightclubs in the city, for dancing and dealing, and he asked George to run them. A robbery, at a bodega, tonight, hours from now; he knew the two guys who planned it, what kind of gun they'd carry, why they picked it, how they knew that the owner's brother, a pockmarked Dominican, carried a .357, and how he was the one to watch, to take out if he moved. One of the guys had robbed a meat market a few months ago, with two other guys. They got five thousand dollars, with at least a grand in food stamps, which they moved through a Chinese restaurant. The shoot-up at the record store was a hit on a guy named True, but since True made his living robbing drug dealers and numbers spots, and had testified against another drug gang at trial, and was messing with some gangster's girlfriend, George hadn't narrowed down who ordered it. He knew about another planned hit on a Brazilian man, a witness in a state case. He wouldn't say more.

It was as if George spread a deck before him and asked the detective to pick a card, any card, but only one. The detective chose the robbery planned for tonight. It was a natural choice: the bodega was in the precinct, and the detective handled robberies. The exchange to be made, help for help, was remarkably frank, brisk, and businesslike. George knew that Danny and Bebe planned the robbery, where Danny lived, and where the bodega was. If a robbery occurred and arrests were made quickly, it would be good; if it could be prevented, it would be better. Either result should be enough to secure his freedom. While it seemed shabby, and even dangerous, to bargain Danielle's distress against the safety of a grocery store, it was just that, a bargain. What was left unmentioned was that George would, in all likelihood, be freed by the judge at his arraignment. Danielle's case was weak, even terminal, with a police witness to her threats and no visible injury. George would have a problem with his parole officer, but that decision would wait until this case was adjudicated, and if history served as a guide, the charges might well be dropped. But George was back in the cage now, and he'd do what he needed to get out of it. It was a line of thought we encouraged.

Calls were made, hours passed. George told me that he had no problem giving up people who weren't close friends and who were going to hurt people. He had hurt people himself, and while it didn't keep him up at night, he thought it a better thing if people didn't get hurt during jobs. It was a thin and abstract pity, as if his victims were the victims of an earthquake in Chile, and his efforts at moral understanding had a rote, calisthenic quality: "You think, what if it's your brother, your girl who gets shot in a holdup, how would you feel?" What bothered him was that he had information of great value and had to spend it on freedom that should be had on the cheap: "I'm in here on bullshit, I know that, Danielle, she *wrong*. I'm not gonna say all I know, I'll give up Danny and Bebe, that's it, that's a *lot*. What if they grab me with a gun sometime, what am I gonna have left to give?" I told him I was sure he'd manage, and he didn't disagree.

The detective ran Danny's address on a computer program that lists every criminal who has used that address. None of the resident perps were named Danny, and none matched the description of eighteen-year-old male Hispanic, five-eight and slightly built. For his own safety, the detective was reluctant to wait in the store without knowing whom to expect, and while George sounded believable, the detective wanted more before he spent the rest of his day on an as yet nonexistent crime. It was after dark now, and the bodega was only open for a few more hours. There was a brief burst of rain. There were countless reasons for the robbery not to happen then: a hangover, a date, the flu, an argument, a bad horoscope, or an arrest. The next night was Halloween, when they could even wear masks without attracting notice. The detective passed the information to Bronx Robbery, and was told in turn that they couldn't find any open cases that matched the meat-market robbery as George described it. The detective sent us on our way.

The password had been spoken, but the gates remained shut. I hadn't quite expected that, and neither did George. Because the information was untested, of indeterminate use, whatever reciprocal favor he was to receive would have to wait. At Central Booking, I put him in the holding cell; he was back with the losers, with their foul smells and sad stories, their tough-guy sneers and choked-back sobs. George leaned close to me and whispered that he wanted to talk.

"About the Brazilian?" I asked.

"About the Brazilian," he said. I loved that part, it was just like the movies. As they say, this is no job for a grown-up.

It was getting late as I went to the Complaint Room, where Danielle was waiting. An ADA told me the caseload was backed up, she would have to come back in the morning to sign the complaint, and if my defendant wanted to make statements, I should take him up to the detectives in the video room. Danielle was amenable to returning, so I thanked her, made sure she got carfare from Victim Services, and went back to the cells.

Upstairs in video, things went badly. It was nearly midnight, and everyone was tired. The detective didn't know me, he didn't know George, and the debriefing began in the irritatingly standard form: "Do you know anything about chop shops . . ." The detective asked George about his most recent arrest, and took an instant dislike to him when he began, "The bitch lied!" And George seemed determined to justify his contempt. When he was asked why he had spent almost ten years in prison, he responded with a lack of hesitation that sounded almost like pride: "I robbed a place. The man tried to grab my gun. I shot him."

"When you say 'the man,' was it someone who was with you?"

"I mean the victim."

I was frustrated with the detective. I was peddling a murder conspiracy, and he was supposed to be in the market. This was no time to act like a human being. But before things could deteriorate further, two detectives from Bronx Robbery arrived, with note pads and cell phones. Their people had staked out the bodega, from a car parked outside, and awaited more detail on the perps. When the car called back to say the bodega had closed without incident, the detectives concentrated instead on the meat-market robbery. Did it happen in April or June? Of the three perps, were any arrested? Who had the guns, were any shots fired? There were four or five robberies that matched their initial, rough outline, and they began to narrow it down. When they left, after midnight, they said they would tell the DA and his parole officer about his assistance, if he wanted. We had good faith on both sides, satisfaction on neither. It was time to go, and I took George back downstairs to the cells. Since I'd have to come back early in the morning with Danielle to swear out the complaint, I knew we could start it all again, and the thought was exhausting even as it brought relief.

Danielle arrived at court in the morning looking fresh and rested, and she remained resolute in her desire to press charges. She walked with a limp, and said that she was told at the hospital that she needed some kind of surgery on her hip. I asked if it was from what George had done to her, and she shrugged, but added that "they'd been telling me to have it for a while." I asked if the doctors had told her whether George had contributed to her condition, and if so how much, but she only shrugged again. When the ADA was ready for the case, I told her the story, then brought in Danielle to tell it again. When they were finished, I was taken aback at the vehemence of the ADA's reaction. "Did you see that poor woman? I've never seen such fear!" she said. "I really want to put this guy away!" She had tears in her eyes.

Ordinarily, I would have been delighted. Time after time, I'd brought in assault cases, from domestic violence more often than not, and seen them dealt down to next-to-nothing. Sometimes you respect the compromise, and sometimes you can't. At last, I'd met a blazing champion of the downtrodden, and it couldn't have happened at a worse time. My peculiar mix of motives—I wanted something from George, so I needed something for him—made me uneasy, but I genuinely felt her reaction was naive and awry. Danielle seemed justifiably angry, but not really afraid. He hurt her, but how much? He shoved her, and trapped her in a room overnight. It was fitting that he spent the night in jail for it, and it would be prudent to provide her with an order of protection, which would allow her to send him back to jail if he so much as raised an eyebrow at her. After a woman from Victim Services had interviewed Danielle, she'd told me, "She doesn't seem afraid of him. She wants him in jail because she thinks he should be there." And then there were her threats, made in front of the cop and, it was alleged, in writing. There are times when your heart breaks for people; this wasn't one of them.

After Danielle signed the complaint, the supervising DA sent me back to the video room, where I met with another detective. He reacted to the story as I hoped, saying we had to move, immediately, and do whatever possible to get to the Brazilian. I took George back upstairs. The night had taken its toll. He'd barely slept or eaten, and his mood swung between sullen resentment and dazed despair: "I don't care, I'll do time, I can do it, I did ten years, man, I know what it is . . . this is bullshit, it's bullshit what Danielle did, and it's bullshit that I gave up a robbery, a robbery that my friend did, and I'm still here. . . ." He agreed to talk and refused to, talking in crazy circles, saying he didn't care, he'd go back to jail, or he'd never go back because he didn't do anything. Once, he broke down, crying with his face in his hands, and I thought we'd lost him. We moved between paying him sympathetic attention and allowing moments of privacy; we fed him, let him call his sister to talk. "Think about your children!" I said. Let me tell you, we were ruthless. He came around, and told us what he knew.

The Brazilian was playing both sides, with the dealer and the law; how exactly, George didn't know. He didn't know if the Brazilian had testified or was scheduled to, if he was an informant or just suspected of thinking about turning. He said he didn't know the man in prison who had commissioned the hit, but the fee would be six thousand dollars, half on agreement, half on completion, and he knew the name and address of the Brazilian. He'd seen a video shot as a kind of prospectus for the hit: footage of the man's block, his building, his apartment. In the last ten seconds, the Brazilian appears, stumbling into the frame as he happens to come out of his home, then smiles and waves at the camera. All this he knew, he said, because he was asked to do the hit. Throughout the afternoon and into the evening, we made the deal. Calls went back and forth between cops and prosecutors, word went up the chains of command; bureau chiefs were consulted. The DA wanted the Brazilian's name, to run it through city, state, and federal databases to see if he was a registered informant, to check with the U.S. Attorney and the other DAs to find out if he was a witness in a case. We were determined to prevent a murder, but the DA, in particular, was terrified of another one, whose headline would read: DA FREES PAROLEE, GIRLFRIEND SLAIN. He asked me about the case, and I told him George hit a woman every month. It wasn't ferocious violence, it was shoving and slapping, never even a punch, but it was habitual. He had Danielle brought back in to see her for himself.

George would not give up the name without a promise from the DA that he would be out, today. The DA said he needed the name, to make sure the information was good. George said he wouldn't give up his friend, who had relayed the order from the man in prison, but that he could show them the tape when he got out, and maybe get them the gun for the hit. The DA said it should be enough, if the name checked out. George gave up the first name, which was all he remembered: Kari. The detectives left to start calling.

I sat with him for a while, as he mused aloud: "I think about these hits people want me to do, and I wonder . . . I always say, 'I'll think about it, let me think,' then tell them, 'Nah, it don't feel right.' I'm not into that anymore, even though it's good for people to think I am. Like this hit in the Heights they asked me to do? That guy, I could walk up to him and he'd be no more. *No more . . .*"

I didn't ask him why so many people were under the impression that he was a contract killer. Somehow I didn't think most record-store clerks get that kind of offer.

The calls went back and forth: "DEA has a Bosnian named Kiri, wants to know if it's your guy."

"FBI has a Corio, from Naples."

"Naples, Florida, or Naples, Italy? Never mind, forget it, but keep taking anything close, Brazilian Kari might be Jamaican Kelly after how many guys are passing along the name. . . ."

By sundown, there had been no confirmation, but after George repeated his information on the robberies and the record-store shooting, there was little doubt about his credibility. The DA agreed to let him out that night, in exchange for the address, with the stipulation that George would accept the terms of the order of protection, enter a batterer's program, and agree to bring them the videotape the next morning. George gave the address in Manhattan, 325 West 57th, and in a few minutes, DEA agents were on a cell phone from a car. There was no such address. How tall is the building? Is there an awning, a light? George was surprised, and described an apartment house. Maybe it was East 57th? Ten minutes later, they called back. The building didn't match, it wasn't even residential. Was it on a two-way street? No? Then it isn't on 57th. "We'll call you back." The DA prodded George for details. He remembered a CVS on the corner. The DA called information, asked for the locations of CVS stores in Manhattan. Bleecker Street, Eighth Avenue. "Give me Eighth Avenue." He called and asked for the cross street. "Fifty-eighth? Thanks!" He called the DEA, and when they called back, they were in front of 325 West 58th Street, a building like George had described. They would call back in a minute, they said, after they went to the apartment.

It was almost half an hour when they called. No one was home, but neighbors confirmed that a Brazilian lived there, and several said he was a drug dealer. They had a name. The Manhattan DA confirmed that he was a defendant in a drug case, resulting from a search warrant executed at his house. And he wasn't the witness of a kidnapping but the victim of one, though those who had released him clearly had had second thoughts afterward. He didn't sound like a very good man, but thanks to George, he would be a living one, at least for a little longer.

George would go back to the cells for an hour, then see a judge and be released. "I keep getting pulled out of there and put back, people are gonna put things together," he complained. The detective told him, "You'll think of something to say." He said nothing, nodding as he left.

Later on, the detective told me that George had delivered the videotape, as agreed. In fact, the hit was supposed to have taken place that night, but the killers were spooked by the DEA presence. The Brazilian was in police custody. There was also news of True, the intended target at the record-store shooting, who had been shot six times. He was alive, but he wasn't talking to police. And Danielle had decided to drop the charges.

Every week or so, I'd run into George on the street, and we'd say hello. I liked him, as far as it went. The feeling was as mutual as it could be, I think; as it can be between two people who wouldn't hesitate to shoot each other. As hit man and cop, the odds of this occurring were less remote than they might be otherwise. Semi-retired hit man, pseudo-retired hit man, it didn't matter. Anyway, we'd both be around, and I was sure we'd be talking.

. . .

THESE CHANCE ENCOUNTERS ALONG FAMILIAR PATHS OF-fered a glimpse of where the Job might lead—to a higher stage, where the stakes were urgent and the players elite, as our gathered forces improvised with a killer to save a life. Other meetings pointed toward a lower road, dull and degraded, and one such meeting took place hours after another cop took his last steps altogether. On a midnight tour in May 1997, cops in Chelsea re-sponded to a robbery in progress. A masked gunman had broken into the apartment of a wealthy garment manufacturer, where he tied up the man and his girlfriend. The girlfriend managed to free herself and call for help, and PO Anthony Sanchez and his partner responded, splitting up between the stairs and the fire escape to seal off the robber's exit. Sanchez met him in the stairwell and was shot in the head and back. He died at the scene. He was thirty years old, married, with two young children. The bottomless shame of it, the poisonous waste, worsened with the arrest of the perp, a failed stock-broker with a cocaine habit named Scott Schneiderman, because his intended victim had been his father. Whether he was dissatisfied with his allowance or wanted to rush his inheritance, he had destroyed the Sanchez family in an as-sault on his own kin.

And so I wore a mourning band, a slip of black elastic that covers the em-blem of the City on the shield, when I took my post the next morning. For a while, I watched drug spots, without success. At around six in the evening, I got a job for a Missing Person. Such cases overwhelmingly involve teenage girls who are out with their boyfriends, or husbands who later turn up with a hangover or lipstick on the collar. But unless I could prove something like that within an hour or so, to make certain that this missing person wouldn't turn up in the East River, I would have to make it an official case and go back to the base for at least two hours of paperwork and phone calls, making no-tifications to the precinct, the Missing Persons Squad, Operations, Transit, and the Port Authority.

When I arrived at the apartment, a painfully sincere woman told me that her fifteen-year-old son hadn't come home. Though I tried to point out that a teenager who isn't even late for dinner yet isn't necessarily a police emer-gency, she protested that her son was an angel who practically ran home from school every day to get a start on his homework. In response to my other questions, she sobbed that they hadn't fought, that he didn't have a girlfriend, and that she had never had any prior occasion to call the police. I was disinclined to believe her, but I felt for her genuine tears, and I didn't want to risk the worst—and by that I mean getting jammed up myself, in part because that's how cops think, but also because whatever had happened or would happen to the boy was out of my hands. One of the ironies of handling an ordinary Missing Person case is that you only look for the person before he or she is declared missing. And so I took a picture of the boy, instructed his mother to call 911 again if he returned, and set out to check the usual haunts. After the playground, the schoolyard, and the busier corners, I went to the Community Center, where the gym was crowded with basketball players. I walked along the sidelines, hoping to spot my kid. And then one of the ballplayers ran up in front of me and started yelling, "Get out of here! You can't come in here, this is our place! Get out!"

I stopped, glared at him, and told him to get out of the way. He stepped back a pace but went on shouting: "Cops can't come in here! Leave us alone, get out!" I thought about locking him up, and I had a solid disorderly conduct and even a plausible misdemeanor—obstructing government administration—but mostly I had a loudmouthed jackass who was keeping me from doing my jackass job. And it hooked me a little, the out-of-the-blue, fact-free rudeness of it, the doubly deluded posturing as victim of the Man and hero of the 'Hood. And it was in part because I was starting to lose my temper that I didn't lock him up, after I stepped up to him and he stepped back, which in our impending dogfight was a sign of submission as distinct as a lowered tail. I continued to canvass the gym before hitting the streets again. Although it was probably the better way to handle it, I was bothered by how much it bothered me. He had a familiar look to him, and if I was setting up the next cop, that cop would most likely be me. That was the mixed blessing of a beat: you got second chances with people, and they got them with you.

After an hour had passed, I went back to check the apartment to see if the boy had returned. He had, of course, and when I began to lecture him about consideration for his mother, he said, "I'm fifteen years old, and she calls the cops every time I go to my friend's house after school." I looked at her and she turned away. I gave back the job: "Mark that a 91, Central, missing returned." The code meant "condition corrected," but it didn't feel like what had been wrong was in any way righted.

Not for the first time, I began to suspect that this is what my father would have warned me against. But how could he begin to convey the maddening circularity of patrol, the daily diet of bullshit, the smallness of people and the grandeur of their demands? The danger was not in corruption but corrosion. I stewed: *They call it the beat for what it does, not what it is—it beats you down . . . for all that, I take home seventy-five dollars a day . . . and I did go home, unlike Anthony Sanchez.* Such was the drift of my thoughts as the sun set and then the skies opened, dousing my self-pity with cold, blind rain.

After I was soaked to the skin, a sector car came by and I hopped into the back. Some beat cops rode like that fairly often, if their post was slow, or to back up the sector, if we had only one car to cover the precinct, but I liked walking by myself. The cops in the car were Chris Meyer, who was a couple of classes ahead of me, and John Timpanaro, who was in the class behind me. As was typical for cops who were no longer quite so new, I didn't really know Timpanaro; it was as if I was a second-grader, and while I knew most of third grade, the first grade was a blur of babies, indistinguishable to anyone but their mothers. I sat quietly in the back as they talked about the Job, bitching about the bosses and laughing at the gossip. We drove around for a few hours, and the downpour seemed to drown out the complaints. As the tour wound down, the rain stopped, and the radio woke up again for a domestic dispute. The three of us responded.

A crowd of teenagers had already gathered at the building, immediately back in position after having been deprived of hours of hang-out time. There had been frequent complaints of dogfights there, and two guys in the crowd had pit bulls. In the past, they had told me that they didn't fight their dogs, they just "faced" them, holding them on the leash as they strained to attack, snapping and barking, inches apart. While I didn't expect them to know that they verged on violation of the animal-cruelty statute, an unclassified misdemeanor in the State Agricultural Law, I thought it shouldn't be such a stretch for them to realize that they were a nuisance, especially late at night. It was the kind of rebuke I had to make daily, often to hostile incomprehension, whether a man decided to relieve himself beside a busy playground or a woman lit her cigarette in an elevator packed with children. "You can't tell me what to do," I'd hear, and, "But there's no sign. . . ." I knew others in the crowd, and they knew me, and they knew that when I told them to leave, I meant it.

"All right, that's it, no hanging out in front of the building," I called out, and we went upstairs to the job. A couple had fought, or rather a wife had taken out her frustrations on her husband, who had called us to calm her down. And it was an actual, legal husband, with a real job as a union electrician. In this neighborhood, working husbands were a small and respectably eccentric fraternity, like the Freemasons. Though he was somewhat the worse for wear, he insisted he didn't want his wife arrested, and so we calmed her down, wrote our report, and went back out. The group hadn't moved.

"Let's go!" I called out. "Everybody move! You don't, you get locked up!"

The teenagers looked at each other, reading the cues from those inclined to stay and those beginning to go, until the momentum built among the latter and the groups began to walk off. And then a few guys turned back and started to mouth off. One in particular seemed to have a lot on his mind, and he broadcast his opinions of the police with some volume. The general theme was that as individuals, we were pathetic cowards of dubious manhood, but together, we were worse than the Gestapo. I recognized him from the basketball courts, that afternoon. We started to walk toward him and he backed away, going on as he went about how it was a great thing when the people took matters into their own hands, and the cops got what was coming to them. We walked a little faster, hoping to gain before he broke into a run, when he bellowed, "And that's why your buddy got scraped last night!" And then he turned and ran, with us hard after him, as the crowd let out a cheer.

A few inches of rain had fallen in the past hours, and the ground was a sea of mud. The terrain didn't favor him any more than it did us, and in fact he fell down as we chased him, though he recovered quickly. But I knew we were no match for the skinny young guy in his "felony fliers," loaded down as we were in our equipment and heavy boots. He fled across the lawns of one project, across the street to the projects on the other side, ducking out of sight behind a building and heading toward the next street beyond. Timpanaro proved to be a great sprinter, however, and held his pace, with Meyer following gamely. I slowed to a jog, figuring that he might double back, because he was more likely to live in the projects on Webster or Washington Avenue than in the tenements by the park, where he was now headed. And so I was less surprised than he was as he rounded the corner, almost running into me, and I was close on his heels as he fled back toward the crowd. We skidded though the wet lawns until he hit a fence which he could not clear, and he went down into the mud, with me on top of him. As Timpanaro and Meyer joined us, the crowd moved forward, yelling and jeering, but I was too winded to notice. "Okay, okay, you got me," he said, as I cuffed him up. *No shit,* I thought, *we got you.*

The crowd was getting jacked up and ugly, so we hauled the perp back to the car. I looked at them: for one girl, I'd collared a gang leader who had threatened to shoot her; for others, I'd been in their houses, trying to help when their mothers were sick or their brothers had disappeared. They were rooting for this criminal, who had taken such pride and pleasure in the death of a young cop. When we got back to the precinct, I realized that I'd been to the perp's house as well: his brother had called after his ex-girlfriend had threatened him on the phone. The perp reclined on the couch as I took the report and explained the procedure for obtaining an order of protection, and had even called the girlfriend to tell her to lay off. Why did he hate cops so much, and why did I care? As I checked his record, I found some clue—he was a crack dealer—and as I wrote out the summons for Disorderly Conduct, he recovered his perp composure. He paced in the cell, saying he wouldn't let us plant drugs on him, that he would sue us for what we'd done. All of us were muddy messes, and he had a lump on his head, and he demanded to go to the hospital. I told him he could go if he wanted, in handcuffs, now, or I could wait for the warrant check, give him his ticket, and send him on his way. He said he'd wait. As I saw it, I couldn't really charge him with Resisting Arrest, though he deserved a night in jail, because running isn't resisting. Moreover, I was just as glad to go home. The tour had ended, Timpanaro and Meyer had gone, and once the warrant check came back, I cut him loose, suspecting, however, that I hadn't heard the last of it.

Some months later, I was called down to Internal Affairs. The interview was routine and, in fact, anticipated, as Meyer, Timpanaro, and I were notified at the same time. They don't advise you of the allegations beforehand, nor do they inform you of their findings afterward, unless you are charged. Two detectives interviewed me in "good cop, bad cop" style, though the vaguely embarrassed tone of the younger one may not have been purely tactical. I certainly was embarrassed to be there. I did note for the record that management later told me that my accuser had been banned from the Housing Authority for dealing drugs, and that his family had signed a stipulation that permitted them to keep their apartment as long as he stayed away. The man claimed we beat him, which was expected, but he also alleged that I had robbed him of his jewelry. As we left, Timpanaro said, "So that's why you've been sporting that four-fingered gold THUG 4 LIFE ring."

"Hey, I gotta have something to show for this."

While I appreciated the necessity of process, just as I do for audits and root canals, it didn't mean I had to enjoy it at the time. In any case, I heard nothing afterward, which I had to assume was to the good. When I was called down to the Civilian Complaint Review Board, I felt I had rounded out my education. Again, I had only been told to bring my memo book for a particular date, but since I was assigned to a "conditions car" that day, to look for arrests and summonses, instead of a full page of entries for building checks and jobs, it said little beyond "exterior patrol." The investigator was a pleasant young guy who appeared to be straight out of college, who shook my hand, turned on a tape recorder, and asked whether I had choked a child, nine months before. At IAB, I had been nervous and angry, appalled that the lies of some random criminal would leave a permanent mark on my record; here, I was simply intrigued. It was not my habit to choke children, and I was curious about how it was construed that I had. Specifically, it was claimed that two kids were play-fighting in front of one building, when a cop of my general description mistook it for a real fight, and used excessive force in breaking it up.

"How about that!" I said. Most of this investigator's interviews consisted of gruff, defensive, one-syllable denials, I was sure, much as mine had been at IAB, but at CCRB, I was a cheerful participant, as if we were playing a game of Clue. I told him what I did in general and on that day, and said that breaking up fights between kids was routine. While I might not recall one instance from almost a year before if I'd only had to yell at them, I thought I would remember if I'd had to use force, however slight. "Can you help me out here? Were they black, white, Spanish?" If he'd asked to hypnotize me, I might have consented; as it was, we were equally confused, which was not the worst situation to be in. He told me he would talk to the complainant again, and might have to put my picture in a photo array for her—my mug shot among five others, in the standard form—which I found a bit offensive. The interview ended, and when he turned off the tape recorder, we both saw there was no tape inside. We shook hands and I left. Some six months later, I received a letter from CCRB, informing me that I had been "exonerated," in that I was the officer in question and had used force in the event, but that my actions were appropriate. Yeah, whatever.

Veteran cops often warned us, "If you're out there as an aggressive cop, sooner or later you're gonna get jammed up." Sometimes the implication was to expect punishment as much as reward for your efforts; sometimes it only meant, "Watch your back." Another one said to me, "The way you're going, you're gonna be burnt out in five years." When I first got on the job, those remarks struck me as embittered and exaggerated; now, they were beginning to make sense. I had to make sure that the last comment wasn't true, at least—I only had two years on patrol, and I was already starting to get a little crisp around the edges.

After the night with Timpanaro and Meyer, I had two weeks off. I needed it. In the NYPD, the pay is bad but we get more time off than Frenchmen. On my first day back, I left Sunday dinner at my mother's house for the four-to-twelve, and I filled in a sector with another cop from my class, Gina Fredericks. Right after roll call, we responded to a job for an EDP in one of my buildings. An elderly woman told us her grandson had drunk a bottle of liniment—she showed it to us; the liquid was thick and pink as shampoo—before he began to break the furniture and talk to God. We wrestled him all over the bedroom, knocking over the bed, and when Gina blasted him with mace, he licked his lips as if it was whipped cream. After we finally subdued him, we both went out for the rest of the day with line-of-duty injuries. I had been back at work for an hour, and I was off again. *Vive la France!*

As my third summer in the Village approached, the weather was getting hot again. One sweltering afternoon, an Aided case came over for a pregnant woman in front of a building. When I got there, I saw it was Tonya, sitting on the curb, about to deliver another one of George's children. She hugged her belly and moaned, surrounded by neighbors. I didn't know what to tell her, to sit or stand or walk, so I said, "It's okay, take it easy!" The ambulance was long in coming, and people began to complain about the police: "They don't do *nothin'!* They *never* around!" I put a second call in for the ambulance, and a third, and then George walked by, eating an ice cream cone. He stopped to watch, at the edge of the crowd, with an expression of idle curiosity. Tonya was about to give birth to his child, literally in the gutter, and she might have been a stranger, or even a strange dog, about to drop a litter of pups. I'd heard that when a cop delivers a baby—in a cab, on the street, wherever—the mother often names it after him. Would I deliver my informant's child, and would he be named after me, or at least code-named? Were there special forms to be filled out, or notifications to be made? A woman began to complain about the police again, and I snapped at her, "The police *are* here, lady, whaddaya want me to do, carry her to the hospital on my back?" George finished his ice cream cone and shook his head. "Man, this is one hot day!" he said, and then he walked away. *I have much to learn from him,* I thought, and when the ambulance came and took Tonya, not long after, I walked away, too. It was time.

FOUR

When I was in the Academy, a detective came in to give us a talk about trouble. For years he had worked undercover in organized crime and narcotics, to great effect and at visible cost. Pacing the stage and chopping the air with his hands, he warned us of hot-blooded crackheads and cold-blooded dealers and how each could kill us, and speaking of blood, how the random prick of a junkie's needle could leave us dead from AIDS in a few miserable years. He couldn't have been more alarming if he had a flashing light on his head, and sometimes I thought the Job put people like him out in front of us to say, "Are you sure about this? You better be—it's your last chance!" The near-paranoia of his tone, warranted as it was by the assignment, bumped up a notch—for all of us—when he told us how his undercover career came to an end: a fellow cop gave him up. "I don't care what you did before, if you used drugs, stole cars, whatever it was—maybe you can use it to become a better cop," he said. "But you're cops now, and a cop who does any of that is a piece of shit."

The last epithet silenced the room. Had we been inclined to speak, I doubt that anyone would have argued with either the harshness of the line, or its finality. But it made me wonder about what pasts were gathered around me, what winding roads had been taken to this place—and whether they would straighten out entirely for all of us, from this point onward. My own path had taken a few odd turns along the way. Whenever I'd dwell upon my great-grandfather's litany of sins, suspected and certain, I could imagine old Pat Brown cutting me short: "At least I never got arrested." Though I never thought of myself as a symptom of declining standards in the NYPD, if they didn't allow people with criminal records to join, I wouldn't be here. *They were different times, back then.*

The detective was on to something when he said our juvenile delinquencies could be transformed in maturity, whether it meant a deeper understanding for those who had done wrong, or a more discerning eye for how wrong is done. One cop I later worked with told me, "When I was a kid, my mother found weed in my pants pockets when she did the laundry. I told her that I was holding it for a friend. Now, I know it's the lamest line in the world, but it's really what happened—God's honest truth! So when I hear it, I have to think twice, because I know it's bullshit ninety-nine times out of a hundred, but it did happen to me." Another told me that a cop in his precinct had a true gift for spotting stolen cars because, as a teenager, he was responsible for a few of them.

Arthur Niederhoffer, an NYPD lieutenant who became a distinguished sociologist, observed of his former colleagues that "the more maladjusted tend to be more satisfied with their work than the less maladjusted." There was a lot to consider in the phrase, from the coppish cynicism in the formulation—none of us are "the better adjusted," only "the less maladjusted"—to the loop-the-loop logic of unhappiness lending the only hope of happiness here, and vice versa. How do you see yourself, and what should you wish for, if the dark clouds are drawn to the silver lining? I wondered how it could effect screening, or even recruitment: *Are you irritable and withdrawn? Do you have trouble sleeping, or maintaining relationships? You may be just crazy enough for the NYPD!* As for myself, I was troubled enough to believe I might one day be a detective.

The idea that you could benefit from beginning on the wrong foot, or at least profit from having made a few missteps along the way, is not new: the reformed sinner is at once the most typical and the most powerful character in our culture, whether in religious terms or those of self-improvement, with the newly thin, sober, solvent, or self-esteeming among the traditionally born-again. Counselors for addicts and ex-convicts routinely work their way up from the ranks of their clients; no one else can command the authority, or extend the empathy, of a veteran among veterans. We admire the self-made more than those who have it all from the get-go, and we'd rather hear about a roundabout journey, full of setbacks and pitfalls, than the express trip from good to better. As St. Augustine prayed, before he found his calling, *Make me holy, Lord, but not yet.*

While most of us are moved by stories of people who find religion in prison, few look as kindly on those who happen upon their redemption in the police department, whether during or after their term of employment. Movie-hero cops are almost always rule-benders but rarely lawbreakers; in real life, when bad cops confess to how and why they crossed the line, the audience—myself included—tends to be dubious of their sincerity and unhurried to forgive. Hackneyed stories of the "slippery slope" that leads the innocent rookie from the proverbial free cup of coffee to the all-out, two-fisted, steal-a-hot-stove take are part of our training, and in the past, especially, there was no shortage of little seductions and large pressures to accommodate the freewheeling style of the City. But the reverse has been true as well: some of us have slipped up the slope, or scaled it, less from serious crime than from lives low in purpose or prospects, which we sometimes stooped to fit. And while the history of policing has seen unimaginable changes in what we do and how we do it, from the rattle watch of New Amsterdam to the SWAT teams, DNA tests, and digital fingerprints of today, the stories of individual police officers are no less miraculous in the distance traveled and the directions taken.

· · ·

IF MY FIRST EXPERIENCES WITH POLICE OFFICERS OUTSIDE my immediate family foretold any contributions I might make to the NYPD, it would be as a source of arrest overtime. One night in my senior year of high school, I went out with my best friend, a Hispanic immigrant I'll call Eddie. Spring was approaching, and so was graduation, if we needed reasons to be spirited and stupid—and we went to a club in lower Manhattan. While we waited to get in, a bouncer walked along the line and told a number of people to leave. When he approached us, Eddie got the same non-invitation. We walked away without protest—democracy is as alien to New York nightclubs as it is to North Korea—and though it took me about a half a minute to see the rule of thumb at work, Eddie had it figured out in an instant: nonwhites should pursue nightlife elsewhere. So we did, heading back to the neighborhood in upper Manhattan where he lived. I'll shorten the story to say that our fiery mood increased with the consumption of flammable liquids, and our new dedication to the cause of breaking down barriers was commemorated by my shattering the plate-glass window of a Greek diner. And then we ran away.

We got about a block before an unmarked police car rolled up on us, and two plainclothesmen jumped out. I froze and raised my hands, as ordered. Eddie danced a little, stepping up to protest and deny—we hadn't done anything, they couldn't stop us, and so on (a speech I've heard many times as a cop, never from the innocent)—talking fast, and with his hands. The cops talked with their hands, too, popping him in the face a few times. I was untouched. My instinct to freeze had been instilled by years of education by my father: do what you're told; do not argue with cops; do not say anything at all, in fact, except that your uncle is Chief McNulty—which was not, strictly or loosely speaking, true. We were charged with Criminal Mischief, and since our arresting officers were Transit cops, we were taken to an underground precinct. The rumble of the trains lent the cells a feel of steerage, as if we had been shanghaied, along with the other mutts, skells, and drooling lunatics, to the bottom of a cargo hold bound for Shithead Island. Since I was more afraid of my father than the cops, I waited it out, without calling home or dropping the name of my newly adopted uncle. We were released at dawn the next day, and I had a track meet in the morning. Still charged with adrenaline, I showed off my handcuff marks and set a school record in the quarter mile. My teammates were impressed, and none were rude enough to point out that if I'd run as well the night before, I wouldn't have been arrested. In truth, I don't remember how much it worried me at the time: trouble then meant trouble with my father, for wanting to stay out late or not doing chores. Justice would not be rougher in the streets than at home. Whatever his warnings about the gravity of a criminal record, I knew that an eighteen-year-old who broke a window would not be cast out of society altogether. I had a court date six weeks later, and a family vacation in between. The family vacation scared the hell out of me.

The court date was set for the day after we were to return from our first real trip, on a plane, to a foreign place. My mother had finagled a package deal to the Bahamas, where seven of us—Mom, Dad, Johnny, Eddie, Regina, Stephen, and Marianne—would share two rooms for the week for around five hundred dollars. The trip was carefully orchestrated and long anticipated, and I'm not sure how my mother managed to persuade my father to spend money on a trip to a faraway beach. We were budgeted for one meal a day, and we carried the rest of our provisions in two enormous suitcases—perhaps the same ones my father had taken to summer camp—that were filled with tuna fish, peanuts, and Tang, the orange-flavored drink powder famously marketed as the beverage of astronauts. The moon for them was not as far as the Bahamas were for us, nor as hazardous. I had been stupid, but I was not suicidal, and I was not about to confine myself on an island with my father for a week-long discussion of what was wrong with me.

Although for most of my life I have gotten along quite well with my brothers and sisters, at the time they had the burden of being relatives, and so were not my first choice of company. Steve, my thirteen-year-old brother, was a different story altogether—I loathed him. He was finicky and complaining and disinclined to movement, preferring to spend his time reading and watching television, except when in pursuit of that which both consumed and provided his energies: Coca-Cola. When he didn't have it, he wanted it, and his increasingly devious thoughts were more and more directed against moments when he might find himself without it. For Steve, it was still made with cocaine: he had secret caches of soda, like a guerrilla army has its buried rifles, or a squirrel its nuts. Cans and cases were hidden under his bed, in his closet, and even underground, in the yard.

At the airport, he set off the metal detector. Though my father would have been angrier had his youngest son turned out to be the more conventional kind of coke smuggler, this was embarrassment enough. Cans were produced from pant legs and shirtsleeves, to the amusement of security. Though my father often attempted to ease difficulties by mentioning the fact that he was an FBI agent, he did not do so then. The flight was otherwise uneventful, and the trip turned out to be a mix of the advertised tropical pleasures and typical family strains. The days at the beach were beautiful, and we swam for hours, fortified by tuna and Tang. In the little room we shared, my brother bounced off the walls when he found that his beloved refreshment was a gift America had given the world. On the last morning, my sister Regina determined to take home as dark a tan as possible. Another tourist advised her to use baby oil, and a few hours later, she was loaded on the plane in a wheelchair, shivering beneath her blankets, sun-poisoned and in shock. When we were back in New York that night, and the last empty suitcase had been unloaded from the station wagon, I somewhat offhandedly broached the subject that had been on my mind but, thank God, not yet his: "Dad, are you going to work tomorrow?"

I could see how he half-consciously registered that something was afoot, but he brushed it aside as he headed toward the bathroom.

"Of course I'm going to work tomorrow, it's Monday, I work every Monday."

"Because, uh, I was wondering if you could go to court with me. . . ."

The story then poured out of me, and my father asked why I hadn't called him from the cells. I said I didn't want to bother him, or to spoil the vacation. I think he said, "You've spoiled it now," but we both knew that wasn't true—the vacation was over; it was my life that was ruined. He asked a few questions and made a few statements. His voice hit me like a gale. What he said had the force of reason and rage together, and because I'd never heard him shout before, it was as if he'd saved it all up for that moment. I would have confessed to anything, but I had already done so, and it was best for me to be quiet then.

The next day, when his manner returned to a more familiar low-boil anger, he was no longer interested in my opinions. We went to court with my co-defendant, Eddie, and his father, as well as Mr. DiMichele, a favorite teacher, and the grown men all greeted each other with plentiful apologies and thanks. Eddie's father spoke little English, and though Mr. DiMichele had coached numerous national debating champs, he was there more or less as a stage prop, to attest to our bright futures and blameless pasts. Eddie and I were to sit quietly, in visible contrition. The arena was my father's, to do whatever he could. He could do everything, it seemed, and though I was relieved that the drama was ending, I was enthralled by his performance. Though the conversation was largely out of earshot, he was quick to elicit the educational background of the assistant district attorney—she went to Fordham Law, did she, why, he did too!—and her father, it appeared, was also an acquaintance from the NYPD. And then he re-created the crime, for the judge and the ADA, moving like a dancer to show Eddie and me pushing and pulling back, play-fighting, and the inadvertent smash of the poor man's window, for which he would be reimbursed immediately, of course. The case was Adjourned in Contemplation of Dismissal, which meant that if we stayed out of trouble for six months, the charges would be dropped. It was a fair sentence for a first offense and a minor crime, probably no different from what we would have gotten without the pantomime and the belabored name-droppings. In the course of twelve hours, I had seen my father transformed into a thunder god and then a Tammany shyster, and each shift brought its own revelation.

As with the case of St. Augustine, however, there was a certain interval between revelation and reform. A month or so later, I broke another window.

Or rather, one was broken with me. I went to a Jesuit high school called Regis, on the Upper East Side of Manhattan, which drew students from neighborhoods ranging from Scarsdale to Bedford-Stuyvesant. Occasionally, friction would arise between us and kids from Yorkville, the neighborhood to the east, where there were still a dozen bars where German or Hungarian was spoken, as well as the remains of an Irish neighborhood. My friends and I met some of our local counterparts one night at a bar, and somewhere along the way, a few words and then a few punches were exchanged. Though the matter was soon settled, some of us took the radical step of calling it a night. One of our side had been a friend of mine since the beginning of our freshman year, and I'd felt a certain guilty closeness to him: we were from similar backgrounds and nearby parishes, and both of our mothers had become ill with ovarian tumors at the same time. Though my mother had been told to prepare for the worst, her condition proved to be benign and readily operable, whereas my friend's mother had died. Afterward, he became a kind of willfully innocent kid, and I believe that night was his first at a bar. The first skirmish sent him rushing to his father's car, which was parked in front, and his sudden departure was interpreted by our rivals as an attempt to bring in reinforcements. The bar emptied into the street, and a couple of them pounded on the car and prevented it from leaving, and someone punched him and someone else said, "Your mother!" and the combination more or less did him in. I tried to break it up and calm them down, but I might as well have tried to make my case with geometry proofs. Another one of their gang, unfortunately a much larger person, happened by, and I wound up fighting with him. We each threw a punch and then he grappled me around the middle, pushing me back. Behind me was a beauty parlor with eight-foot-tall plate-glass windows. I shattered it with my back, then raised my hands as the glass rained down, and one shard pierced the center of the palm of my right hand. Alarms sounded and the street cleared as the flashing lights of patrol cars approached. I ran, with a couple of other guys, and as the cops pulled over and stepped out, one said, "This guy's covered with blood," and I responded, "My uncle's Chief McNulty, and I have to go to the hospital." The cop asked, "What hospital do you want to go to?"

That particular dust-up sidelined me, and I was able to avoid trouble for a while. The median nerve of my right hand had been severed, and even after extensive physical therapy, the hand remained somewhat stiff and numb, scarred from knuckle to wrist. My father tried to take some comfort in my presumed disability: "Well, it's your shooting hand, so if there's a draft, I guess you're safe. And at least it'll keep you out of the police department."

So much for that prophecy. I was hard to predict, which may have been a great part of my father's frustrations with me. I defied his expectations, high and low: I would be going to Harvard in the fall, but with an arrest record; I won the city championship in the half mile, and would become a pack-a-day smoker. My avowed interest in becoming a writer was similarly troublesome; while no one who read as my father did had anything less than respect for authors, as a livelihood, writing required too much luck. My father's sense of caution was so profound that he once warned me about speeding, in a canoe. He suggested teaching, publishing, speechwriting, and advertising; any salaried approximation of what I wanted to do. My ambitions were less confusing than conflicting to him, I think. He was a great junk collector who also despised the fact that I smoked; nonetheless, when he came across a brass ashtray in the shape of a horsefly at a garage sale—with wings that moved!—he bought it for me.

Likewise, our family ate for free at our uncles' restaurant at the World Trade Center, and for years, birthdays, anniversaries, and every other special occasion that merited a meal outside the house took place there. We ate nowhere else that had metal utensils. When the World Trade Center opened, it was desperate for tenants, and my father got the uncles an extraordinary twenty-year lease. There were three uncles—Joe, Herman, and Victor—and three businesses: a bar called the Trade Inn, a coffee shop, and a restaurant called the Commuter's Cafe. The Tretters were Austrian immigrants, and the three who owned the restaurant weren't really uncles; a fourth brother, Nick, a doctor, had married my father's sister, Theresa, a nurse. Their meeting was a coincidence, their romance a secret, and their wedding a surprise, at least to my father. Theresa broke the news to him the day before, by way of a request for assistance with Nick's citizenship papers. Joe and my father had been close friends since the 1950s, when Joe had owned another restaurant downtown, also called Commuter's, where my parents had their wedding reception. When Nick and Theresa married, Joe and my father vowed to remain friends, family notwithstanding. My father took a fee for the lease, but soon afterward, he felt that the volume and variety of requests—the calls about a cook's drunk-driving arrest, a job for a waitress's nephew, a complaint about an inspection—suggested that the half-blood, half-money ambiguity of the relationship promised a lifetime of mutual resentment. He decided to set forth a rule that he would do what he could for them, as he saw fit, without charge, and that he and his own would eat, *gratis,* in perpetuity.

From high school onward, I had an open tab at the restaurant, which was a dangerous thing for a young man. My father's work and my uncles' generosity translated into regular feasts of shrimp cocktail, Wiener schnitzel, and imported beer for my friends. I felt like a tycoon. If these visits became excessively frequent, or just excessive—*This round's on me, boys, and try the veal, it's excellent. Hey, could you believe that Latin test?*—my father would be quietly informed. My father didn't drink, and he struggled more to contain his disapproval of alcohol than his desire for it, and in any other circumstance it would have brought on a stern and lengthy speech. But at the Commuter's, my extravagance was his revenge, and he could only offer a few casual and half-smiling words, "Be careful . . . be polite . . . and don't forget to tip."

As Senator Daniel Patrick Moynihan observed, "Harvard men were to be checked. Fordham men were to do the checking." Though he was talking about government service in the 1950s, it was also true in the Conlon house. When I arrived at college that fall, my first scuffle showed I hadn't learned much since the spring. Again, a friend for whom fistfights were as foreign as bullfights found himself being roughed up, completely unprovoked—this time by the most substantial resident of a ten-man suite that was hosting a Halloween party. Ten-man suite! I was always bad at math. I quickly emerged as the silver medalist in that conflict, though my being knocked cold apparently didn't dissuade my opponent from continuing to swing away. But the pain lasted for only a day or two, whereas the college needled me for months, as they conducted a bizarre and exhaustive investigation with a special subcommittee, and finally concluded that I was somehow at fault. I was placed on disciplinary probation for the rest of the year. Thereafter, out of disgust at the college more than anything else, I did try to stay out of fights, with mixed but increasing success.

What struck me at the time—aside from enormous, drunken thugs—was the rarity of physical confrontation for the young men around me. For some football players and other jocks, brawls were ordinary enough, but I would guess that three-quarters of the rest hadn't been in a fight since the third grade. At home, I knew people for whom most Saturday nights brought a few rounds of beers and a few rounds of punches, and they often felt the former more than the latter the next morning. Having learned the two essential drawbacks of fighting—bodily harm and litigation—I began to take the position I hold now: that it is to be avoided until it truly can't be, and that on most occasions you can give people enough room and reasons to agree with you. But my altercations had given me a reputation, which was neither very comfortable nor deserved (my record had not seen many recent additions to the win column): that I was a useful person to look for in the event of trouble. A female friend who found herself followed by a pervert and a male friend who had been threatened with a beating each came looking for me. I had to spend several weeks, almost without interruption, with another friend who was being stalked by a boyfriend, who threatened persuasively that he would kill her. (He was a genuine villain and went to prison several years later for molesting children.) She had to move from room to room in various dormitories to stay hidden, and I escorted her to classes. There was one little scrap with the stalker, but he was neither a big man nor a brave one, and he left quickly. Neither the college nor the courts were any use—one judge urged them to reconcile, because they were "such an attractive couple," and if the college took any position at all, it is probably noted in the minutes of one of its subcommittees. For me, violence was a language that I wasn't fluent in, but I knew enough to get by in the places where it was spoken.

As a cop, I wouldn't exaggerate the value of being reckless or quick to fight, young or not, and I would recommend even less the kind of wildness that I definitely enjoyed back then. I lost some fights when justice was on my side, and I won others when it wasn't, and the lessons to be drawn from them are not ones I'd like to teach. I made plenty of trouble for myself for no other reason than because I was good at it, more or less. Every now and then, some friend will reminisce about some evening that I had forgotten and which I neither regret nor wish to explain in a job interview. "Remember the lady who complained about the noise at the party, from the apartment behind the yard?" it begins, and from there it goes on to the pith helmet, the catapult, and the herring. I wish I could say that the evening had been the germ of some later innovation, the development of a device to control crowds of unruly sailors or to counteract fish piracy, but it would be a big, fat lie. Education has a point, but experience doesn't have to.

Although I'm sometimes tempted to view old misdemeanors as a necessary link in a chain that led to my present job, if there was some force of fate or anything else at work, I did not see it. Whatever I did as a young man could have prepared me for a life on either side of the cell bars, and I now know firsthand which side I prefer. There is something to be said—everything, by some lights—in that preference, that choice, which has to be made daily, for what you want to do and be. I don't see how I've changed, but I can feel it sometimes, not as a chain of necessity but like the escape rope a convict would make in his cell, handmade from the scraps of his mean and small surroundings, a lifeline from old ways to new.

. . .

IT WAS A STRANGE THING TO HEAR HOW PEOPLE COULDN'T believe Eddie Conlon had died. He was my uncle, and I was named after him. At his wake, a man on the other side of the family said, "When I first heard, I thought it was you." The implication was that he wouldn't have been surprised—or would have been less so, at any rate—had disaster struck any of my brothers or sisters or cousins. It was the fall of 1988, and employment had eluded me for several months. I was a scholarship kid, but school had been out for a year and a half, and, in terms of my prospects, my coin was still in the air. I wasn't out robbing banks, but my teenage years were over in a numerical sense only, as if I'd found a good accountant who could keep the deductions going. If bets were taken on whether, in ten years, I would have some extra money in my pocket or I might be asking for yours, the odds would have favored the latter. But if becoming a criminal was highly unlikely, becoming a cop was completely unreal. If there were two Eddie Conlons, there was one "Eddie the Cop," and the line had ended there. For me, cops were still people you ran from. It was an adult line of work, in several ways. Cops were firm and fair and mad at you, a lot of the time, for good reason. Cops were fathers.

I had never seen Uncle Eddie in uniform. And while he embodied the Job for me, in his steadiness, his thick skin, and the pleasure he took in the raw comedy of street life, I knew next to nothing about him as a New York City police officer. I couldn't imagine him saluting without rolling his eyes and winking at you afterward. I have a hard time picturing him writing reports or tickets, let alone chasing anyone, although he did all three—the last at least once, when he tore his knee for his efforts. In a way, his old-time coppishness contradicts much of the daily reality of the police life I know: he worked from the gut—and it was a considerable gut—in a way that is increasingly rare amid the technologies and bureaucracies of today. For that matter, Eddie was less of a father to me than a kind of counter-father, offering boat rides instead of assigning chores.

Eddie was heavyset, easygoing, and outgoing, and he seemed to have the stolid permanence of the civil service, or of the apartment he'd lived in for fifty years. When he made a change, it was a big one. His death devastated my father. It had been a long time between deaths for his family, and this first breach of his generation was not only early but out of order. As the oldest, my father must have felt guilty and lucky at once, the survivor who could not afford to die. The two of them had shared a bed until they left home, and as adults they still spoke every day. When two days had passed without hearing from him, my father went with my older brother John to check the apartment in Kingsbridge in which the family had grown up and which Eddie had never left. They found him there. He had recently been diagnosed with prostate cancer and had died of a heart attack, not long after their last conversation. I didn't see my father shed a tear—I never did—but later I watched him say, quietly and to no one, "The poor kid, he died alone."

Don't we all, though, I thought, even at the time. And that aspect of his death never struck me as especially sad. My father had urged Eddie to marry his girlfriend, Susan, whom he had been seeing for as long as I could remember, not least because he could leave her his pension, which was probably the only argument that carried weight. Eddie had only recently retired, after having worked to nearly the maximum age allowed by law. You might call it a superstition among cops if it wasn't so commonplace; the guys who do "twenty and out," leaving on the first day of full pension eligibility, die happily of boredom in Florida in their dotage, whereas lifers in the NYPD are just that, gone soon after they go. But Eddie was not a sentimental man, nor likely to change his life when it had suited him for so long. Maybe when you start life sharing a bed, you want to finish it with a little more elbow room. Eddie lived as he pleased, without regret. But my father and Eddie had faced most hard things together, and maybe that was what he was talking about.

My father and Eddie were true partners, complementary in type and in temperament. One planned, one improvised; one saved for you, one emptied his pockets; one got the calls when your career was in jeopardy, the other when a sunny Saturday afternoon was going to waste. Within the family, they tended to fall into a kind of "good cop, bad cop" routine: my father would urge you to take things more seriously, while Eddie would convince you, in fewer words, to lighten up. When my father told stories about the odd jobs he'd worked during the Depression, delivering newspapers or helping the super, he cast himself as a plucky orphan who was glad for the chance to earn his gruel. Eddie once worked as a "mutt" for Western Union, delivering telegrams for three dollars a day or some such starvation wage. When we chimed in, as if it were one of my father's stories, "But that was a lot of money for the time, right, Uncle Eddie?" he replied, "It was lousy money for the time." He carried a sack of telegrams through Harlem, trudging up and down the tenement stairs, until one day he decided he'd had enough, and threw the entire bag into the river and went home. And if we had any doubts as to whether the story had a message or moral like one of my father's, he put them to rest: "What do they expect from me for three bucks a day, I'm gonna climb up six flights of stairs just to give some poor bastard his draft notice?"

If you ask any cop what his partner means to him, or what's best about him, or why he is his partner, the reply will almost always be, "I can depend on him." You have each other's back. For my father, he could depend on Eddie in all the usual ways, but he could also depend on him for surprise, for some relief in laughter. After their parents died, Eddie and my father raised their younger sister and brothers, and continued in that role at home throughout their careers. My father was the image of a G-man: tall and prematurely silver-haired, with a trench coat and fedora, a profile in sternness and probity that masked a playful curiosity and a devious sense of humor. Eddie also might have been sent from central casting, if the picture was set in a coal mine or on the docks: he was shorter and heavier, with a perennial crew cut, a pug nose, and a quick, skeptical smile that could seem devilish beneath his broad V of an eyebrow. Eddie was a patrolman for most of his life: twenty-eight years as a non-cop, thirty-three years as a cop, less than two years as a retired cop. He was "Eddie the Cop" to many, himself maybe not least. And for Eddie, the Job, the family, and the neighborhood ran together, whether loosely twined or tightly knotted. My father's interests, however, strayed beyond the dominion of the Bronx Irish, the familiar parishes and precincts—strayed beyond, and sometimes fled from them, though never without the exile's bittersweet regret for the loss of the hoary certainties. He also kept a door open to the old world, an escape hatch, should the newer, wider world go to hell. Eddie set his course early and stuck to it, stiff-arming his way through any setbacks.

The setbacks came soon enough: as a youngster, Eddie would "walk a beat" in front of the family's apartment, carrying half a broom handle on a thong as his nightstick. One day, a man walking past stopped to watch him, then opened up a conversation.

"Hey, kid, whatcha doin'?"

Eddie told him he was on patrol.

"That's your billy club? Lemme see it—"

Eddie handed it over, only to get it back across his jaw, breaking the bone.

My grandmother dragged him from the hospital to the precinct, where the incident was duly reported. As my father recalled it—Eddie never told me the story—they were again beaten to the punch, so to speak. The man's girlfriend had a brother who was a detective, and expecting some repercussion from the assault, had already filed a complaint. My uncle was charged with carrying a concealed weapon, a violation of the Sullivan Law. His admiration for the cops brought him a criminal record.

When Eddie later applied to become a police officer, that record presented a problem, which was resolved in part because my father, already an FBI agent, had the authority to persuade the Department that the record was at odds with the truth. (Eddie and I filled out identical forms, in 1952 and 1994, to explain our arrest records.) And even though I accept this version of the anecdote, I wonder about the details of the encounter that have been lost not just to time but in the retelling, as simple, pointed stories are more likely to survive the natural selection of family lore. Maybe the man remembered Eddie as having egged his car some previous Halloween, or maybe some exchange occurred along the lines of the man jokingly saying he might want to keep the stick, and Eddie suggesting where he could shove it. Eddie sometimes gave advice like that.

Like his namesake, he prepared for his life as a peacekeeper by being a troublemaker, only more so. He ran away at the age of sixteen to join the merchant marine, and he spent some time in the brig after knocking out a superior officer. The incident was typical of the kind of broad farce that Eddie ordinarily thrived on: he had a habit of sleeping with his eyes open (which I did also, when I was younger) and one day, while he was in bed, his boss ordered him to hop to it and do some job. When Eddie's response was an expression of peaceful indifference, and perhaps a snore, his superior grabbed him to show he wouldn't tolerate such insubordination, whereupon Eddie woke up and flattened him. When my father was in the Marine Corps, in 1945, he received a letter from his brother Joe relating that, while on leave, Eddie had made some qualified progress toward entering his chosen profession: "By the way, Eddie and Dave are still doing crazy things. Their last escapade was to rent cop uniforms, they rented them for a week for five dollars. They went up to Yonkers and White Plains impressing girls with them. It really was quite funny. Eddie would go into a bar and have a beer, then Dave would come in with Mike Mikanko handcuffed to him and say to Eddie, 'What am I gonna do with this prisoner?' Then they would have a beer before they took the prisoner to the station house. Mike would just stand there with that dopey expression on his face. The uniforms are turned in now so don't say anything to Dad he doesn't know." Eddie's apparent belief that the way to a woman's heart is through prisoners and beer may explain why he never married.

But once he became a real cop—a dream come true, at the expense of a gag—that role fell from his repertoire. The theme of the impostor ran through my uncle's relentless practical jokes, and in a letter to my father during the war, he wrote, "I met a nice girl in the U.S.O., she comes from Texas. I told her I came from Arizona, we get along pretty well." Of course, there was far more to Eddie than his jokes, and his other signal qualities—his generosity, his devotion, and his love of the macabre—are all in evidence in the same letter, written from San Juan in 1943. He sends money for my father's college graduation ring and money for his mother, with the stipulation that she spend it on herself. He promises he will buy a suit and have his picture taken for her, and he offers to pick up cigarettes for his father, since they are six cents a pack. He also gives assurances that he is going to church, and describes at length the bodies he's seen in glass coffins in the cathedral, as well as that of "Ponce De Lon, the fellow who was looking for the water of youth."

Eddie spent his life on the water, from his adolescence in the Merchant Marine to his leisure hours on his outboard motorboats, the first named after my cousin Maureen and the second after my sister Marianne, the first- and last-born in my generation of cousins. Though he started out in precincts in upper Manhattan and the South Bronx, in the Three-Four and Four-One, he spent the largest part of his career, from 1961 to 1975, in the coveted Harbor Unit, on patrol in the waters of the city. If my view of his cop life on land is somewhat hazy, on the water it is completely lost in fog, and even now I'm not sure what cops in Harbor do for eight hours and thirty-five minutes a day. In Eddie's NYPD files, I found a few letters of thanks from people he helped after their boats capsized, and in one of my father's scrapbooks— Eddie favored the scrap heap over the scrapbook—I discovered a *Daily News* clipping, from July 19, 1965:

SHOWER AIR CONDITIONS
THE CITY

A violent thunderstorm which struck the metropolitan area yesterday afternoon drove temperatures down 8 degrees in one hour, knocked out power in five sections of Staten Island and flooded the Belt Parkway in Brooklyn for three miles.

In Coney Island an 8-year-old boy was struck by a piece of masonry knocked off a building by lightning. A 24-foot sea skiff . . . owned and operated by Joseph Derrico, 53, of 2132 LaFontaine Ave., Bronx, exploded and burned off the northwest end of Hart Island at 2:45 p.m.

Derrico, who was alone on the craft, said he was in the rear and that the explosion occurred up front. He thought it must have been caused by lightning. He leaped overboard and was picked up by a police launch.

Patrolmen Edward Conlon and Charles Bengston, in another police launch, saw Derrico jump and went aboard the burning craft to make sure no one else was aboard. They suffered minor burns and smoke poisoning. Derrico was unhurt.

Cops are awarded medals for this kind of incident, and deservedly so. But since we have to write up these exploits ourselves for commendations, Eddie would have been disinclined to bother, out of both laziness and modesty. *Why would I want everybody to know that I jumped onto a burning boat, when the guy on it already had the sense to jump off?* It happened, and no real harm was done, so why dwell on it? When he told the story at the bar, or to his nieces and nephews, he could embellish it with pirates and sharks. Such stories were not for medals or to impress bosses, but for a few laughs before you went back to sea.

In Harbor, these rescues are not only of the living. Every year around tax time in April, the winter jumpers become the spring floaters; the holiday suicides undergo a bodily sea change in the warming water and rise to the surface, as if prompted by second thoughts when the days grow bright and long again. Eddie liked to wander around on Hart Island in the Sound, which has been the city's Potter's Field since the Civil War. The unknown and unclaimed dead are buried there by prisoners from Rikers Island. When my family went out on his boat, we would sometimes pass by the flat and green haunch of land, where bones fell from the little dirt bluffs around the shoreline.

Those years when Eddie was in Harbor were tumultuous ones for the City and the Job. Narcotics flooded the streets and crime surged, and racial tensions and civil unrest broke out into violence, while he sat it out on Launch #13, maneuvering through the swells. When the City nearly went bankrupt in the mid-seventies, he returned to shore, to the Four-Seven, in the north-central Bronx, a neighborhood that changed from the old trio of Irish-Italian-Jewish to West Indian during his time there. Though he finished his career on land, I still think of him as a helmsman, as much at ease in the ebb and flow of street life as he was on the tides, a steady little vessel in the great, mercurial element. He was never a "collar man," but he took care of what came his way, whether it was an armed robbery or a family dispute. He often drove his lieutenant, Eddie Donovan, who became a close friend. Donovan told me a story about a time they were parked outside a nursing school on a winter night, having a cup of coffee. There was an abandoned car beside them, and when a sleepy derelict stirred within the car, it startled them. A nun then came out from the school to tell them to drive the man off, complaining that he was a loud drunk and an obnoxious panhandler. Donovan told me, "Eddie then gave the nun a lecture on Christian charity that made her blush. By the end, she went back inside and brought the man blankets, and Eddie gave him five bucks out of his own pocket. Things like that were continuous with Eddie, he was such an easy touch for people who were down on their luck. When he had the cells, he would sometimes add his own money for the prisoner meals, so they could get something decent."

For Eddie, to be a cop was to have a lot of fun and do a little good. If you missed out on either, shame on you. Because his pleasures and his labors were so simple and so long-standing—in the same apartment, in the same job, with his free time spent in his boat and the bar around the corner—his theater of identity served a purpose; he was a kind of reverse Walter Mitty, supplying daydreams to lives that needed a jolt or a twist. Eddie's sense of play came from a denial of the seriousness of things, a view of fate that says, *Don't kid a kidder,* as the polite version of the saying goes. At his wake, there were stories that began, "I never knew he wasn't a lion tamer," and others that ended, "And it was only when the plane landed that I realized he didn't have a pilot's license." They went on for two days at the funeral parlor on Broadway in Kingsbridge, told by patrolmen and officers of high rank, guys from the boatyard with names like "Pinkie," and people from the neighborhood, then and now. But even when the stories were told, by men red-eyed with laughter and grief at once, they often had a "you had to be there" quality that was pronounced even for the circumstance. Eddie was the subject of stories more often than the teller of them, an actor who improvised for the moment. He had a talent for making things up as he went along, and he had come to a full stop.

At St. John's Church, across the street from Vanity Court, six officers in dress blues carried out Eddie's coffin, snapping a final, white-gloved salute as he left for Gate of Heaven to join his parents. It was an Inspector's Funeral, and many cops would argue that he died in the line of duty, in his way, passing away so soon after serving so long. His commanding officer, Inspector Thomas Mullen, was there in uniform, lending the ceremony an air of purpose and belonging, as if Eddie had at long last been promoted after decades on patrol. Mullen lived in the neighborhood and was a friend of my parents'. When Mullen was a patrolman, my father introduced him to his friends, and Mullen in turn looked out for Eddie the Cop. Mullen later went to Bronx Narcotics, and he helped me get there, when it was in Eddie's old precinct, the old Four-One, the "Fort Apache" of legend. At the time, I thought that if I'd died then—had my other uncle been right—I don't think the other messengers or copy-machine operators I had worked with could have mustered up much of a send-off.

But the NYPD had not yet entered my thoughts as a possibility of livelihood, still less a life. It was a private world, like that of Eddie's apartment—which hadn't been painted since the New Deal, and probably hadn't been cleaned since the Kennedy Administration—and it intrigued me mostly because I wasn't allowed inside, rather than because of any obvious allure of its own. Within weeks, however, I was living in Vanity Court, and the Conlons would continue on Kingsbridge Avenue for another decade. But if the Job didn't appear to be the life for me, at least not then, it became increasingly clear that I had to find what was, or would be. I had enough of my father in me to know that it was time to move on.

And I had enough of Eddie in me to go where I wanted, indifferent to reproach and immune to regret. Near the end of his life, at some family dinner for Easter or Thanksgiving, we were all watching old Super-8 movies from the '60s and '70s that had been transferred to videotape. The jumpiness of the hand-held camera gave the old footage an accidental vitality, as if the juice, the tempo of those days, could barely be contained on film. My uncle had no children and little time remaining, which would incline most people to a retrospective mood. But he stayed on a couch on the far side of the room, indifferent to the fishing trips and First Communion parties that had enlivened the past decades. I went over to him and sat down, asking if he wanted to watch the tape. "Nah," he said, a look of calm bemusement on his face. "I never look back."

· · ·

MY FATHER KNEW THAT HISTORY NOT ONLY REPEATED IT-self, but often spoke louder the second time around. Strange as it seems now, I looked up to cops more than he did. Not all of my friends' fathers were cops, but a number were: Rich Ferrari, Mike Gilchrist, and Brian O'Connor all had cops for fathers, and there were other men like Inspector Mullen in the neighborhood. Beneath the surface of the uniform, I saw a uniform sub-stance, strong and caring and fair, if not always welcome when you were out with your friends. FBI agents don't wear uniforms, and my father's job was often not like theirs, though the difference was more pronounced in the past. My father had been a police officer briefly, after the war, though I don't think he spent a day on patrol. He took a leave of absence after the Academy to go to law school. In his scrapbook, I found a clipping from the July 2, 1948, *Journal-American* of his graduating class, which expresses a sense of nearly ra-diant patriotism and achingly local hope. The caption quotes from the address delivered by Commissioner Arthur W. Wallender, who "ordered the new policemen to 'use rough tactics with criminals and kindness with the general public.'" My father is somewhere amid the sea of faces in the photograph—all men, all veterans, and mostly white, though with more black faces than might be expected—whose diverging horizons draw the eye back like the crosses of Arlington Cemetery. But its broadcast of a great, collective "Attaboy!" is under-cut by my memory of my father's ambivalence. Wallender would resign in a few years, driven out by the Harry Gross scandal, as would his boss, the ex-cop and friend of the family Mayor William O'Dwyer. As my father told it, the Job was a kind of safety net, and he had just begun to climb the ladder: "I was a veteran, a Marine lieutenant—acting captain, for a while," a college gradu-ate for whom the GI Bill offered still more opportunity, in a city and country and a time of promise as none other in history. He could do better than the NYPD, he felt, and ambitious men in the police department faced their own peculiar risks: "People would tell me, 'With your background, we'll get you on the Commissioner's Squad, no problem—you'll get rich!'" He wanted no part of it. My father had many friends in the NYPD—a few retired cops have told me, with some vehemence, that my father was the only FBI agent they ever got along with—but he felt it was not the place for him.

The NYPD was a more human institution than the FBI, for better and worse; more varied in its actors and aims. The NYPD was subject to the pressures and compromises of local politics, whereas the FBI was led by a man who, regardless of his other qualities, had led an independent and professional organization for decades. Nonetheless, there was ample room in the field of play for honorable men, and because those men were the ones I knew, their characters reflected the character of the Job. The stories of villainous police officers that sometimes appeared in the newspapers were seen as rarities, and their portrayals in movies and TV were silly cartoons. Men like Pat Brown were figures from a distant and long-dead age. And so when Eddie's old friend Davey—his partner in crime from the impostor prank that Uncle Joe had described in his letter—came over to the house after the wake and reminisced about his time on the Job, he brightened our dark days with some very strange light.

Davey was wiry and fair, in a checked tweed blazer and a Bavarian-style hat, with a narrow brim and a jaunty green feather. I noticed the hat because he wore it indoors, but also because I'd heard he'd killed a lot of Germans during the war—he was highly decorated, and even captured a U-boat—and I was tempted to check the lining for a Nazi scalp. Davey had availed himself generously of the spoils of war, which was apparently a habit he'd picked up in childhood: his mother was the Democratic district leader who likely arranged my grandmother's audience with Boss Flynn, and she and Davey were the caretakers of various historical sites. My father told me that they sold many of the beds that George Washington was said to have slept in, several times over. As Davey sat in our living room, slight and quick as a ferret, he told cop stories of such plain and unapologetic corruption that any comment by my father would have been pointless, like taking a cannibal to task for his table manners. On television, when a crooked cop spoke of his misdeeds, it was usually in a haltingly pious, broken-backed apology, a confession from the bowels of shame. By contrast, Davey was the cat, as he might have put it himself, who ate the canary.

My father told me that Davey once led cops from Internal Affairs in a high-speed pursuit, which led to his tossing a load of guns off the George Washington Bridge. I don't know if he heard it third- or fourth-hand, if Eddie told him, or if Davey said so himself, still less what truth or embellishment accompanied the source. When I read a few articles from the summer of 1958, there was no doubt that much had been left unsaid; the question was whether they even told of another escapade entirely. The *Daily News* broke the story:

POLICEMAN HELD IN PISTOL THEFTS
6 TAKEN FROM PROPERTY CLERK IN BRONX—
SPECIAL SQUAD TRACES MISSING ARMS

A Bronx policeman was held on $7,500 bail yesterday on charges of stealing six pistols from the Bronx office of the Police Department property clerk. He was also charged with possessing two other weapons stolen from a policeman's locker in 1955.

Patrolman David . . . was arrested Thursday after a three-week investigation by a special police detail. The police said that [Davey] who has been on the force eleven years, had traded the six pistols to a Yonkers dealer for merchandise, money, and two other pistols. In addition, the investigators said, two pistols stolen from a policeman's locker at the Bathgate Avenue station were found among thirteen unregistered weapons in [his] possession. . . .

Two days later, the *Times* ran an update:

2 ARE ARRAIGNED IN POLICE ROBBERY

With the arrest of two more cops, however, the gun dealer in Yonkers reconsidered his identification of Davey, who apparently bore a strong resemblance to one of them. And three days later, the *Times* reported that this doubt had borne fruit:

PATROLMAN CLEARED OF STEALING PISTOLS

Though Davey still faced charges relating to the theft of guns from another cop's locker, his luck held, and within two weeks, it was all sorted out:

POLICE THEFT JURY INDICTS 2, CLEARS ONE

They had a witness and a lot of guns, and then they had nothing. Now, especially, I would have loved to hear how Davey beat the case, but it also seems rude, like pestering a magician to explain a trick.

In ordinary police procedurals, a clever sleuth finds the culprit, as his unerring instinct guides him through a maze of obstacles. In Davey's version, there was something of this, too, in form if not content. "It happened on the Upper West Side, an old lady kicked the bucket," began one account, as he settled into his easy chair, the children gathering around him on the floor. "She was a junkie, it turns out, there's more of them like that than you'd think. The sergeant called me in to help search the place, which was a wreck—piles of magazines, stacks of laundry, books up to the ceiling." When someone dies alone, the police have to search the scene to secure valuables, safeguarding them until the next of kin can be located. "These other cops were sick of it, ripping through her old underwear and coming up with morphine—what a disgrace, the old bitch!—when something told me to take a look up on the top shelf of the bookcase. It was a thick medical book, and I climbed up and opened it. It was a fake book, with a pocket inside, and there was thirty thousand dollars in cash!" Davey sat back and smiled modestly, as if he were Sherlock Holmes discovering the Duchess's necklace in the maid's pantry. I don't remember if he smoked a pipe, but when I imagine him now, that impression grows stronger. "After that, they always called me in for DOAs. I always knew where the money was."

In Davey's chronicles of larceny, he was a figure of canny aplomb, favored by fortune and making the most of his luck. For most of his career, he was a motorcycle cop: "A lot of times in a car wreck, people get knocked right out of their shoes," he went on. "Now there was one wreck where a priest was killed, thrown clean from his car, and he's lying dead in his socks. You know how well priests dress, and I found the shoes, they were better than anything I'd ever seen, and brand-new. And wouldn't you know, they were my size, exactly! I thought, is this a sign from God, or is this a sign from God! When the sergeant came to the scene, he asked where the shoes were, and I said, 'You know, Sarge, how a lot of times in a car wreck . . .'"

I didn't want to brood over what Davey might have prayed for, or how his prayers were answered. There was much to take in. St. Augustine said that evil was not a phenomenon in and of itself, but an absence of good, much like cold and dark have no physical reality beyond the absence of light and heat. And yet you could see this creeping nothingness, like an eclipse. Was there something more than something missing in this man, who came to the wake to tell funny stories about robbing corpses? He had no fear, no shame, and not enough money, plainly and in no particular order. Maybe he did only lack things, as if he had a hole in his pocket that he kept on trying to fill.

But why did we welcome him, even in our home? Again, I thought it better to listen now, and think about it later. I knew from my father that Dave and Eddie were friends from childhood, but they had never worked together. Though I don't doubt my uncle's integrity—I doubt if he even would have liked the stories—he knew Dave well and long and remained fond of him. And so we listened with some trepidation when Dave began a story that cast them both as police officers, when the uniforms they wore weren't rented. "I had a partner who thought he could ride a motorcycle better than me, poor man. One night we decided to have a race in Central Park," he commenced, and then proceeded to recount the curves and straightaways as the two men flew through the park, with Davey allowing his partner to stay close enough to appear to be competitive. Then, rounding a turn into a transverse, the man tried to take the lead, and collided head-on with a taxi. "The driver was an old Jew, he came out crying, 'My God! I've killed a policeman! Oy vey! Vat vill I do?'" Davey knew that that the accident wasn't that bad—he'd get no new shoes that night—and took the driver aside. "I tell him, 'He's not dead, my friend, but this is very serious business. If you do exactly as I tell you, you might make it through this all right.' Now I happen to know there's a problem with this kind of motorcycle, a manufacturing defect—there's a weakness in the front struts and they sometimes give out. I says, 'Now try to remember, and be very clear. Did you see, as my partner and I were driving along at a moderate rate of speed—slowly, even better, you saw us drive slowly—when you saw the front of his motorcycle buckle down. . . .' And he says, 'Ya, ya, I can see that, I remember, that is exactly how it happened. . . .'"

His partner suffered a broken leg and was brought to a hospital on Fifth Avenue ("a very boola-boola joint," in Davey's phrase), which distressed the partner in its way as much as the injury. At that point, Davey called Eddie and apprised him of what had developed. That night, Eddie went to the hospital and announced that he was a police surgeon and would require a stethoscope and surgical gown. So costumed, he clamored for a nurse to escort him to the cop's room, where he viewed his patient with alarm and dismissed her: "My God! What kind of hospital are you running here, anyway!" He lit a cigarette and ominously reviewed the chart. After a period of study, he took his cigarette and placed it between the man's toes, which protruded from the end of his cast. Putting on the stethoscope, he listened to the man's pulse, in his chest first ("Mmmm, not good"), then moving on to his head ("Brain waves very weak"), and leg, newly plastered and smoking from the toes: "No, no, no. Officer, I don't know what these quacks told you, but this leg has to come off, toot-sweet." With fierce dispatch, he tossed the chart away, collected his cigarette, and marched out of the room. The terrorized cop called his wife, who raced to the hospital and had the car waiting as he hobbled out to escape. For my uncle, at least, the Job came with great benefits.

For Dave, however, the story had a bittersweet ending: "The motorcycle company paid out sixty thousand dollars for the accident, split between my partner and the old Jew. Did I see a nickel of it? No, I did not!"

The first shock was that these things happened; the second was that we learned of them in what was more a boast than a confession; the third, far longer in coming, was that we didn't even hold it against him. Davey's tales were a kind gesture, in their awful way, making us laugh as we prepared for a burial. And it was not the first time he had done such a thing for my father. In the first days of 1952, when he and Eddie buried their father, Davey came to the funeral. Their mother had been dead for seven years by then, and their youngest brother, Gerry, was eleven years old. What a winter it must have seemed, to be orphans and parents at once. Requiem means rest, but not for them; as they left the church, all the hymns and prayers, the promises of God in a dead language, faded in their ears. They would have mustered on the cold, familiar sidewalk in their black ties and fedoras, smoking cigarettes, as they readied to leave for the cold, familiar fields of the cemetery. And then Davey arrived, in uniform on his motorcycle, at the head of a delegation of cops on bikes, helmets gleaming and engines roaring, in formation at the head of the cortege. They led the hearse and the line of cars northward through the city streets, as other cars pulled aside to let them pass, and the drivers must have wondered which dignitary had died and deserved such splendid ceremony. They did not stop at the city line but drove on, commanding the highways until they reached the place called Gate of Heaven and saw my grandfather home. And so my father must have been glad that Davey had been there then, as he was now, and glad he had not seen much of him in the intervening years, and gladder still that it was not his place to judge.

· · ·

IF DAVEY SHOWED ME THE KIND OF COP THAT MY FATHER feared, a few months later, one of my closest friends provided a dramatic counterpoint, offering the Job such talent and heart that it hardly knew what to do with it. And when Mike Kelly took up his beat in Spanish Harlem, my father was angrier with him than he ever could have been with Davey. Mike Kelly had gone to Regis with me, and then on to Williams College. After graduation, he worked for the Chase Manhattan Bank, and seemed destined for a steady ascent through the white-collar world of the city. Which, as my father saw it, was as it should be. Our families were close: my parents looked on Mike as a son, and I was at the Kellys' in Brooklyn with their seven children almost as often as at my own house.

My father had a particular fondness for Mike, not just as a surrogate son but almost as a surrogate self—the resemblance between them was stronger, in many ways, than it was between my father and me. Mike even had a younger brother, Pat, who also became a cop, and he reminded me of my Uncle Eddie. Both Mike and my father were strivers, with a seriousness of purpose and a self-sufficiency that I lacked; from an early age, the Kelly boys worked as teamsters during the summer, covering the cost of their education and helping with household expenses. Both were readers, especially of history. Now that I think back, both had the quality that Father Callahan, our sophomore-year Latin teacher, tried to describe when he talked about "pious Aeneas," who founded Rome after the defeat of Troy. By piety, he didn't mean its modern sense of something fussy and narrow, an almost fearful clinging to old conventions, but a steadiness and strength that came from its roots in the past. Aeneas was a man who carried the stones of the old city until he found the place to build the new. When it turned out that, for Mike, the new city would be Spanish Harlem, it wasn't exactly what my father had in mind. Mike received no offers to get rich by joining the Commissioner's Squad, but that's not what mattered most to my father. The move was not only against common sense—to leave a bank for a beat when you have loans to pay off—but a violation of something deeper, a derailment of our progress in America that was closer to a crime against nature than a bad career choice. From the hardscrabble West of Ireland to the docks of Hell's Kitchen, to the apartments in the Bronx and then our house in Yonkers, where we moved when I was young, the generational trend in the Conlon and Kelly families had been to move up and out. For Mike to choose as he did, he might as well have announced that he was going back to Ballinrobe, to tend a few sheep and dig potatoes with a stick. For months, my father was mad, and I had to hear about it. "If you have any influence with your poor friend Mike Kelly," he would begin, as if I could have talked Mike out of it, even if I'd wanted to.

For one thing, I thought it was funny, in the way it's funny when any of your friends does something stupid. For another, Mike was happier than I'd ever seen him. At the bank, he looked as if he was going gray from within, but the Job brought out a sense of fervor and mission. In the Academy, he was somewhat self-conscious, and glad that no one had heard of Williams College, one of the "little Ivies," to spare himself the questions and complaints of his classmates, who by and large would have taken the same position as my father. Given that he was a twenty-four-year-old Irish kid from Brooklyn, the gap between him and the other rookies was not exactly unbridgeable, but there were moments when he slipped up. One day in law class, the teacher asked him to explain the Fourth Amendment, and since he was dozing or daydreaming, his response was unguardedly good:

"The right of the people to be secure in their persons and their homes, their papers and effects, shall not be abridged, except . . ." As he rattled off the text, he noticed that the rest of the class was staring at him. "And shit like that," he concluded.

Mike graduated first in his class of two thousand, which gave him his choice of precincts. A cousin was a lieutenant in the Two-Three, which covered 96th to 116th Street, from Fifth Avenue east to the river. It was a bad neighborhood, except for the lower extremity, which touched on the Upper East Side and the yuppies—a term that was new at the time, and the group to which Mike might otherwise have belonged—and the remnants of an Italian enclave at the northeast edge, which I called Very Little Italy. It was a good choice, for Mike: bad enough to keep him busy but not unrelievedly poor, and, for him, the closest bad neighborhood in Manhattan, the center of the world as we knew it. Mike worked steady day tours, which allowed him to go to school at night for a master's in criminal justice at John Jay College. Day tours—the second platoon of three, following the midnights and leading to the four-to-twelves—are usually the slowest, in terms of crime, but the most engaged with the neighborhood, at its most benign and routine. School opens and lets out, the streets are full of *mami*s on their errands. Men who work have left for work, and the men who don't aren't up until at least midway through the tour. More than at any other time of day, you see the people who are happy to see a cop, and with Mike, their expectations were fulfilled. After his tour ended, he volunteered at a community center called the Oasis, tutoring and playing basketball with the kids. Although the stories he liked to tell were not action-movie arrests but adventures in absurdity—"Did I ever tell you about the time I nabbed the infamous cheese bandit of 103rd Street?"—Mike's belief in the white knighthood of the Job never abated.

That belief was what Mike was most afraid of losing, I think—I never heard him talk about his personal safety, as a real concern that lasted beyond a few moments of danger, fighting an EDP, facing a volatile domestic dispute, and so on. The threat was to his faith in the Job—what the Job meant, as a whole; what it would do to him, and with him, in the event of some crisis. And the crises we read about usually came in the form of racism or corruption. In a sense, he expected to encounter them in the NYPD not because it was an especially crooked or racist institution, but because these evils were part of the human condition, and to be a cop meant you would experience humanity at a level of skinned-alive intensity. The fact that a Brooklyn neighbor was one of the cops involved in the "Buddy Boys" scandal, which involved a ring of drug-dealing thieves and became a book by journalist Mike McAlary, didn't make him rest any easier. But the fact remains that he never saw any corruption, never saw a cop take a nickel or even heard of any who did.

Racism was another matter, not nearly as simple, and if what he saw wasn't enough to shake his faith, there was much to challenge his reason. Mike was from a part of Brooklyn that had reconvened from other parts that had "turned"—turned bad, or turned black, which to the shame of liberals and the bitter delight of bigots often meant the same thing. But in the aftermath of racially charged killings in Bensonhurst and Howard Beach, the attitude of simply being fair in how you dealt with people, and figuring it out as you went along, didn't seem to be quite enough, either. After Mike went to the Two-Three, he was sometimes partnered with an old-timer who used racial slurs almost as if they were punctuation marks. Mike didn't like it, and tried to explain why the best he could—which, in a rookie-veteran partnership, is somewhat like an altar boy preaching to the Pope. In most ways, the old-timer was a plainly decent guy, and his treatment of people was respectful, no matter if it masked an abstract contempt. On the street, or responding to a job, he handled matters with the amiable pragmatism of the veteran city cop, and face to face, he was an effective public servant. But once they retreated to the car, it was all color commentary, so to speak: "Would you believe how these niggers . . ." and "It reminds me of the time this spic . . ." Suffice it to say that they agreed to disagree, Mike being a fair guy who figured it out as he went along. And then came a day that made it all the more confusing. Mike was at court or on vacation—not on patrol, in any case— when his partner went into a burning building, alone, and saved an elderly black woman. Mike was never able to reconcile his partner's constant and audible prejudice with his act of color-blind heroism. In the old-timer's case, the divorce between word and deed was wide enough that there's at least one black person who is grateful he worked as a cop.

Mike's own call to arms came at an unexpected time and place as well. He was in his apartment with his fiancée, Tara, in the Bay Ridge section of Brooklyn, which was mostly middle-class Irish and Italian. Late one night, Mike and Tara were awakened by a loud disturbance on the street, and when it became clear that they would not sleep again soon, Mike took a look out the window. From his third-floor room, he could make out five or six white guys surrounding a Hispanic man on the street, closing in on him, then stepping back as he brandished a screwdriver. Mike shouted at them to knock it off, and when they didn't, he threw water at them, which sometimes works on dogs. It was the summer of the riots in Washington Heights, which Mike had been sent to: three nights of burning and looting after a cop killed a drug dealer who was trying to kill him. Mike dreaded the thought of Bay Ridge joining Howard Beach and Bensonhurst on the martyrs' trail, of riot duty at work followed by protests at home, of having to push past the Reverend Al Sharpton and the cameras to get to his dinner. Whether the Hispanic man was right or wrong, whether he was coming home from the job he worked at for a hundred hours a week—turning screws, I suppose—or whether the white guys caught him stealing hubcaps, it didn't much matter—or it wouldn't, as Washington Heights had proved. And so Mike picked up his badge and gun, told Tara to call 911, grabbed the first piece of clothing at hand, and headed down to the street. As soon as he entered the fray, he stopped it cold. It might have been the badge, and it was more likely the gun, but it was even more probable that what shocked the combatants into détente was the fact that Mike was wearing Tara's nightgown.

When you see a statue of Justice, remember: she usually carries a sword but she always wears a dress. Though Tara's message to 911—"Mexicans . . . screwdrivers . . . Sharpton . . . *and tell Michael that I love him!*"—may not have been entirely lucid, the situation must have been powerfully confusing to the responding officers. Mike shouted that he was a cop, but he wasn't the only one shouting:

"Put your hands up!"

"Put the gun down!"

"Don't move! Don't move! *Don't move!*"

One cop approached Mike, grabbed his outstretched hand—which still held the gun—and it went off. Mayhem broke out, briefly, but Mike gave up his gun and assumed the position. The other cops moved in, and they put everyone against the wall till the collective blood pressure went down. The bullet had gone through an apartment window across the street, but everything was spared except a pane of glass and the peace of mind of the old woman who lived there. The duty captain arrived—a rotating assignment for precinct commanders, covering the borough—in time for Mike to recover his composure if not his pants. When a cop shoots his gun, either punishment or praise is allotted, as a matter of course: either you get a medal or you lose time, from a loss of vacation days to a potential prison sentence. In this case, which entailed an accidental bad thing happening during a good deed brought about in a deeply weird manner, no easy judgment was available, and so Mike was simply told not to do it again. Sometimes, Justice wears a blindfold because she'd rather not know. And so the city held together, that night and for many to follow, with our many warring tribes gathered in enforced harmony beneath the soft skirts of Patrolman Kelly.

My father couldn't remain mad at Mike for long, and as it happened, things got better at home for me, too, not least because I left it, weeks after Eddie's death. My father eased up on me; maybe he'd lost some of his fight, as if part of him had gone into the ground with Eddie, or—as I prefer to think—because he kept something of Eddie with him. Things between us had never been terrible, in retrospect, but after I left home, they were positively good. When I was in high school, he once threatened to throw me out of the house—at the same time, I threatened to leave—and though neither of us threatened lightly, it came to nothing, when tempers cooled, and my father asked me to stay "for your mother's sake." After Eddie's death, he realized that what time we had together would not be well spent on lectures, which never had much of an effect on me anyway. We would not be partners, as he had been with Eddie, but he would have to trust me to find my place in the world. It would not be far away, or long in coming: within a month, I moved into Eddie's apartment in Vanity Court and found a real job. It wasn't as a cop—in a sense it was the opposite—but now I see it as taking a step back, readying myself for the big jump. From the time of the wake, I began to realize that the NYPD, which could employ Davey, Mike Kelly, and Inspector Mullen, not to mention Uncle Eddie, offered entry into a drama as rich as any in Shakespeare. And I didn't want to hear the story as much as I wanted to tell it, and I didn't want to tell the story as much as I wanted to join it.

. . .

A FEW WEEKS AFTER UNCLE EDDIE DIED, MY COUSIN SISTER Patricia Daly, O.P. (aka "Patty the Nun"), offered me an extra ticket to a big fund-raising dinner. Not one to turn down a free meal, I went, and I met a friend of hers, a Jesuit priest named James Joyce, who introduced me to a friend of his named Janet Storti, who ran a small social-service agency in Brooklyn called Consultants for Criminal Justice Alternatives. The position of Court Liaison was available—it had been most recently filled by Meyer Lansky's nephew, but I wasn't to make too much of that—which involved meeting indicted or convicted felons, writing up their life stories, and proposing alternatives to prison, usually some combination of community service, counseling, education, and job training. Though the undertaking would have pleased my predecessor's uncle more than mine, my father was more than content that I had a job of any kind. And so it was by a chance meeting, a few words, and a handshake, amid echoes of Irish writers and Jewish gangsters, that I started on the road to the Job.

Consultants for Criminal Justice Alternatives was a mouthful to say, and it suggested something massive and shadowy, as if what we did took place in an outbuilding on the grounds of the Rand Corporation. There were as many people employed there, in fact, as there were words in the title, which was shortened to CCJA. There was Janet the boss; Sheryl the secretary; Liz and Louis and me, who had different titles but did the same thing. When a defendant in a criminal case cannot afford a lawyer—which in New York City is in the vast majority of instances—they are represented by the Legal Aid Society or a private attorney, paid by the state, from a list known as the 18B panel. We worked for 18B, and other defendants were referred to us by judges who knew us—usually in cases in which they were inclined to give a defendant a break, and wanted us to give them a reason to do so. We handled fewer than eighty cases a year, and as there were some fifteen thousand felony indictments annually in Brooklyn at the time, we had the luxury of choice. As one defense lawyer told me—he was also a Jesuit priest—"After you get your third baby-killer in a row, you don't want to go to work anymore." We were engaged on behalf of people whose guilt was not in doubt but whose futures, hopefully, were; we would try to cut a deal for the deserving. The idea was a good one, however slight its effect on the raw volume of cases in the system, and as I saw it, it worked—though there were surprises in our successes and our failures.

My first case was my best case, and my hardest. It involved a great kid who became a bona-fide bad guy, quite suddenly, but who looked as if he could be turned around again. Jack was "a rare case with a real chance," as I later told the court, precisely the kind of defendant we should be fighting for. His case was also, on the face of it, a loser: Jack had been arrested three times for robbery within a year, all of them "wolf-pack"-style muggings, in which a group of teenagers had roughed up another teenager and taken a hat or a chain or a radio. Jack had pled to a misdemeanor on the first case; the second two were still open. After the third arrest, his mother wouldn't bail him out, and he was sent to Spofford, the juvenile jail in the South Bronx, where he had been for a few months before I got the case. He was fifteen years old. Judges tend to feel in these cases that the defendant hasn't been getting the message, and a stronger one has to be sent. They are right.

Until the year before, Jack had been a good athlete and an excellent student, popular with adults and other kids. At his parish grammar school in Bushwick, St. Barbara's, he had led the youth group, and he'd been selected as a delegate to Washington for a conference sponsored by the Kennedy Center. From there, he'd attended a special junior high school, in which all students were required to pass an entrance examination, and his mother, Maria, proudly showed me the trophies he'd won at graduation, for English, Science, Physical Education, and Community Service. Both his science teacher and the assistant principal raved to me about Jack, and they even went to visit him at Spofford—the only time I've ever heard of teachers making jail visits, before or since.

This transition from honor student to inmate was occasioned by three events, in the span of a few months: his family left Bushwick for Brighton Beach, a better neighborhood but a move that left St. Barbara's behind, along with his teachers, counselors, and friends; his special junior high school was superseded by a huge, chaotic, and gang-infested high school in Manhattan; and a reunion with his long-absent father took place just before the father's death from AIDS. "I changed," Jack said. At home, he became withdrawn and argumentative, eating little and sleeping often. At his new school, his grades were poor and he began to cut class. He also hung around with a wild bunch of kids who called themselves "the Decepticons," and he got into fights. Two months after Maria had a heart attack, Jack and a few other Decepticons took someone's radio, and he was arrested again.

When I first met Jack, it was painful to witness his nostalgia, especially when it was so well-earned. He was a fifteen-year-old kid in prison coveralls, talking about his trip to the Kennedy Center and how the hotel had "HBO and rugs and everything." He was handsome and well-built, with an openness to his expression that usually doesn't last long in jail. He was at once a regular kid—his mother described his interests, before things changed, as "weights, basketball, and girls . . . he spent a lot of time smiling in the mirror," and a special kid, personable, articulate, and bright. He knew what he had going for him, and he knew what he was up against.

Jail proved to be just the place for Jack. He picked up a lot of his old, good habits, and his new teachers and counselors began to repeat the accolades I'd heard before. His social worker told me, "It's a good thing he was in here. It shook him up—he feels he let a lot of people down." His dormitory supervisor was even more enthusiastic: "He's a beautiful kid, a great kid. Of all the kids I've seen come through here, and I've seen a lot of them, Jack is one of the best. He has tremendous, tremendous potential." Everyone I spoke to thought Jack could readjust to life outside, as long as he was provided with a significant degree of structure; I wanted to make sure the structure wasn't made of cinder block and barbed wire.

I found a residential school in upstate New York for "gifted but troubled youth," which would have been ideal, as Jack excelled in both categories. I got him admitted to the school and found a way to pay for its fifty-thousand-per-year tuition. I amassed statistics, showing that the juvenile prison system was not only significantly more expensive, but utterly disastrous for kids like Jack: for fifteen-year-old urban minorities with multiple violent crimes, the recidivism rate was over 90 percent. At the school, where Jack's record was not regarded as abnormally or unworkably grave, the recidivism rate was under 15 percent, and three-quarters of their graduates went on to college. If they listened to me, I would argue, Jack would be saved, and if they didn't, he was doomed. I had convinced myself, at least.

In my report, I wrote about the Decepticons, the gang Jack had joined in Manhattan. The childishness of it struck me—they were named after the villains in a cartoon called *The Transformers,* in which cars and trucks turned into missile-shooting robots—and I thought the silly juvenility of it all would show that we were hardly dealing with Murder, Inc. On the day of the sentencing, the front page of the Metro section of *The New York Times* led with the headline A GANG GIVES A NAME TO STUDENTS' FEAR: DECEPTICONS. The article said that the gang was organized so loosely that no one quite knew who or where they were, and this anonymity helped feed the legend of its menace in city high schools. As I entered the courtroom, I felt a little sick.

The judge had many shortcomings, but alas, he wasn't illiterate. He had read the *Times.* He read my report, too, but his interpretation of it wasn't mine. "So you're saying, because he's bright, he shouldn't be held responsible? Because his home is a good one, he shouldn't do time? These are arguments *for* a prison sentence, not the opposite." He asked me if I had anything to say, and, heart in my throat, I made a stammering, angry speech. I didn't insult or provoke him, I think, but in truth I don't recall exactly what I said. The judge sentenced Jack to two to six years in the maximum-security version of juvenile prison. I felt nauseated. Jack looked sad but stoic. "It's all right, Mr. Conlon," he said, touching my arm. "Thanks for everything. You gonna be okay?"

After Jack, I kept my distance from my clients. The cases tended to fall into two categories: people like Jack, who had led ordinary and even good lives that fell apart in a short period or through a single act, and found themselves as far away from the familiar as if they'd swum into a rip tide. These sudden derailments were easier to work with than those in the other category—those of the non-starters, who seemed to have been doomed from the outset, and who arguably deserved a break from the system, since they had never had a break in life. For some of these, the debate was chiefly over what kind of cage they should be in, as when I visited a guy named Dwayne at the prison hospital at Rikers Island. He believed he needed his sneakers in order to breathe, and he had a habit of exposing himself and assaulting interviewers. He had been picked up in the subway for carrying a Molotov cocktail, and CCJA hoped to put him in a hospital instead of prison.

Or Frank, a cheerful, chubby, and middle-aged Italian man with the mind of an eight-year-old brat and the body of his great-grandfather, and whose heart disease, diabetes, and hypertension required a dozen medications that didn't mix well with lithium and mixed worse with crack. Frank had tried to make off with a refrigerator from a construction site. Because of his lifelong history of such offenses, he was in jail, where his chances for survival were slim. There are places for mentally ill people, and places for addicts, and places for the physically ill, but I could find only one for all three, and they didn't want him because, years before, he'd set a fire in another institution—after, he told me, he had been raped. Arsonists aren't welcome anywhere. But if I could get him admitted to Kings County Hospital, and then transferred to a state hospital, he could be evaluated and placed from there. I went to court and offered to take him in myself.

"Okay," said the judge, and he released the big lunatic into my custody. Frank was like a two-hundred-and-fifty-pound puppy, not nearly ready to be let off the leash, which I wished I had thought to bring. He wore oversized hospital pants that kept falling down. I called Mike Kelly, who was a rookie cop then, and he picked us up. Frank liked Mike. He liked lots of things—me, crack, and other people's refrigerators—and he gabbed away as we sat in the emergency room of the massive gothic red-brick hospital, amid the survivors of car wrecks and gunshots, and howling schizophrenics who made Frank look as grounded as Harry Truman. After five or six hours, Frank was seen by the attending psychiatrist, who asked him if he wanted to hurt himself or anyone else, and whether he heard voices. Frank was feeling quite chipper at that point and said so, after which the doctor promptly dismissed him. It was not what was supposed to happen, and I protested to the doctor, explaining my predicament and insisting that Frank's moment of clarity was no reason to disparage his first-rate résumé as a loon—which was the only thing keeping him out of jail, and alive. I couldn't call the cops—he'd committed no new crime—and I had no real power to make him wait with me overnight and then surrender to the judge. The doctor was unimpressed, even as Frank's pants fell down again. We would have to try again later, with another doctor. In the meantime, we decided to take him shopping for pants.

Thus began a long night for the three of us. At a department store on Flatbush Avenue, Frank tried to put things in his new pockets even as security followed us in a man-to-man defense. At a McDonald's, Frank said he wanted to drop by to see an old girlfriend—not to worry, he tried to assure us, he'd just meet us later. Back at the hospital, we were told to wait until the morning, when we could again make our pitch to the day staff. There, Frank helped us stay awake by engaging his brother John in a lively debate, notwithstanding the fact that John had been dead for fifteen years. Frank stared fixedly at a spot on the wall as he said, "No, Johnny, you know I never did that, it didn't happen!" and "Yeah, I know, I miss you, too!" as Mike and I gazed at him with weary dread. Then he turned to us and grinned: "Had ya goin', didn't I?" Yes he did, we had to admit, and we persuaded him that the quality of his performance was such that it would be wrong to deprive the next doctor of it. And so when morning came, it was Frank's ability to act crazy—and perhaps Mike's and my appearance of losing our grip as well—that won his admission to the hospital, and our final freedom.

It's hardly worth mentioning that there is no formal training for this kind of work. The massive, interconnected systems of cops, courts, and corrections, physical and mental health care, social service, community service, and educational facilities, public and private, religious and secular, would take a lifetime to learn, or you could just wing it. Although I'd had a mother who was a psychologist, a father who was an FBI agent, and a brother in law school, each of whom was consulted constantly, the responsibilities to which I was entrusted now seem laughably large. I had been an English major, with a postgraduate résumé that included messenger, elevator operator, and guy at the copy machine. Now, I argued in court; I visited jails, and homes that were worse; I learned to ask women how many fathers their children had without embarrassment or accusation, questions which would have been fighting words where I came from. This was in the late 1980s, when New York City was breaking its homicide records, and I would walk into neighborhoods that led the city in that statistic—Bedford-Stuyvesant, Brownsville, East New York. Once I asked a cop for directions in East New York, a precinct where there were one hundred and twenty homicides in one year, and he looked at me, shaking his head, and said, "You go three blocks that way, if they don't kill you first." My clients included a three-hundred-pound Czech Gypsy crackhead, whose father kept weeping on my shoulder while trying to stuff fifties in my pocket, and a charming little girl gangster, who used to go to church and announce that various relatives had died, to take up collections. I had a woman who'd put a butter knife through her boyfriend's heart, men who killed each other barehanded in street brawls, a thirteen-year-old who had thought the gun didn't work.

The thirteen-year-old was named Dondre, and he stood just under five feet tall and weighed less than a hundred pounds. He was at once an ordinary child and a working criminal: he had an imaginary friend and loved to watch Saturday-morning cartoons; he sold crack, carried a gun, and at the age of eleven had been discovered hiding in the ceiling of a bank, after closing. He lived with his grandmother, and his best friend, named Kataun, was her boyfriend's grandson, making them "cousins." Dondre's father was unknown, and his mother's rap sheet listed burglary, assault, arson, and other generally masculine felonies, as if she was trying to be two bad parents at once. One Saturday, after a morning of cartoons, Dondre and Kataun went out and bought a forty-ounce bottle of malt liquor, which they shared, after which they played with the gun Dondre had recently bought—he was told it contained three "dead" bullets, which wouldn't discharge—and they began to horse around, wrestling in the hallway outside Kataun's apartment. When Kataun got him in a headlock and wouldn't let him loose, Dondre took out his gun and put it to Kataun's head and pulled the trigger, once—*Click!*— twice—*Click!*—and a third time, which covered the wall with Kataun's head. Dondre ran to his own house and went to sleep for a long time. Odd details of that case have stayed with me: for some reason, I was more irked by the fact that Dondre, who looked like he was eight years old, was buying beer than that he was selling crack. And I was struck by the conversation with

Kataun's gently sorrowing grandfather, who remained with Dondre's grand-mother afterward, and from whom I hoped to obtain some statement of support for our claim that it was neither an adult nor an intentional act. Instead, he told me, without anger but with deep conviction, that he hoped Dondre would be charged with murder and remain in prison. But what I remember most about that case was talking to Dondre's grandmother in her favorite chair in the living room, a stack of paperback books on one side of her and a bottle of brandy on the other, and how she was reading the spy novels of John le Carré. I wondered what she made of them—their chess-game of subterfuge and betrayal in foreign capitals, their patterned world of clever rules and lofty purpose—and how it all appeared from an easy chair in a housing project in Brooklyn, amid dead bullets that came to life and living children lost forever.

What I did not see was the crime. CCJA rarely disputed the facts of a case—even for Dondre, who we argued should be sentenced as a juvenile—and our remoteness from the violence in which we trafficked could give it the blandness of a statistic, like a bad report card. The closest I came to the reality of a killing was when I happened across a crime-scene photo showing a young man who had nearly been decapitated, his spine completely severed and his head loose on his neck like a chopped-down tree. My client in this case was a hapless little old man named Cecil, an immigrant from the tiny island of Montserrat in the West Indies, and the cause of his clienthood was his stepson Keith, the youngest of his wife's five children from a previous marriage. The first four had grown up on the island, and in America they were distinguished and professional people—teacher, banker, and so on—whereas Keith, who had grown up in Brooklyn, had become a crackhead and subjected his mother and Cecil to years of terror, breaking in, beating them, and stealing everything in sight, including wedding rings and wedding pictures. One night, after Keith begged for hours to be let in the apartment for a shower, his mother relented and opened the door, and once in, he blew up, shouting threats and tearing the phone from the wall. Cecil picked up a kitchen knife and took one swing at him, which connected with a force that, in photographic retrospect, was amazing to consider. Initially, both Cecil and his wife argued that Keith was to blame for his own death; it was what cops sometimes call a "public-service homicide." But during the year that it took to litigate the case, his wife had a change of heart and a change of story, out of natural remorse and pressure from her other children. Keith was now a blameless angel whom Cecil had murdered in cold blood. When she made dinner, she would set a place for Keith but not for Cecil, who lost his job as a dishwasher and sank into a depression, responding to most questions by muttering, "I would not be able to say." For Cecil, the bloody reality of his act was offset by the surrounding circumstances, and although the jury found him guilty of manslaughter, he was sentenced to probation on the condition that he go back to Montserrat.

But there were other cases which no past wrong or present optimism could explain, crimes which I hoped I would never begin to understand. One night I worked late in the office and got a call from Rikers Island, from a woman who was on trial for killing her infant. (My phone number must have been on the wall of the murderesses' washroom.) I told her that I might have been able to do something before she went to trial, or could perhaps do something after, if she were found guilty, but that I had little to offer innocent people, as such. She was a lost, lonely person with a sweet voice, and, as the trial went on, her calls became increasingly friendly, and we spoke less about the case, which had to do, sketchily, with a baby and a bathtub, and which she insisted was an accident. One day, her lawyer called, an Indian man with an accent so heavy that I could barely understand him. The verdict was guilty, he said, because the prosecution was able to show that the water in the tub had been heated on the stove. I had been chatting with a woman who had boiled her baby to death. She called, half an hour later, when I was still a little dizzy from the revelation, and I said abruptly that I would not be able to do anything for her. As when I became a cop, I found myself entwined in lives I could barely imagine, and I wondered if theirs were the better for it, or how mine, in time, would be the worse.

. . .

SOME OF MY COP FRIENDS DIDN'T THINK MUCH OF WHAT I did at CCJA, but others respected it, whether because they took a larger view of the system, or because I told them the stories, or just for my sake. As I said, my father liked my job primarily because it was a job, but also because he saw that I was taken with it, how it drove and stretched me. There was no obvious next step in sight: I had no interest in leaving the field for an administrative position, and since I got to play lawyer without the burden of law school, or the awful caseload—numerical and moral—of real defense attorneys, pursuing a degree made little sense. And so it came as something of a surprise when my father mentioned, offhandedly one afternoon, that I might think about becoming an FBI agent. It happened not long before he died.

We were outside in the yard, on a warm afternoon. I think I might have nodded, or said, "Hey, yeah, maybe." I had begun to take a zealous interest in La Cosa Nostra, and I had a fair command of its history in America. I thought of his angry reaction when Mike Kelly joined the NYPD, and I wondered if his suggestion implied that he thought things were looking down for me, or up. Given all that had passed between us, the adolescent storms and the recent years of grace, the remark struck me as a gift: you could do what I did, and it would be good. He also told me that when he'd worked on the docks, loading freight, he knew that some of the men there would sew razor blades into their caps. When a cop approached one of them, he would take off his hat, feigning humility, and then swipe it across the cop's eyes to blind him. Later on, as an agent on the waterfront, when my father confronted a man who took off his hat—"Geez, Officer, what's the problem?"—he knew to step back, gun out, and tell him to drop it. Because he had seen it before, he would see it again. That's what he thought I should know.

There is a scene in *The Godfather* when Don Corleone tells his son Michael how the other families will come after him. The Don has survived a shooting, but he is in semi-retirement, having handed down power to the son whom he hoped would do better. He tells him he is not ashamed of his own life, that he felt he had done what was necessary, but that Michael had gone to college, and might have been "Senator Corleone . . . Governor Corleone . . . I don't know. . . ." He mutters and meanders when he talks, but he makes himself clear. There is no sense that Michael shares his regret, though he will later on. All he says is, "I know, Pop. I know."

Until the very end, when my father spoke of his career, it was often with a distinct note of remorse; though he was proud of his service in the Bureau, he began to question whether he would have been equally proud had he stayed there for ten years, or fifteen, or twenty, instead of the twenty-eight he was permitted before mandatory retirement at the age of fifty-five. When he retired, the eldest of his five children was fifteen years old and the youngest was seven. He made another deeply cautious choice by becoming a security consultant for Con Edison, which supplied power to New York City and was as close to the civil service as any job there was. He declined the opportunity to become head of security there because he would have had to be available twenty-four hours a day, rather than be a deft, daylight fixer of such problems as arose. Because his responsibilities came so early and heavily, the cultivation of opportunities for their own sake—whether for financial or intellectual rewards—had an air of vanity about them, of selfish pride. And during the time when he expected to live a long life, to endure with the thrifty eternity of the civil service, it troubled him. But when he began to suspect he was going to die, soon, and for no reason in particular, the fact that he lived well and had loved his life restored his perspective like the clouds breaking below the North Star to a sailor lost at sea.

In 1991, the last year of his life, my father had a minor prostate operation in the month of March. It was a routine and successful procedure, after which he walked out of the hospital and resumed work without impediment. But something entered his mind in the next few months, lightly at first, but then with the grip of a premonition. He had always been in good health, and I can't even remember him having a cold, though when he did suffer some physical ailment—a cut on his finger that turned septic, say—he made an uncharacteristic fuss. By June he believed that he was going to die, and though he maintained a dignified skepticism on the outside, the increasing strength of his belief led him to consult five different doctors in the week before it proved true. The last referral was on Friday, to a company psychiatrist, who prescribed valium despite his protest that he was not depressed: *No, I like my job, I love my wife and kids, my life is good—I just think I'm going to die.* On Saturday afternoon, he sat on his red fake-leather easy chair in the living room, watching television as my mother was in the kitchen putting the house together and planning the remainder of the day—the Mullery boy's graduation party, then five o'clock Mass, then a drive to the Poconos, where they would spend the weekend. There was something in his manner that made my mother ask, "John, do you want to skip the party?" And he said, "Yeah, Betty, why don't we?" After a little while in the kitchen, she came in to look at him and said, "We could go to Mass in Pennsylvania in the morning," and he said that might be a good idea. A few minutes later, she returned and looked at him again, and asked, "John, do you want me to call an ambulance?" And he said, "Yeah, Betty, I think maybe you should. . . ." She held him as he dozed off, and he never woke up again.

At the funeral, I gave my father's eulogy, and I had secretly arranged for my friend John Rowland, a Transit cop, to play the bagpipes outside the church. As we followed the coffin down the aisle, the organ played "Jerusalem" and the bells pealed, as the drone of the pipes rose from the street. John played the "The Minstrel Boy," because it was a sad, Irish song:

The minstrel boy to the war has gone,
In the ranks of death you'll find him.
His father's sword he has girded on
And his wild harp slung beside him . . .

And then he played the Marine Corps Hymn, which my father loved, and then "Going Home," because that was the usual way it was done. I thought I had done well by my father. There were over a thousand people there, and I saw none who were not weeping. I hugged Uncle Gerry on the sidewalk, and he shook his head and smiled.

"There's nothing like the pipes to get you. I love them, I could hear them all day."

I nodded, as I loved them too.

"One thing about your father, though. He couldn't stand the bagpipes, I never knew why. Well, go figure, you can't please everybody."

• • •

THREE AND A HALF YEARS LATER, THERE WAS SOME DEBATE over whether I was in the picture. After the first row, and maybe the second, the faces began to dissolve into the grid of dots. The caption above the photo in *Newsday* read NEW, BUT TRUE BLUE, and it told how we were the last class of Housing cops to be appointed, as the long-rumored merge of Housing, Transit, and the NYPD would take effect in April. We had our hands over our hearts as we were sworn in as officers, in the auditorium of the Police Academy. My brother John said that he couldn't see me there, and it did take some imagination to make me out in the third row, where individual features blended into the background. If my family had doubts about whether I was there, they were utterly mystified as to why; I wasn't sure myself, but it felt right. My circumstances were different from those of my father, when the *Journal-American* snapped the picture of his class, with their hands on their hearts, forty-seven years before, but my reasons were fairly similar: I needed a job, and I thought I might like this one. A couple of days later, a friend called to say, "Hey, I saw your picture in the paper!" It had to be true, though it didn't seem so at the time.

The Academy was to last six months. There was a moment a few days in—the first several were spent in an auditorium, filling out forms—when the guy next to me, Kenny Wade, whispered, "How do you spell 'deceased'?" I pointed to my form, where I had written it, though he was already looking at it anyway, as I was looking at his. Everyone was watching how everyone else filled out the forms, as if knowing the Social Security number and next-of-kin of our neighbors could spare us from failure. As it happened, this particular answer was the same for Kenny and me, and the flash of affinity was a consolation. We had dead fathers, and that connection was more apparent than any other in the auditorium, where four hundred individual responses to the term "business attire" suggested that business ranged from ditch digger to pimp: jeans, T-shirts and work boots, and pajama-like suits of pumpkin and purple. To look around was to learn what "motley" meant.

Some of the instructors made a show of drill-sergeant bark and bravado, making public examples of those of us who returned late from lunch or otherwise showed a lack of seriousness. I wondered if it would have been faster for them to pick out the biggest guy in the room and knock him flat. There were questions from the audience that might have warranted it:

"I have a twenty-six-inch neck. Do they have a uniform for me?"

"I expect to get a lot bigger from working out; should I buy a uniform for my size now, or for the size I expect to be?"

"I had stuff to do during lunch. Mind if I pop out for half an hour and grab a quick bite?"

In the past, cops who were recruited for long-term undercover assignments skipped the Academy altogether, so that the NYPD sensibility wouldn't rub off on them. The risk seemed minimal, as far as I was concerned. In the months before I was sworn in, I had told only two people that I was going to become a cop: Mike Kelly's brother Pat, who reminded me of my Uncle Eddie and therefore seemed like the most typical cop I could imagine, and John Driscoll, my smartest friend. Pat thought it was hilarious, and John thought it was good, and their opinions showed at least that I had chosen my confidences well, as there were few other endorsements when the decision became known. One friend called it "the worst career move since Rudolf Hess parachuted into Scotland." Though my brother Steve was intrigued, the rest of my family thought it was awful, that it would be dull and depressing work.

Initially, they were right: even before the Academy, I had to make repeated three-hour subway trips to Queens for my background investigation, bringing in heaps of paper to explain my career so far. When I brought in my college diploma, my investigator made me return with my high school transcript, to make sure I was educationally qualified. When I brought in my passport, he told me I didn't need it, and then changed his mind later, making me spend another day bringing it out. I took to bringing in information by the boxload—when he asked for taxes, he got all the receipts, too—which deterred further interrogations along those lines. I had to explain my criminal record, which no one made too much fuss over. As I had no license, there was no driving record that needed explanation—unlike the recruit in the next cubicle over, who defended one summons by saying, "That was the time I sneezed and missed the stop sign."

But these tedious chores, necessary or not, became bearable when you viewed them as halting steps toward the destination. A lot of the Academy was degrading, or at least recalled a degree of humiliatingly close regulation that I could barely remember from childhood. The day would begin on the muster deck, the open roof where we would form into companies for drill and inspection. Strangers would denounce you for the quality of your shoe shine or haircut. When actual cops walked past you on the stairs, someone had to call, "Make way, recruits! Make way!" signaling us to press to the side to let them pass. Our gray polyester uniforms made us look like Cub Scouts. Discipline was enforced through demerit cards, or "Star Cards," and administered in the dreaded Room 512, where General Patton himself would have been berated for the quality of his posture and salute. Stairways were specifically designated UP or DOWN, and there were lanes painted in the halls. Seats were always assigned, as were the places we stood in for Gym. After Gym, a hundred men would stand in line for the three working showers, nearer to each other's sounds and smells than we would have liked, but preferable to the course chosen by the stinking shy-guys who skipped the showers altogether. On that note, I discovered that the Department employs men for what has to be one of the most awful jobs in the world, and though I don't know the formal title, "piss inspector" describes it plainly enough. For drug screening, we had to fill a bottle at a urinal with a slanted mirror at the top, so the piss inspector could tell it was produced from the genuine article. Those who were afflicted with "stage fright" were given coffee, water, and all the time they needed—some lasted through the night, I was told—so that it could be ascertained that the delay was prompted by embarrassment over what was in the pants and not what was in the bloodstream. One guy in my company failed, a postal worker who had left his old job "because of the stress." The drug test was given the day after St. Patrick's Day, and I wondered if it was a coincidence.

My classmates in Company #95-04 were older than I'd expected—a third of us were my age, thirty, and above—slightly more white than black and Hispanic, and substantially more male than female. The youngest was a twenty-year-old guy named Kris Cataldo, who rarely spoke, and the oldest was the once and future postal worker. By and large, we were an earnest and studious group, who had been mechanics and teachers and toll takers before, married as often as not, sometimes with several children. I got along best with two white guys from Long Island, Wade and Breitfeller, and two black guys from Queens, Ford and Casey, and though we sometimes talked about going out after work, we never did. I was surprised when I asked Ford to go to lunch one day and all the other black people in the company came, too, but if we had any kind of social life together outside the Academy, I never heard about it, and our old friends and other responsibilities claimed our free hours. We never called each other by our first names. A number of instructors went on about the importance of keeping our old, civilian friends, so that we had a wider and healthier perspective on life, and wouldn't live completely within the Job. We seemed to have weathered that danger.

During training, we were force-fed massive amounts of technical detail, some of it powerfully moral and logical, some microscopically petty. I worked far harder than I did in college, copying out homework assignments on loose-leaf each day for each class, in proper 49 format. This was one:

POLICE DEPARTMENT

CITY OF NEW YORK

May 24, 1995

FROM: PPO Edward Conlon CO#95-04
TO: Sgt. Alvarado
SUBJECT: Homework, Lesson #63

1. State the rules regarding Environmental Control Board "Notice of Violation and Hearing" summons and return locations.

   ECB, 1250 Broadway, 7th Floor, NYC 10001 for
   a. Food vendor regulations
   b. General vendor

   c. Health code violations
   d. Public health law
   e. Noise code violations
   f. Sanitation provisions
   g. Air code provisions

2. State rules regarding an incident where there are both ECB and Criminal Court offenses.

   A Universal Appearance Ticket can be issued for summonsable Administrative Code offenses not covered by list at Desk.

3. State the provisions of the Canine Waste Law, Unleashed Dog Law, and Unnecessary Noise Law.

   a. Any person who owns, possesses, or controls a dog must remove feces from public area.
   b. Dog in public place must be on leash no longer than six feet.
   c. 1. Involving sound reproduction device:
        Seize and write voucher.
      2. Not involving sound reproduction device:
        Attempt to correct, write, advise Desk Officer.

5. Apply the general procedure regarding the "Notice of Violation and Hearing."

   a. Inform violator of offense.
      1. No enforcement v. blind in Canine Waste Law
      2. Discretion in re elderly/handicapped
   b. Request proof of ID and residence
      1. Escort offender to Station House if proof refused or dubious
   c. Separate Notice of V & H for each offense
      1. Complete captions in block letters, ballpoint pen
   d. Insert violation code, section of law, mail-in and maximum penalties on Notice as determined from Common ECB Offenses at Desk
   e. Make notice returnable to ECB, 1250 B'way, 7th Fl, NY NY 10001
      1. If food/property removed, make return date 21 days on next business day
      2. If none removed, return date 30-37 days
   f. Violator gets pink copy
   g. Arrest log entries
   h. Entry on certification of summonses served

      i. White (ECB) copy: precinct of occurrence
        Yellow & cardboard: retain with certification
      j. If violator cannot be ID'd, confer with Desk Officer
      k. Effect arrest only when criminal sanctions committed in addition to
        ECB violations (Civil jurisdiction only.)

6. For your information.

Edward Conlon
Probationary Police Officer

I notice in that homework assignment, which only in part discussed dog-shit, I skip from number three to number five, and I suspect that I put one over on the otherwise vigilant Sgt. Alvarado. Though the Academy felt like an odd combination of kindergarten and boot camp, I was nonetheless buoyed by a sense of mission, a heart-lightening hope that I was becoming part of something unexpectedly strong and large and good. My instructors were excellent, on a par with any I'd had in college in terms of their dedication to the subject and to their students. Sgt. Alvarado, our immediate supervisor and Police Science instructor, was a forbidding man, at least initially. He had a rabbinical devotion to the *Patrol Guide,* the four-inch-thick manual of procedures for everything from how to handle Emotionally Disturbed Persons (EDPs) to the dates when short-sleeved shirts were authorized, with exceptions for specified temperatures and the discretionary power of commanding officers to alter same. Sgt. Alvarado told us he kept separate folders of Revision Notices and Interim Orders, even when they became obsolete, so that he could observe the evolution of NYPD thought on matters like tow-truck notifications. It was up to him to impart the procedure for every phenomenon the police officer is likely to encounter: the sick, the lost, the crazy, the dead, cars, traffic, accidents, dogs, bombs, crowds, missing persons, runaways, juvenile delinquents, domestic disputes, gangs, arrests, hospitalized prisoners, community policing, investigations, tactics, victims, complaints, complainants, civilian complaints, corruption, and the storage and disposal of found and seized property, from drugs and cash to body parts—as well as the forms and formalities by which the Department governed itself; its structure, protocol, conduct, and discipline; times and charts of tours of duty, overtime, night differential, off-duty employment; the kinds and terms of sick leave, military leave, terminal leave, bereavement leave, and death benefits; uniform and equipment regulations and maintenance, radio codes, and all manner of in-house record-keeping. As such, Sgt. Alvarado was the man for the job, and we learned everything. He was especially severe at first, as if he were breaking horses, and then increasingly open and easy as we learned our paces and marks. He began to display a surreptitious sense of humor, asking us, during the lesson on civilian complaints, what was the one word cops use with the public that gets them in trouble most. We shouted out in unison, "Asshole, sir!" He nodded and smiled.

PO Rickard, a young Housing cop who taught us Law—constitutional law, case law, criminal law, and procedural law—was equally methodical and fervently enthusiastic, and she tried to convey the seriousness of the material while making it fun, with occasionally unintentional success. In the "justification" lesson, which outlined when a police officer could use deadly force, she ran through scenarios where shots might be fired: "What if you hear a burglar alarm, and you see a guy running down the street with a television?"

"No."

"What if he sees you and says, 'Let me go, or I drop the TV'?"

"No."

"What if he pulls a gun, and is gonna shoot a little girl if you don't let him go?"

"Yes."

"All right, forget about the burglar. What if the little girl comes up to you with her old, sick dog, and says, 'Please, officer, I need you to put him down!'"

There was a pause, and a few mumbled negatives.

"It's the sickest, oldest three-legged dog, howling in pain, and she begs you to please put it out of its misery. . . ."

A few votes shifted to the affirmative, and then Rickard tried to pull the rest of us in.

"What if she's a little blind girl, and she comes tapping up to you with a cane, and . . ."

Breitfeller interjected, "Since she's a blind girl, couldn't you just yell 'Bang!' and tell her it was dead?"

Sgt. Solosky, who taught us Social Science, would open, close, and interrupt classes with the motto "Remember, we're the good guys!" and the ringing phrase rose to mean whatever it needed, whether the curriculum covered bias crimes or poverty. Our instruction on discrimination was no different from what would have been taught at a liberal-arts college, but Solosky's street-corner regularity and surpassing decency stripped even the touchiest subjects of controversy. He asked the black students what they thought of the way black people use what's called the "N-word," and got the widest-ranging and most civil debate I've ever heard on the subject. The one person who thought it was unobjectionable to use in a casual, friendly way was my friend Casey—he'd call me a "crazy nigger" in conversation—and he surprised me later as well, when he had to do a presentation on an ethnic group. He chose the Irish, and announced that their favorite food, drink, and music were corned beef, whiskey, and bagpipes. I began to wonder if he'd missed the lesson on stereotypes, and then he concluded, "I know all of this because my grandmother told me, and she's from Wexford, in Ireland." We listened to Sgt. Solosky because he was a good talker, but also because he told us things we hoped we'd never learn but knew we might. Once such lesson had been imparted to him, some eight years before, when an accident of roll-call assignments put a rookie named Eddie Byrne on his post, guarding a witness in a drug-related homicide. Four men crept up behind him and shot him in the head. Sgt. Solosky could keep things light because he had seen things that were not.

For each of the three academic classes, we had to fill out biographical forms with education, work and military experience, languages, and other special skills. I had written where I had gone to college in a cramped scrawl, and the best guess for what it said would have been "Howard." Sgt. Alvarado and PO Rickard must have wondered why I'd gone to a historically black school, but Sgt. Solosky interrupted himself in the middle of class to say, "Hey, wait a minute! Conlon, there's a rumor going around that you went to Harvard! Didja?"

I made a derisive sound. "Not lately, Sarge."

After class, I approached him and apologized, saying I didn't mean to mislead him but I preferred to keep that quiet. He slapped me on the shoulder and said, "Don't worry, Conlon, it's nothing to be ashamed of."

The Academy also got us in shape. In one book I read, a cop recalls being told in his Academy Gym class during the 1920s, "We've studied the various physical-culture systems of England, of Sweden, even of Japan, and we think our course here combines the best features of each." The Anglo-Swedish elements seem to have been dropped since, and, for us, Gym combined running and calisthenics with self-defense, first aid, and CPR. Our instructor was Detective Washington, who had taught there for most of his career. He was a superb athlete and a black belt, and he sought to hone our survival skills by providing all kinds of so-far-unimagined motivations:

"You know what's gonna happen if you get killed on the Job—if you're too fat to run up to the thirtieth floor of the Polo Grounds projects on a gun run, and you're gasping for breath on the fifth, too wiped out to do anything but throw up, you can't even lift your arms, forget about remembering this wrist hammer-lock we learned today—and *Bam!* You are done! And everybody's gonna be sad for a while, and the Mayor and the PC will go to your funeral, and a few months, a year later, your partner, your *best friend,* the one who said he'd look out for you, he's gonna be looking out for your *wife!* He calls to see how she's feeling, and he's the only one who understands, and the next thing you know, they're on the beach together in Martinique! Martinique! My favorite place in the world, and they're gonna be drinking mai tais and daiquiris and saying, 'Should we have another?' and 'Yeah, why not!' because you're paying for it! They're living *fat* on your pension money there, and speaking of fat, you're gonna look down and say, 'Shit, she's looking good, why couldn't she lose those fifteen pounds for me! She does it for him, and not for me!' So do yourself a favor and stay in shape, and remember what I'm teaching you today so your partner can buy his own mai tais for his own fat wife. . . ."

Each of our instructors stressed that his or her subject was the most important part of the Job—that if we didn't know the *Patrol Guide,* we were finished, or if we didn't know the law, or how to deal with people, or how to defend ourselves, or drive, or shoot, we might as well go home now—and all these things were true in their way. We were force-fed acronyms to help us remember mandatory memo-book inserts (DICES: Domestic Violence, Auto Identification, Corruption, EDPs, Spanish phrases), circumstances when you couldn't carry a gun (FAVOR: Family court as a respondent, Alcohol, Vacation, Off-duty employment, and, of course, "R"), the felonies for which a juvenile could be charged as a Juvenile Offender (MARK ABRAMS: Murder, Arson, Robbery 1, Kidnapping, Assault 1, Burglary 1, Rape 1, Aggravated Sexual Abuse 1, Manslaughter, Sodomy 1). We did role-plays, acting out good guys and bad in family fights, car stops, drug sales. We took a class trip to the morgue, and though no one embarrassed him- or herself amid the filed corpses, most of us thought the smell stayed on us for a few days afterward. We were appointed to the New York City Housing Police, but Housing merged with Transit and the NYPD in April of 1995, so we would graduate as NYPD. No one seemed to care. As the months passed, the mood became less autocratic, but we were both exhausted and increasingly anxious to get out. During one lesson—I believe it was on authorization dates for tire chains—Breitfeller, Wade, and I took turns banging our heads on the wall to pass the time. I got in trouble once, or near-trouble, after our schedule changed and I went to Meal while the rest of the company went to Gym. My absence was immediately reported, and an investigation commenced, with a thorough examination of my background and disciplinary record. I returned from a pleasant fifty minutes with a cheeseburger and the newspapers to meet the Integrity Control Officer, who had a death-in-the-family look in his face.

"Where were you?"

"Lunch?"

"Where were you supposed to be?"

"Not lunch?"

To be AWOL is a serious matter, but as he led me up to Room 512, he had a hard time keeping a straight face. He asked, "Where did you go to school again?" He also mentioned that if I had been inclined to rob a bank, the Police Academy would have provided a wonderful alibi. In Room 512, another lieutenant looked at me, my record, the report of the incident, and said, "Oh, get the hell out of here."

When I did—when we all did—it was on a bright and warm afternoon in June, and we quick-stepped to Frank Sinatra's "New York, New York." Three blue columns poured into the auditorium from the entrances, stage right and stage left, and the production had far more Broadway flair than military pomp, as if the reigning spirit of good-natured wiseguy had finally transcended the bureaucratic weight of the Department. Mayor Giuliani spoke, as did Commissioner Bratton and several others, and I don't remember what anyone said except Sinatra, who belted out, *I want to be a part of it, make a brand-new start of it, in old New York!* That much was true for me, and I laughed to think of the aptness of the old standard, sung by the mob-guy wannabe whose heart was in so many places, both right and wrong. *You got a problem with that, pal? I didn't think so. . . .* We stood in our new dress uniforms, and saluted with our white gloves, then took them off and tossed them up, and they filled the air like a flock of birds.

FIVE

The Street Narcotics Enforcement Unit and Anti-Crime were considered the elite teams of the precinct, each a local version of the citywide Narcotics Division and Street Crime Unit. The SNEU sergeant, Tom Messer, had told me that if another spot opened up, he'd like me to work for him. "I told the captain, I need you since you know how to get search warrants," he said, and I don't think he was kidding, but with Messer, it was hard to tell sometimes. Messer was a legend at the precinct. He spoke his mind indifferent to rank, above him or below, and there was a perennial debate among the cops as to whether he was crazy or only acting. One recent story had it that Messer had been working behind the desk while another cop was about to eat lunch, when a woman came in screaming that she wanted to make a Civilian Complaint. Messer listened to her thoughtfully and said, "Those are very serious charges, Ma'am. Tell you what—I'll give you a choice: I'll take the complaint, or I'll give you this nice cheeseburger." Messer handed her the cop's lunch and she walked out of the precinct. Someone else told me that when Messer was a cop, he saw a drug dealer counting a fat wad of cash and asked him, "Want to double your money?" Before the dealer could reply, Messer took the wad, tore it in half, and handed it back to him. I knew better than to ask him if either story was true. When Messer left SNEU for another assignment, most of his cops went with him, and there were only three holdovers from the old unit: Kris Cataldo, from my Academy class, who picked up the nickname "Stix" because he was a distance runner; Alicia Hall; and Sammy Maldonado.

When Sgt. Mike Carroll took over the unit, I asked him if I could join. I liked him: he was bright and driven, with an attitude that had a nice balance of enthusiasm and sarcasm. On patrol, I'd had one experience with him, when I'd asked him how to handle complaints about a man who was selling fireworks to kids in one of my projects. Carroll had been a cop in Housing, and whether it gave him a belief that procedure was dispensable, or that the dignity of a police officer should be, his remedy was to send me in there "undercover." He cobbled together some ridiculous getup—I believe it was an Army coat and a Con Edison helmet, worn over my uniform—and dispatched me to the apartment. I suppose I should have been grateful that there wasn't an Avon Lady costume around. It felt like I was pledging a fraternity, and the people didn't even open the door, but it apparently showed Carroll that I had the right stuff.

For the first few days, Stix, Alicia, and Sammy were somewhere else, in training or on vacation, and so Sgt. Carroll and I took the lay of the land together, driving around the public housing of the five South Bronx precincts covered by PSA-7. It was mostly new territory for me. At my old post, I'd rarely driven, because even when they gave us a car, it made me realize that while walking the four-by-five-block grid of the Village got dull after a couple of years, driving went stale in minutes: up Webster, down Washington, up Park, down Third, One-Six-Eight to One-Seven-One. We called the route "the Claremont Village 500." Sgt. Carroll and I drove around the major projects in the Four-O: Mitchell Houses, Millbrook Houses, along One-Three-Seven Street, and then Patterson and Mott Haven, the adjacent low-rise and high-rises around One-Four-Three, and then Betances, with its smaller, scattered buildings in the upper 140s, from Willis to St. Ann's Avenue, then Adams-St. Mary's, along Westchester, and Melrose-Jackson, by the PSA, from One-Five-Three to One-Five-Eight, from Courtlandt to Morris. The numbered streets made it easy, as the evens went east, the odds west—with a few exceptions—and I began to memorize the avenues: Lincoln, Alexander, Willis, Brook, St. Ann's, Cypress, and Jackson, west to east along One-Three-Seven, gave me LAW BAC Jackson, with the second A for St. Ann's, and I didn't include Brown Place, a three-block street between Brook and Willis, since I remembered it anyway, because Jose Velez from field training lived there, and we'd hung out one night on his stoop and had a few beers. Learning the buildings—which ones had roof alarms, or exits in the back, or working locks on the front doors—would come in time.

Just after midnight one night, Sgt. Carroll and I went to the roof of 169 Cypress, in Millbrook, and looked out over the grounds, the familiar red-brick towers and wide green lawns. A few young men loitered in a lobby, and a fat man sat alone on a bench along the pathway, but otherwise it was desolate, unusually so for a night in the city, as we eased into the summer heat. "Quiet tonight," Sgt. Carroll said. I waited a beat and added, "Too quiet," because that was the line that usually follows in war movies, which was a bad idea: seconds later, three or four shots were fired, and the rounds passed just over our heads. We hit the deck, a decent impulse and yet a pathetic one, as if we could have dodged the bullets. We laughed nervously as we crept back inside the building.

To have a boss, and especially to drive one, was a novelty. On patrol, most of the sergeants had regular drivers, and the assignment was prized to the degree that the sergeant was; as a driver (a "chauffeur," technically, though only the very old bosses or the slightly delusional ones used the term), you tended to work less but to see more, as you made the rounds of beat cops and sector cars to raise them for the scratch, and to respond to heavy jobs, complicated jobs, or arrests. You had to call a boss for a Missing, or before you could force entry into an apartment where you heard a brawl going on inside, or if you couldn't make head nor tail of a situation. As with any partner, you had to pass the eight hours and thirty-five minutes of the tour sitting eighteen inches away from each other, and if there was a lack of sympathy or shortage of small talk, the time crawled by. But even if there was no mismatch between cop and boss, there could be for the rest of the precinct: some drivers saw themselves as junior supervisors, and others saw themselves as lobbyists for the rank and file. Usually, a kind of lopsided fraternity developed, and if their respective personalities and experiences fit the big brother–kid brother roles, a partnership as strong as any might be formed. Sgt. Poplaski was "Pops" to Richie Henderson, and Sgt. O'Hagan was "Hagie" to Joey Castaldo, but it was some time before Sgt. Carroll became "Mike" for me, and usually only off-duty even then. I was at least as old as any sergeant in the command, but most had ten or more years on the Job, and their experience as much as their rank earned my respect.

I liked my boss, and I was ready to try out my new partners. Partners in a squad car could almost seem married, in their devotions and divisions, in the conversations they could pick up from months before, as if they had never stopped talking. The two-cop team became customary when the patrol car came into use, and this accident of technology led to what now seems the natural arrangement: wolves run in packs, cattle in herds, cops as partners. When long-term partners broke up, that was the term people used—"Didja hear, Mike and Joe broke up!"—and it was spoken in the sorrowing, fretful tones usually reserved for news of divorce. Partners faced the street together, and the sheer size and variety of what they encountered intensified their bond. With a partner at your back, you were free to think about the street, the radio runs, and the pick-ups; to look outward and ahead.

On a team—or in a squad, or in a unit, which SNEU was, though we called it a team—it was different from patrol. In a team of one sergeant and five cops, one and eight, one and ten, the odds were better when you faced the street, but the perspective was different as well. We usually worked in vans, not cars, and so the social model was not marriage but a family, or a pack of kids with a single parent. The teams didn't chase the radio, taking what came to them, but instead largely picked their own targets—drugs for SNEU, stolen cars or guns for Anti-Crime. As much as cops can, they engaged the world on their terms. But in deciding those terms, there was a lot of talking among themselves, and of themselves. In the precinct, or driving around in the van, as much attention was focused inside as out: there was always someone complaining that they had to go to the bathroom every half hour or had missed a meal, or making everyone else complain because they had just gone on a protein-shake diet and they were stinking up the place. Even if the boss was a dictator, there was always a rowdy democracy to a unit, if not concerning when or where they worked, then at least how. If the police department was a paramilitary organization, as we were frequently reminded, the units stressed the "para."

I kept quiet at first, but keeping to myself was out of the question. After I joined Stix, Sammy, and Alicia in SNEU, Tony Marcano and Orville Reid, who had been partners before, came onto the team. We got along well enough, but there were disparate personalities in play, and, in terms of background, we were like an updated version of a unit in a World War II movie—Orville, or "OV," the strong-minded Jamaican Christian; Stix, the cagey, quiet Italian kid from upstate; Tony, the down-to-earth Puerto Rican guy from the

South Bronx; Sammy, also Puerto Rican, even-tempered, modest, and older; Alicia, the princessy but tough-as-nails black woman; and me, whatever the hell I was. In real terms, I was the newest guy there: Stix and I had the least time on, but he had been in the unit for six months already; Orville and Tony had occasionally worked with the unit when Messer was the boss. Moreover, everyone else knew the Four-O: Stix had worked in Betances and Mott-Pat, as had Sammy and Alicia, and Tony and Orville had been beat cops in Melrose-Jackson.

If I didn't have the least to offer, I certainly had the most to learn. When Orville said later, "You should have a game already when you come to SNEU. You're not supposed to come here with nothing, expect us to teach you," he wasn't talking about me, but I kept my mouth shut anyway.

A SNEU team makes arrests for "observation sales," and the way it works is by dividing into an observation post, or "OP," and a catch car. One or two of us go to the OP—if you're in it, you're "doing ops"—on a rooftop or in a vacant apartment to watch a "set," or drug operation. The set might be one teenager standing on a corner with one pocket full of crack and another full of cash. Or it could be an organization of complexity, with lookouts, managers, money men, steerers to guide customers, and pitchers for the hand-to-hand transactions. The dealers might send out phantom or dummy buyers, who appear to have bought narcotics but have not, to see if they're stopped. There were systems of such intricate subterfuge that you'd think their purpose was to deliver canisters of microfilm from double agents to covert operatives instead of ten-dollar bags of junk to junkies. We would watch, and give descriptions of buyers for the catch car to pick up, a few blocks away, on a radio frequency dedicated to point-to-point communication within a range of a few blocks.

As the catch car, we usually had a van, and though we preferred an unmarked van to the blue-and-white, in reality we were so well known it made little difference. Once you got the description, or "scrip," and the buyers' direction of flight, you moved toward them, allowing a distance from the set, but not too much, or else you'd lose radio contact, or they'd get home—in neighborhoods like this, you didn't have to travel far for hard drugs. Sometimes they'd run, and sometimes they'd fight, and sometimes they'd toss the drugs, and sometimes they'd eat them when they saw you coming. You'd want a scrip with something distinctive, something beyond the "white T-shirt, blue jeans" of warm weather, "black jacket, blue jeans" of cold. You didn't want "Male, walking three pit bulls." You were glad to hear hot pink or lime green, T-shirts with legible writing on them, "Female in purple-and-yellow track suit, with a Cat-in-the-Hat hat, riding a tiny bicycle." For crackheads as much as any other species, protective coloration was a successful evolutionary strategy.

When we had a handful of buyers, we'd move in on the sellers. Most of the spots that we hit were well-established, patronized and pursued on a regular basis. Others would pop up and disappear, as a player for a day picked a spot for the day, sizing up his prospects with an expert or rookie eye. You might drive around, to see who was out, the faces at the places, the traffic pattern of steady customers and usual suspects. Sometimes you felt like the man on the catwalks over the casino floor, scanning the tables for the sharps and card-counters, looking out for luck that's too good to be true. Other times you felt that you were in a nature program, some *National Geographic* special on the felony ecology of the streets.

Though I'd watched from an OP before on my post, I had little experience with a catch team, which may have explained my limited success with drug collars in the Village. Generally, if you were looking, you would do verticals until you ran into someone with drugs on them. If I saw a sale, sixteen floors or twenty floors below, it was unlikely that I would get down in time even to get the seller. I stumbled into most of the decent collars, like when I watched a playground from a rooftop for a few hours before I gave up and came down, then walked into a guy smoking a blunt whose knapsack was filled with bundles of crack and heroin. My eyesight was less than perfect, and I wore glasses at night; staring for a long period of time through binoculars gave me a headache. Tony rarely went up into an OP, and Alicia almost never did. Stix, Sammy, and Orville went up most often, and Orville, especially, had an eye that approached genius. Orville could survey a crowded playground and say, "The guy in the green shorts has it in his right pocket."

On our first day out, we watched a building in Mott Haven from a school across a street. I was with Sgt. Carroll in an OP in the gym, peering through the window to see who made thirty-second visits to the lobby. If drug dealers ever hired consultants to find the best defense against arrest for observation sales, they'd probably recommend this kind of set: a dealer in a lobby with a locked front door and the stash nearby, usually in the stairwell, concealed in a light fixture or over a doorjamb. Any change in the variables—if they kept stash on them, or if the front door was broken, or if we had the key—made an arrest more likely, but in general we couldn't take them for sale, as we rarely saw the transaction inside. We could pick off buyer after buyer, rattling off the scrips for the in-and-outs, and stopping them to ask what they were doing in the building. If they had no answer or a false one— "Um, I watched a movie at Maria's house, I forget her last name, and where the apartment is,"—after we'd seen them spend less than a minute in the building, we got to search them. But once we hit the lobby—creeping up, then rushing in, maybe when the door opened for someone to leave, hoping that an unfriendly neighbor wouldn't blow us up on purpose, or that a friendly neighbor might betray us by their astonished look or questions—if they didn't live in the building, the most we could charge them with was trespass.

A young Hispanic guy worked the door, in a white shirt and black tie, greeting customers like the maitre d' of a restaurant. After filling the van with buyers, we moved in and grabbed him, and though he wasn't holding drugs, he had several hundred dollars in small bills. The maitre d' was a great ex-plainer, unfailingly polite, maintaining a patient and sympathetic tone as he attempted to correct our benighted delusion that he was a drug dealer. It was as if he understood that we were limited people presented with ambiguous circumstances, and he could hardly fault us for coming to foolish conclu-sions. At the precinct, his explanations were endlessly elastic, and we asked more and more questions just to see how far he could stretch: no, he didn't live in the building, but his aunt did, and he waited in the lobby because he didn't think she was home, and he let in those people because they knocked, of course, and it was the civil thing to do. Why did they all turn up with heroin in their pockets? He had no idea, but he had some of the cash because he had just been paid, from his job as a stock boy in Manhattan, and yes, it was more than a week's pay, but the rest was from his wife's baby shower, and he had to buy a crib. . . .

Sgt. Carroll laughed in his face. I didn't believe him, either, but there were times when I found myself wavering—not because of his technique as a liar, though it was excellent, but from the sincerity that welled up in his voice when he talked about his wife and baby, and how he could never, ever have anything to do with drugs because of them. It wasn't my first drug collar any more than it was the first lie I'd heard, but it always amazed me to witness the passion and nerve that addicts brought to their falsehoods, though they often lacked skill. Once, a huge woman bellowed at me as I took a crack vial from her open hand, "You planted that there!" It reminded me of the Richard Pryor line about a man whose wife catches him in bed with another woman,

"Who are you going to believe, me or your lying eyes?" My perp followed up with an unassailable truth, as she lifted up her shirt: "You can't take me to jail, I don't got no bra—look!"

But we charged the maitre d' with sale, arguing that the pattern of conversation and movement, the recovery of cash and identical product—in this case, heroin stamped AIRBORNE—from all of the buyers, gave us probable cause for the charge. It was certainly true that he was the seller—he even admitted it, months later, when I saw him again in the precinct after another arrest—and it should have appeared so to most people, in most places, but as a sale case in the Bronx, it was dead on arrival. No transaction was witnessed, no contraband was recovered from the defendant, and inference alone, no matter how obvious, would not warrant prosecution. He was out the next day, and if he did have an aunt in the building, not even the trespass charge would stick. That bothered me a little, not because I had any vested interest in whether the maitre d' spent ten minutes in jail or ten years, but because it meant our work meant nothing, or we didn't, and all the hours of labor and risk were for our benefit alone. The gap between what we did and what it meant seemed to widen, though the work engaged us enough that we didn't bother dwelling on the big picture.

Within the team, that kind of arrest occasioned a frequent debate over "splitting collars." If three perps were collared for robbery, of course, one cop would take the arrest, but if two cops saw two people trespassing in a building, they sometimes tried to split it up into one for each. The pressure for "activity," specifically arrests and summonses, was always on the increase. On my beat, I didn't like writing summonses, and I eventually stopped writing parking and moving violations altogether, but since I made a lot of arrests, the bosses never minded. Since crime was rampant, it seemed ridiculous and even dangerous to take a day's pay out of someone's pockets because they parked in a Housing lot without a sticker, or their registration had expired last week. The people who had cars tended to be the people who had real jobs, and I wanted to keep them on my side. But other cops had slower beats, and others worked in sectors where they raced from job to job, and some were simply lazy, and for them a month or two could easily pass without an arrest and twenty summonses, which was a rough average of what was expected. As Compstat pressures increased, those cops could have days off denied them, or have their weekend switched to Tuesday and Wednesday, or be transferred to another post or even out of the precinct. Quotas were illegal, but the Job needed some concrete measurement of performance, and so the Job usually won the argument.

As SNEU was an arrest-oriented unit, the problems were slightly different. We were all eager to collar, on most days, and so our concern was to keep the numbers roughly equal, both for the activity and the overtime. If Orville had five for the month but Sammy had none, Sammy was up. But in a maitre d' situation, you could say either you had five misdemeanors and one felony, with one arresting officer, or you had six misdemeanors, with six A/O's. After arraignment, you would have six misdemeanors, regardless, so the decision rested on whether you wanted the felony statistic, which benefited one cop, the sergeant, and even the captain, in some tiny increment, or for every cop to get a collar. When a team worked together, taking their time and evenly distributing the labor of paperwork, fingerprints, vouchers, and prisoner search and transport, the time passed quickly and the quality of work was better. If one person took all the collars for that day, the rest of the team would help, certainly, but not in quite the same way, all the time, and each piece might not be done precisely as the A/O wanted. More to the point, the non-arresting officers might be sent home to save on overtime. Alone, your paperwork for six collars could be overwhelming, late in the day, if one of the perps got sick or went crazy, or a computer broke down, or a DO started to scream at you that your prisoners were in the precinct too long. For us cops, it was better to split things up, as much as possible; for them—the boss, the precinct, and in some thin and theoretical way, society—it was better to wrap everything into one case.

I wasn't sure whether I was us or them. Carroll was them, certainly, but he wanted the felony for the catch-of-the day satisfaction more than anything else, the pride of taking out a set to throw to the lawyers and say, "We got 'em. Now, it's up to you." I agreed with him, but I wasn't going to go against the team. I couldn't say, "Felonies are more fun, guys!" and I couldn't say, "Our purpose is to drive out the scourge of narcotics that has bedeviled Three-Eight-Three East One-Four-Three since they piled up twenty-one stories of cinder block and sheetrock and stuck a fucking junkie in every fourth apartment." And I couldn't tell Carroll, "Who are you kidding? We'll work hard, and we'll get our numbers, but why go crazy when we're not backed up by the DA or anybody else?" When Messer was the boss, he was less involved in the street operations, often covering the desk or supervising patrol while the team picked up bodies. When they were ready to go, they would raise him on the radio to head into the Four-O, and he would take care of whatever was necessary to process the arrests. Carroll was in the mix, as much as any of us, sneaking up into an OP or rolling around with perps on the street. It was a change, and change did not always go smoothly.

. . .

WE WENT OUT TO COLLAR ALMOST EVERY DAY, EXCEPT WHEN we had court, training, or some other contingency, or when the boss was out, in which case we would fill in patrol cars or take footposts. Sometimes they let us work together in a van, but technically we weren't supposed to mount a SNEU operation without a supervisor. For some reason, however, setting up to pick off trespass collars was not considered SNEU work, and if we came in with a van full of prisoners, no one complained. If something went wrong—an injury, an escape, or anything that invited scrutiny—we would have been in trouble, so when Carroll was out, they mostly stuck us on patrol. And I'd had enough of patrol to last me for a while.

The change from a beat to SNEU was exhilarating. For one thing, you only dealt with criminals. There were no more domestic disputes, EDPs, or DOAs, the morass of negotiable and non-negotiable difficulties people had with their neighbors or boyfriends or stepchildren. On patrol, you dealt with the fluid whole of peoples' lives, but usually when the tide was going out: people who had the cops called on them weren't happy to see you; people who called the cops didn't call when they were having a good time. In SNEU, all I did was catch sellers of crack and heroin, and catch their customers to show they sold it. The rest of their lives, the parts unaffected by coca- or opiate-based products, was none of my business. Patrol was politics, but narcotics was pure technique.

There were rules like in chess, percentages like in poker, moves like in schoolyard ball. We called dealers "players." When we drove around to set up, early in the tour, we'd read the street, looking at who moved and who stood still, the solitaries and small groups, their reactions and relations to one another. Most people occupy their environment blithely, with only a slack and occasional awareness of their surroundings. A store window or a noisy garbage truck might distract them for a moment, and they might look around before crossing the street, but the ordinary pedestrian is a poster child for daydreams and tunnel vision. Not so in the narcotics trade, where the body language of buyer and seller alike reads of outward focus, a taut awareness of opportunity and threat. There are distinctive addict walks, such as the prowler, who might be new to the spot or sussing out an operation that has shifted to a more favorable corner. His pace is slow and his progress is roundabout; he wanders, floating around like a flake of ash above a fire, looking out, alert for the deal. The addict on a "mission walk" moves with double-quick footsteps, leaning forward, as if against a strong wind, so as not to waste an extra second of his wasted life. Many players have a way of carrying themselves, a body language that is as plainly open or closed as a hand. They have a watchfulness, a containment, a false repose like a cat sunning itself on a windowsill, eyes half-closed but ready to pounce. Attention must be paid, and we had to outspend them.

A street set operates through an odd combination of aggressive marketing and strategic defense, with simultaneous needs to broadcast and deny its function. The young man on the park bench needs to look like a high school senior from thirty yards but has to show he's a merchant at three, to have the drugs near enough for convenience but far enough away to be out of his "custody and control" should he be stopped. If he's holding the drugs, he has to have an escape route, through a hole in the fence, to an alley, to the building where his grandmother lives. The kid on the bench is a kid on a bench regardless, and it takes time for his context to prove him to be anything more. You watch who he watches, who approaches him. And as you do, figures emerge from the flow of street life as coordinates on a grid, as pins on a map.

Say you have a street with three young guys on the corner by the bodega, a couple with a baby in a carriage by the stoop, old men with brown-bagged brandy bottles by the vacant lot. A man on a bicycle moves in a slow lazy slalom, up and down the street. The cornerboys are the obvious pick, but I have to wait. A buyer is easier to recognize, and his arrival on the set sends a signal, a vibration like a willing fly landing in the spiderweb. The buyer is the bellwether and bait, who draws the players out and makes them work, prompts them into visible display.

The buyer walks past the old men at the lot, the family on the stoop, to the cornerboys, as I thought. One cornerboy takes the buyer aside and palms his cash, the second stands still, watching up and down the block, the third goes to the family on the stoop, has a word with the woman with the baby. The woman steps inside the lobby for a few seconds—thank God, I think, the stash isn't in the carriage—returns and hands the cornerboy something, and he meets up with Player #1 and buyer, handing off the product. The buyer walks away, retracing his route. The man on the bicycle follows him, slowly.

I put the buyer over the air: "Hispanic male, red cap, blue Tommy Hilfiger jacket, blue jeans, south on Willis. . . . Be advised, you got a lookout on a bike, white T-shirt, blue jeans, black bike, tailing him to see if he gets picked up, let him run a couple of blocks if you can. . . ."

Now I have a three-player set, with Mama and Cornerboys #1 and #3 down cold. The buyer should be taken, the lookout only observed, for now. Mama's short time in the building tells me the stash isn't in an apartment, but either on her person or right in the lobby, in a mailbox or a crack in the wall. Player #2 is the one to watch, to see if he's the manager or a lookout, up a rank from them or down. His position will become clear, through watching the group dynamic, the choreography of who stands where, who talks and who listens, who tells the jokes and who laughs, who's the one who runs to the bodega for the chips and soda. Until he participates in the exchanges, taking money or product, he's legally safe from arrest for an observation sale. If he's a manager, he's the one we want, to try to turn, moving up the organization; if he's a smart manager, touching neither cash nor stash, he's the one we're least likely to get. In a sense, we both want the spot to get busy: with more buyers, they're less likely to get away, popping into a nearby building before we can grab them, and the players will be less wary as they get greedy, bringing out more product, paying more heed to the customer and less to us. The manager might have to step in and lend an incriminating hand. When the spot is slow, the cops and the players both have to be patient.

Even when nothing happens, there is much to interpret: are they out of product, and will they re-up within ten minutes or an hour? Are they "raised," afraid we're around, and if so, is it because they saw our van, or one of us creeping into the corner building to peer over the roofline, or is it because three patrol cars raced by, to the robbery a few blocks away? Did they turn away the last customer because he wanted credit, or because they thought he was an undercover cop, and were they right? Is it worth waiting, is it worth watching?

Watching isn't always easy. I've spent hours on tar rooftops, crouched down till my legs cramp, sweating, shivering, wiping the rain from my binoculars every ten seconds. There have been times when I've forgotten to look down before I kneel by the ledge, and seen piles of dog shit, broken glass, or syringes beside me. On one rooftop, there was an ornate Victorian bird cage, five feet tall, bell-shaped and made of brass. Chained to it, still on a rotten leather leash, was the skeleton of a pit bull. You walk up dirty stairs to a dirty roof to watch a dirty street. At night, even the light is dirty, as the sodium-vapor streetlights give off a muddy yellow haze. But when it's happening, sometimes, you realize how perfect your concentration is, you feel the cool, neutral thrill of being completely submerged in your task. And when it's not, you can still be caught up in the beauty of the view, the hallucinatory strangeness or the small, random graces of the landscape:

An incinerator chimney shoots out a lash of black smoke, which loops into a lariat before dissolving into the grimy sky.

"Gray livery cab, buyer in back seat, passenger side, possible white with white sleeves, U-turning now to the left . . ."

A soap bubble, then two, then dozens rise up in front of me, iridescent, shimmering in their uncertainty, floating up to be lost in the blue sky. There is a child, two floors below me, as rapt at the view above as I am with the view below.

"Arright, we got one, he's beelining to the player, they just popped into the lobby . . . now he's out—that's fast, he must have the stash on him. Arright, buyer's walking off, now—hold on, he's just kind of idling across the street—it's not an I-got-my-rock walk, I don't think he got done. Stand by . . ."

A man stands on another tenement roof, whirling an orange flag, making it snap like a towel. His flock of pigeons takes flight from the coop with a whoosh like a gust of wind, spiraling out in broadening arcs, the smoky gray of their backs as they bank out, the silver-white of their bellies as they circle in, rising up all the while.

"Player's walking off, he sent the last two away, he's out, he's raised, I don't know, but—*Go! Go! Go! Go!* Hit the set!"

When you hit a set, there is always a charge of adrenaline, arising from the jungle-war vagaries in your knowledge of the terrain and the determination of your adversary. There are elusive ones, explosive ones, and lots of sitting ducks. Some dealers opt for a businesslike capitulation, aware that it's the way to go through the process with the least fuss. Others, especially lobby dealers with access to an apartment upstairs, tend to make a mad dash for freedom. In brief, it could be a surrender as slow and dignified as Lee at Appomattox, or it could be bedlam, a roil of running, struggling bodies, and airborne stash. When you can't count the evidence at the scene, you at least have to control it, the hundreds of dollars in small bills, fistfuls of crack slabs, loose decks and bundles of dope, and you jam it in your pockets like a handful of ball bearings, when there might be a crowd screaming, or perps for whom the fight-or-flight reflex is not a simple either-or proposition.

The smarter dealers carry nothing on them, but you await information from the OP, sometimes with distaste that verges on dread: "It's in his sock—"

"It's in the cast on his right hand—"

"It's in his cheek—sorry, guy, the other cheek, check between 'em. I mean it's in his ass, you copy?"

There was nothing quite like watching someone sniff a bag of dope that was fresh from a dealer's ass. Stash could be hidden under a bottle cap or in a potato-chip bag, strewn amid the liberality of non-criminal trash. It could be wedged in a light fixture in a hall, or tucked inside the bumper of a car; in a magnetic key case, stuck to the iron bolt beneath a park bench, or on a string, taped to the wall and dangling down the garbage-disposal chute. It was the last part of the game—the triathlon, or pentathlon, plus or minus one—of a SNEU op: Watch and Catch; Chase and Search; Fight and Find.

No day passed without some little adventure or eccentric encounter that made us wonder, or made us laugh. Or in my case, that brought up something to keep in mind for the next time: to check the player for keys, to see if one fit a mailbox; to pull a buyer around a corner or into a lobby, to limit public attention to the stop; or to check for the stash inside of the hat brim, or behind the leather brand patch on the waist of the jeans, or under the tongue of the sneakers. It was Stix, I think, who picked out a kid in the park and said he had just hit someone off. I stopped him and searched him, coming up with nothing, and then Stix said, "Open up and smile," and he grimaced to expose a dozen black-topped crack vials that filled his mouth like rotten teeth. Tony once pulled product out of one guy's ear, like a magician.

There was one spot we'd hit that we called The Hole, a huge, abandoned factory where they sold heroin. It occupied a large corner lot, and they pitched from each side of the building, through a blocked-up front door on one side, and at a sidewalk-level gap in the wall below a loading dock on the other. Until recently, the South Bronx had been full of such buildings, burntout and falling down, with a shell-shocked look, like the war was over and the other side won. Inside, it was more like a haunted house, with vast, dark, high-ceilinged rooms where your footsteps would startle pigeons and rats into sudden flight, and vice versa; if you walked up the stairs, they'd creak and give ominously; if you walked down them to the basement, the growling of pit bulls would stop you in your tracks. You might find a half-dozen junkies sprawled out on the floor, moaning a little, or moving a little, but there was something wrong with how they shifted, or made sounds, or didn't, as if they were in intensive care and someone had turned off all the machines. The Hole was run by a crew from down the block, and the junkies bought from them and sold for them, and the healthy, happy fatness of the dealers stood out as they hovered on the corner to supervise or to bring in new supplies to their cadaverous charges. On Saturdays, a busload of white Christians would park there, handing out sandwiches and pamphlets, and the dealers and junkies gathered around to blend in with them. The half-dead and the overfed mingled with the well-scrubbed missionaries, eating free baloney and talking about Jesus as they peddled their dope. When we'd hit the set, all of them looked at us like we were Cossacks.

We had spirit, and we had standards. There was plenty to do in the Four-O, and we didn't have to scavenge for collars. We didn't bother with marijuana, and we rarely took the buyers just for trespass, as it didn't seem sporting—if they beat us, they beat us. The dealers didn't catch that break, of course, and taking them in for trespass gave us the opportunity for a more thorough search at the precinct. And like most cops when they had a little time on, we left bums alone, mostly out of sympathy, mostly for ourselves—what good was done by taking a street guy off the street for a day, having to pick through six layers of year-old underwear for a slab of crack, while he's hacking up hepatitis all over you, and his feet are giving off a stink that could capsize a ship? A police officer was supposed to use Discretion—*a little D*—and if we laid claim to a larger measure than we were entitled to, no one complained:

"Hey, Tony, you get the guy in the black leather? Is he a hit?"

"Mmm, we got 'em, OV, but this is a D. Heavy D."

"How heavy?"

"He puked."

"Ten-four. Let me know when you're 98, we got more."

· · ·

AS WE FUSED TOGETHER AS A TEAM, OUR GROWING DEVO-tion to the idea of all-for-one, one-for-all did not always work to our practical advantage. Some variation of this conversation seemed to take place daily:

"I'm going to get something to eat."

"Where you going?"

"Chinese."

"Could you pick me up a slice from Giovanni's?"

"And could you stop by McDonald's?"

"Could you wait half an hour, and I'll go with you?"

"Me, too, except in an hour, and I don't want Chinese, I wanna sit down, for Spanish."

"You know what, forget it, I'm not hungry anymore."

But God forbid if you just went out and grabbed something. Then the accusations would fly, in tones that insinuated a form of adultery: "You ate, didn't you? *You ate!* Admit it!"

"How'd you get there?"

"I bet you took Brook Avenue, motherfucker, 'cause it's a one-way street."

"One-way streets are all you take. . . ."

In response to our cockeyed communism, Carroll became a kind of mock-democrat. He'd ask us where we wanted to work, and the team would offer suggestions:

"Let's do Mitchell—one-seven-five Alex."

"How about Melrose-Jackson, maybe three-oh-five-oh Park?"

"Or Betances."

"Betances, yeah, one-four-eight and Brook."

And Carroll would listen judiciously and say, "All right, good. So . . . let's go set up for Mott-Pat." In general, Stix, Orville, and Alicia felt more strongly that the team should decide how we worked, whereas Tony, Sammy, and I tended to think Carroll would run the show, as a matter of reality if not natural right. As Tony put it, "Shit rolls downhill." He had a talent for summing things up.

At first, SNEU was a uniformed unit, and over the years, it had gone back and forth between plainclothes and "the bag." Inspector Mullen told me that a few years ago, when he was the CO of the Four-Seven, it was considered a radical step to let the cops in the OP wear NYPD windbreakers over their regular uniforms, which was not exactly deep cover. Plainclothes still had a Serpico-era stigma of corruption, but the more immediate concern was that when you had precinct-level units like SNEU and Crime in the mix with Narcotics, Street Crime, and whoever else was out there, there was a greater chance for mishap if cops failed to recognize one another. As the precinct units were presumed to be less experienced, they were the risk that was reduced. In the bag, you were less effective—sometimes, slipping into an OP while in uniform was impossible—but in plainclothes, there was greater institutional liability. When something went wrong, everyone went back in the bag, regardless of whether the issue was related to uniforms, but as the incident faded from memory and efficiency again became the priority, we slipped back into our own clothes. The cycles went round and round, every few years.

When we started, only the cops in the OP wore plainclothes. Usually, we'd decide among ourselves, in the locker room, but it happened now and then that we all came down in plainclothes, or uniform. Carroll would look at us with hapless aggravation, and we'd shrug—no one can play dumb like a bunch of cops. Some of the guys, like Orville, didn't care whether they were in the bag, but I did—you could get in to the precinct a little later and stroll in to roll call, and you were more comfortable outside without the uniform, especially in the heat. After the regimentation of patrol, from shoeshine inspections to assigned meal times, plainclothes felt grown-up and professional. I grew the white-guy-in-Narcotics goatee, which appeared to be mandatory. But when we all showed up in plainclothes, it was often with an agenda, as we hoped that Carroll would just say, "Oh, the hell with it, let's just go like we are." Eventually, we worked in plainclothes all the time.

Once, we tried to pull that same trick with a tour change, starting at seven in the morning on the last one, instead of at ten. I didn't think we'd get away with it, but since Tony had broken his leg playing football, the menshevik faction was short a vote, next to the bolsheviks. Sgt. Carroll saw through it immediately, partly because he'd heard we'd all come down to roll call in uniform. And he wasn't pleased, to say the least, though he never pushed me to tell him about it, which inspired some relief and greater respect. We got along well, and I went to his house for his son's christening—sorry guys, I never told you—but whether you looked at it as part of the laws of gravity or those of loyalty, the first bond was among partners, cop to cop. The friction with Sgt. Carroll was petty and infrequent, and though I sometimes missed the independence of working alone, I came to see each of my partners as a great asset to the team.

Tony looked black and had an Italian name. He was from the heart of the South Bronx, near Charlotte Street, where presidents since Carter had come to witness the wastelands of the inner city. More than any of us, Tony knew how rough it was out there, and how much worse it had been, and how funny it could be sometimes. Once, we drove past kids playing in an inflatable pool on the sidewalk, leaping and splashing around the gutter, and he said, "Ain't you living ghetto-fabulous." A lot of the team's in-jokes came from Tony, the double- and triple-aged ironies of us and them. When you'd get up from a scrap with a perp, he'd ask, "You ah-ite?" and you'd say, "I'm ah-ite, yo.'" When Sgt. Carroll's wife was pregnant, Tony got us to inquire after her health by asking: "How yo' baby-mother? How she feelin'? How yo' baby-moms?"

Orville also had a way with words, although whether it was Jamaican or just Orvillean was hard to tell sometimes. A scrip from OV might go, "He's got a blue shirt and pants, they're like space pants, I don't know, he's got some kind of space-ass pants on. All right, Space-Ass is getting in a car and going south. . . ." Where someone else might say "John Doe," he would use "Joe Neckbone," as in, "It's not the kind of gun you get from Joe Neckbone on One-Five-Three and Melrose." And once we locked up a guy for buying crack who began to cry, saying he'd never been arrested before, he was only getting it for a girl he liked. "So what's the moral of the story?" Orville asked. "Don't trade crack for ass."

Orville was also one of the more driven guys in the group, quick to say what was on his mind. In contrast, nothing got under Sammy's skin. Sammy was the oldest of us, the father of four children and a sergeant in the Marine reserves, so that the pitch and roll of team life bothered him least. Sammy had an unassuming way about him, and in plainclothes, he could go anywhere without being made for a cop. Part of this had to do with his stature; as we liked to put it, Tony was Puerto Rican but Sammy was "Short-a-Rican."

In the Academy, Stix was even quieter that I was, but he seemed to have gotten over it, at least within the team. The underlying idea behind his jokes was a pretense of innocent confusion, whether his own or that he caused in others. If a squad car was in the way of our ops, he would get on the radio and pretend to be the desk officer, calling them back to the base: *Ten-two, unit, come on in a minute. . . .*" At the precinct one day, in the arrest processing room—a small room in the back, with two cells, a long table for cops to do paperwork, and a fingerprint area—we collared a perp named Trujillo, and Stix subjected his name to ever more inventive mispronunciations, at increasing volume levels: "Which one a you is . . . Trilogy? Yeah, Trilogy, step up, you heard me, I got work to do!"

"Hey, Tally-ho, step out of the cell, we gotta search ya, hop to it!"

"Hey, True Jello! Yeah, you—True Jello! You know who I'm talking to, what's your address!"

There was just enough sincerity in his voice to make it work. He was particular, about his hair and about bathrooms and especially about what he ate. He was a healthy eater, favoring salads and pasta and sliced turkey, and mostly, he would bring food from his girlfriend Anna's deli. If he got South

Bronx pizza, he would scrape the sauce and cheese off it, because he only ate homemade. He would grill you about what you ate as if it were a matter of national security:

"What you get?"

"A hero, sausage and peppers."

"How was it?"

"Arright."

"Arright? Just arright, not good, not bad?"

"Yeah, pretty much—it was arright."

"Would you say it was—"

"Fine, it was great, it was incredible, it was the best fucking thing I ever ate."

"Yeah? Really? That good?"

In contrast, Alicia often maintained a shrewd aloofness toward work. She didn't drive, and she only took misdemeanors, because she didn't like going to court—for every felony, at least one officer had to testify in the Grand Jury, and those cases were more likely to go to trial, though few ever did. While we waited in the van, she would sit in the back and read, which some of the other guys found irksome, although I didn't—probably because I did a lot of reading, too. When she finished her own book or magazine, she'd ransack my bag to see what I had. Because Alicia was petite and female, perps sometimes thought they could get over on her, which was a mistake. On the street, Alicia was as tough as anyone. Tony did an impression of a perp with Alicia's hands around his neck—"The—drugs—are—in—my—pocket!"—as he rolled his eyes and gasped. I never saw that, but I did see that when perps even cursed at her, they were quick to apologize. Alicia was black and Puerto Rican, "a swirl," as Orville would say, or "black and brown, like a Doberman." She was married, with two kids, and one of them would be dropped off at the precinct now and then, and it was a wonderful thing to watch her help him with his homework, tender and patient, and see the contrast between home life, job life, and street life, and how it demanded a different person to meet each.

The natural bonds of police work made us closer, even as the inevitable strains pushed us away from the rest of the precinct. For example, the precinct had only two unmarked vans, and often one or both would be out of service. Our chief competition for vehicles was Anti-Crime, whom we viewed as equals, but we sometimes got the feeling that the favor was not returned. Their boss, Tommy Clark, was one of the guys whose medal rack stretched above his shoulder, and his cops were also a talented and dedicated crew—

Eddie Wynne, Jimmy Rizzi, Richie Hyde, Anna Ramirez, Rob Knapp, Nefti Cruz. We were scheduled for alternating weeks of four-to-twelves and ten-to-sixes to reduce the overlap, but it didn't always work out. One day, as we brought a van full of prisoners to Central Booking, we got a series of calls to return the van to the base. We couldn't, at first, and then we weren't much inclined to hurry, and then we found out that one of our perps had active TB. We'd spent the last couple of hours breathing the same cubic feet of air. When we returned to the precinct, we all climbed out of the van wearing surgical masks, tossed Crime the keys, and said, "It's all yours." They didn't think it was as funny as we did, but as Sgt. Carroll liked to remind us, "We're here to make collars, not friends."

The stronger bond came from what happened in the street. We all knew that if there was a scrap, the whole team was there for it, as far as it had to go. That trust could make you feel extravagantly wealthy, but it was also the minimum wage you needed to work: if a cop demonstrated a too-acute instinct for self-preservation during a brawl—"Go get 'em, guys, I'll find back-up!"—many cops refused to work with him or her again, and their requests were usually honored. At least as often, there were situations that arose that required a common read on things, when everyone's instincts jibed to say, "This one's a little weird, let's do it by the book," or, "This one's a lot weird—let's keep walking, like it never happened." Let's call them hypotheticals.

What if you tossed a guy and came up with a crack stem or a little weed? You didn't want it, or him, and you also didn't want to bother with the vouchering and the rest of the paperwork. What if you just threw it out, and told him to watch his step? On the good side, you'd get a guy who owed you, and he might give you some useful information down the line, and you could get back to doing your real work. On the bad side, you had just destroyed evidence, and if it came up and you denied it, you'd have committed perjury.

What if you found drugs in the back seat of the van, or a squad car? What you were supposed to do was notify the desk officer, and the previous operator would get a Command Discipline for his failure to search the vehicle. Maybe he would get a "Warn and Admonish," or maybe he would lose time, depending on his record, or his relationship with the CO or the lieutenant assigned as Integrity Control Officer. Since squad cars often transported someone else's prisoners, it seemed especially unfair for them to take the hit, when it was the arresting officer's fault for not searching the perp. What kept you from throwing the drugs down the sewer was the fear that they were planted by Internal Affairs, who could hit you with charges relating to the destruction of evidence and possibly perjury, again, if you were questioned and your answers were cute. You tried to guess what was going on by what you found and where you found it—if there was a little slab wedged under a seat belt, it could well have been there for weeks, but if there was a bundle of dope in the middle of the seat, it was a harder call. If the previous driver was still around, you might suggest he look again before he "officially" turned in the keys, but if he had already left, you had to make a decision.

What if you had three or four perps in the van when you rolled up on a dealer, and there was a rumble? The driver of the van has to stay with the prisoners; they are his responsibility, without exception. But who would stay inside a car when his partners were in trouble on the street? What would it matter if all the junkies in the world went free, if it kept your partner from getting hurt? And what if, when the dealer was subdued, you returned to the van to see that there was a little more room in the back seat, with a crowd gathered, laughing? Do you put it over the air, making official notification of escaped prisoners, that will cost at least the cops in the van their spot in the unit, plus a ten- or twenty-day hit? Or will you just pack everyone up and start looking? And if you still don't find them, what do you do? Hope that they aren't collared by a cop without a clue, and that you didn't scratch your shield number on your cuffs? What kind of trouble are you willing to get in to stay out of trouble?

What if you grabbed a lady for buying heroin, and she started moaning and yelling about how sick she was? A lot of people develop sudden illnesses when they're in cuffs, and you do not treat them as if they were relatives who said they weren't feeling well. What if you put her in the van, and she started screaming, "I got AIDS! I got mental problems! I got diarrhea! Take me to the hospital, now!" And what if you knew she was telling the truth about the third ailment, because she stood up on the seat while still rear-cuffed, dropped her drawers and unloosed a fetid green stream into her hands, which she flung toward the front? And the cops dove from the van like it was being shelled, and when they stood outside and watched her, she began to grind her massive, bare cheeks against the windows, pumping out sewage as she moved, smearing it across the windows until you couldn't see inside? Would you take that collar, or decide that maybe cops should have the power to pardon, like presidents and kings, and offer horrified amnesty on the spot?

As I said, these are hypotheticals, and I won't say whether any of them happened to us. I won't even say what I would have done, or defend the merits of any decision, excepting, perhaps, the diarrhea attack, where I would have not only let the lady go, but then poured gasoline onto the van and lit a match. But I will say, at least, that narcotics has been a very funny business for a very long time.

. . .

ALMOST EVERYTHING SAID ABOUT DRUGS IS AT LEAST HALF true. Drug laws are unfair, because vastly disproportionate numbers of black men are incarcerated, while white drug use is considerably larger; the drug laws are reasonable, because the effects of drugs are far more destructive within poor communities. It is hypocritical for us to police the drug-supplying nations, because America's appetite for drugs is their reason for being; we have to go after evil foreign drug lords who have enslaved innocent Americans. Addiction is a disease, and we are wrong to rely on a legal remedy for a medical condition; drug use is a choice, and we have to hold people responsible for their actions. The War on Drugs is a failure. The War on Drugs is a success.

From a police perspective, narcotics falls under the category of vice offenses, which traditionally included gambling, prostitution, and alcohol. No aspect of policing has had as troubled a history as vice enforcement: these were crimes that did pay, often extremely well, and the reasons for prohibition are more abstract than for crimes against persons or property, a distinction that has often undermined public support. In New York, criminal possession of a controlled substance in the seventh degree—for up to five vials of crack, or seven glassines of heroin, give or take—is a class-A misdemeanor, punishable by a maximum sentence of one year in jail. So is assault in the third degree, which differs from felony assault by a lack of "serious" injury or the use of a weapon. And it is hard to argue that beating someone up is just as bad as putting cocaine up your nose. Even when large numbers of people are doing large amounts of cocaine—which tends to drive up the assault rate—couldn't we just punish the assaults in and of themselves, and treat the addiction as a sickness instead of a sin?

Although heroin and cocaine are so contagious that they sell themselves, major epidemics of drug abuse have always been sponsored by organizations of extraordinary dedication and ruthlessness. Long before the Mafia, the Colombian cartels, and the Burmese warlords, there was the British East India Company, against which the first War on Drugs was lost. In the two

Opium Wars of the mid–nineteenth century, the Chinese fought the British to prevent them from smuggling opium into China, which it had done since the late 1700s, to improve the balance of trade. Though there were other issues behind the conflict, the bald fact of the matter is that the British created the largest intentional outbreak of a disease in human history: one third of the Chinese were regular users, and half of those were "sots," hopeless, useless, and nearly lifeless. The Chinese were forced to cede Hong Kong after the first war, in 1842, and to legalize the drug after the second, in 1860. After the British victories, the Americans and the French negotiated their own trade agreements, though the British continued to dominate the market.

By the late nineteenth century, the problems of addiction became a widespread concern in the West, which found outlet in the usual forums of public debate and popular culture. Sherlock Holmes was a great detective, but he probably wouldn't have worked out too well in SNEU. In one story, he defends his use of cocaine to a worried and skeptical Dr. Watson, claiming that the drug provides a worthy diversion when his mind is not stimulated by a case. Cocaine had been hailed as a wonder drug by many eminent figures of the late nineteenth century, among them Sigmund Freud, whose essay "Über Coca" was a "hymn of praise." Cocaine-infused drinks such as Celery Cola, Dope Cola, and most famously Coca-Cola, were touted by the Temperance movement as healthy and stimulating alternatives to alcohol. Cocaine was recommended for treatment of a range of ailments, from sinus trouble to morphine addiction.

Opiate abuse had been commonplace in America at least since the Civil War. Morphine was prescribed primarily for depression, insomnia, and pain, and secondarily for just about everything else, from nymphomania to hiccups. Though the opium dens became locally notorious in the Chinatowns of New York and San Francisco, the typical addict was a middle-class white female whose habit developed from medical treatment rather than recreational use, like the tranquilized housewives of a century later. Americans were avid consumers of the patent medicines marketed with Barnumesque fraudulence and flair, and it was only after the Pure Food and Drug Act of 1906 that people realized that so-called cures for opiate and cocaine addiction were often loaded with opiates and cocaine. At the turn of the century, it was estimated that there were 200,000 cocaine addicts and 250,000 opiate addicts, an overlapping population that may have included one American out of every 250.

Domestic control of drugs began in 1914 with the Harrison Act, and it gathered force through the 1920s with further restrictions and the establishment of a Federal Bureau of Narcotics. Almost immediately, the addict population shifted, from female to male, medical to recreational, and the modern profile of the drug user emerged, of a marginal and transient young man in the city. For the most part, drugs were of a piece with the down-and-out world of the pool hall and the flophouse. They circulated through the traditional vice rackets, at the lower-end bars and brothels, where they were dominated by the same gangsters: Arnold Rothstein was a financier of the opiate trade in the 1920s, which primarily came from legal manufacturers on the continent, and Lucky Luciano's first arrest was for selling heroin.

Somewhat astoundingly, the federal interdiction effort was quite successful by the 1930s. The first head of the Bureau of Narcotics was ousted after it emerged that his son, an attorney, had represented Rothstein on a tax case, and his son-in-law had borrowed money from the gangster. Harry Anslinger then led the agency for the next three decades, and though he is now generally regarded as an empty suit, his first ten years saw a marked decline in the shipment and use of drugs. Opium and cocaine virtually disappeared, and heroin became increasingly more diluted, expensive, and difficult to obtain. By the Second World War, the United States could claim near-total victory over drug use and trafficking, however short-lived.

The Cold War inadvertently set the stage for the return of narcotics, in devastating strength. For the most part, the Mafia had been bitter enemies of Mussolini, and several men who would become leaders of the American underworld, such Joe Bonanno, were driven into exile by the Fascists. During the Allied Occupation, many of the local mafiosi were returned to power by the Americans, who were in need of a leadership that was equally free of Fascist and Communist taint. This resurrection of the Sicilian Mafia coincided with the deportation of some four hundred gangsters, including Lucky Luciano, who introduced their local counterparts to the lucrative narcotics trade. The Sicilians often worked with Corsican gangsters in Marseilles, where the "French Connection" soon supplied 85 to 90 percent of the heroin that arrived in the United States. The French government did little to discourage it: de Gaulle was delighted to thwart American policy, and the problem of addiction was not significant in France at the time. More sinister was the fact that the narcotics trade helped finance French military and intelligence efforts in its about-to-be former colonies, especially in Indochina, where the "Golden Triangle" was the world's great opiate producer, along with the "Golden Crescent" of the Near East, from Turkey to Pakistan.

After the war, heroin use was largely confined to a few, narrow subcultures—among jazz musicians, most famously—from which it spread, like a rumor or a fad, in a geometric progression. The drug was seen as part of a lifestyle that opted out of the mainstream, whether as a protest against the specific exclusion of blacks from postwar opportunity, or as part of the larger, looser cynicism of the counterculture. Some junkies started because they were shut out of society, others because they didn't want to join it, and still others because they believed it explained how Charlie Parker played or Billie Holiday sang. Whether the pipe dream appealed to them or the American dream didn't, once people started, their original reasons didn't matter. As heroin spread through the larger black community, especially in the northern ghettoes, the price went up and the quality went down, even as the addict population exploded. Property crimes skyrocketed to pay for habits, and then violent crimes followed, not only in the competition between dealers, but also disciplinary and debt-collecting functions of the gangs. By the 1960s, changes in the welfare system had accelerated the already extraordinary chaos of the ghettoes, in its disastrous effects on patterns of marriage and work, which remain the two greatest bulwarks against criminality. Heroin created thousands of rich killers and millions of derelicts, whores, and thieves. In short, it created crime as we know it.

In a sense, heroin was one of many white appropriations of black culture, following the same routes of imitation as the blues and hip-hop. But if heroin moved up from the ghetto, cocaine reached down from the white upper classes, offering a mass-market taste of glamour, like designer jeans. Through the mid-eighties, most media coverage of cocaine had an envious quality, as if the chief problem with the party favor of Hollywood parties and Studio 54 was that it was too expensive. Though official anti-drug rhetoric had been fairly constant for decades, it was only in 1986, after the death of basketball star Len Bias, and after crack began to burn through the cities, that action backed up the words. Until then, there was little attention paid to cocaine at the federal level: in 1985, of the hundred agents in the New York office of the DEA, only ten were assigned to cocaine cases, and in South Florida, where the drug had become a seven-billion-dollar industry, the DEA had to have a bake sale to raise money. In other words, until fairly recently, the war on drugs was remarkable for its lack of troops and ammunition, though the casualties certainly abounded.

The modern cocaine business began when George Jung met Carlos Lehder in federal prison, in 1974. Jung, who was from a white, working-class New England background, had developed a sophisticated marijuana business, in which he bought drugs by the ton in Mexico and flew them all over the country in small planes. Carlos Lehder was a car thief from Colombia, who would join with Pablo Escobar and the Ochoa family to form the Medellín cartel. Jung had a hippie's soft-minded indulgence toward drug use, believing it to be kind of harmless and sort of a civil right, whereas the fanatical Lehder saw cocaine as the atomic bomb he was going to drop on America. Cocaine, which had been smuggled by the pound, now began to enter the country by the ton, and the Colombians introduced a degree of violence to the trade that would have made the Mafia blanch. Cops were killed by the hundreds in Medellín, and entire families were murdered, sometimes by the "necktie" method, in which the throat was cut and the tongue pulled out to dangle down the chest. Sometime in the early 1980s, someone invented crack, and business got even bigger than anyone could have imagined.

Cocaine used to cost as much as the best champagne, but crack made the price drop to that of a pack of cigarettes. People fought to buy it and sell it, with more and bigger guns that they sometimes shot without even looking. By the early 1990s, the New York City annual homicide rate had passed two thousand, of which half were estimated to be drug-related. Crack ravaged entire neighborhoods and seemed to claim as many women as men; heroin took a lot of fathers, and now crack took mothers, too. If heroin made the streets unsafe, crack killed people who hadn't even left their homes, and mothers in the ghettoes practiced a kind of fire drill, sending the kids under their beds or into the bathtub at the sound of gunfire. Even as the crack epidemic started to level off, the Colombians began to produce heroin of exceptional quality.

We're not back where we started, by any means, but quitting time—for addict, dealer, cop—is nowhere in sight. Certain countries that used to produce narcotics—Turkey—seemed to have kicked the habit, although others—Burma, Colombia—have picked up the slack. Here, many of the kinds of people who used to take drugs fairly casually in the late 1970s—maybe a third of teenagers, almost half the armed forces—don't use them in anywhere near those numbers. In New York, the expansion of the Narcotics Division was as much a bulwark of Giuliani's crime-fighting strategy as Compstat and the "Broken Windows" theory, though rarely as celebrated, and the eight years of his administration saw the murder rate drop by nearly two-thirds and violent crime by half. As always, most of the money for drugs comes from the suburbs, but most of the blood is shed in the city streets. While some people complain that there are too many people in prison, and others think that there aren't enough, the fact of the matter is that if you got rid of narcotics, you could send half of the cops in this city home. Until then, we take it a day at a time.

And every day, we got to pick: crack or dope, dope or crack. Overall, I'd say I came to prefer dope. It was an acquired taste. Maybe because the players seemed more reachable, as the street dealers at dope spots were often junkies themselves, with a half a mind to clean up and get out, while the hand-to-hands at crack spots were mostly hard-rock younger guys, out to fuck the world and make a buck. Crackheads themselves were rarely trusted with the stash, or even to stand still and look out for the cops. For the most part, they were figures from a famine, bone-thin and filthy. Months in that life took years from their lives, with thirty-year-olds who could pass for fifty, burnt-out almost literally, with a red-hot core of desperation beneath a dead, charred surface. Junkies were a little more human, for a little while longer. Heroin is far purer than it has been in the past, and a lot of junkies snorted it, instead of shooting it, which decreased the risk of disease and also seemed to slow the forward momentum of addiction. They had a longer ride to the bottom, though for all I've run into, the habit gradually slid from being a part of their life to becoming the point of it. But the terminal junkies are even more awful, to me, because they have none of the trapped-rat frenzy of the crackhead, possessing instead a fatal calm, as if they are keeping their eyes open as they drown. When you collar them, they can have a look of confirmed and somehow contented self-hatred, as if the world is doing to them what they expect and deserve. Maybe I didn't prefer heroin, after all.

There is something authentically tragic about addicts, in the way the wreckage of their lives is both freely chosen and somehow fated. They are both casualties of a condition that is believed to have a genetic component, and committed collaborators in their own downfall. They deserve pity, always, and often they inspire contempt. We collared one crackhead, bumping into him by accident as he stood in a lobby counting out a handful of vials. He was a street peddler who sold clothing, and he had about eighty dollars in his pocket. He had the shrink-wrapped look that crackheads get, as if his skin was two sizes too small. He moaned and wept for his infant child, who would starve without his support, he told us. Yes, he acknowledged, the baby lived with the mother, but he was the provider. They were only about ten blocks away, in a playground, and so we drove to meet them. The mother was a pretty and well-dressed woman, though her soccer-mom demeanor was heightened by the contrast with her handcuffed spouse. We called her over, and her look of mild confusion became one of mild dismay as she saw our back-seat passenger. She didn't look surprised and didn't ask questions. He took out his wad of cash, peeled off three dollars and handed it to me to give her. "You gotta be kidding me," I said. "You give me all this father-of-the-year shit, just to throw her three bucks?"

"C'mon," he said. "When you get out of Central Booking, you're hungry, you want some real McDonald's or something."

I gave him back the three dollars and took the wad for the mother. "The Number Two Special, two cheeseburgers and fries, is $2.99," I told him. "It's what I get, and it's all you can afford." For an addict, the priorities are never unclear.

For dealers, the pull of the drug trade is obviously financial, but most make surprisingly little money. The economics—call it crackanomics, or smackanomics—generate vast amounts of money, but it is rarely shared with the front-line pitchers. After talking to one dealer I arrested, I worked it out that he sold three-dollar vials of crack and made five dollars for every twenty he sold. Though he usually averaged around fifteen vials an hour, the day we grabbed him had been slow—all told, he'd worked four hours for fifteen dollars. His proceeds, which were confiscated, were less than the minimum wage.

"Do you realize you'd make more with a paper route?" I asked. He shrugged. He'd had a job at Blockbuster, once, but he stopped going because his shirt was dirty and he didn't have a chance to wash it. His father was in prison for drug sales, and he'd sold since he was thirteen, he told me, as if it was a habit he was unable to break.

Because the "victims" of drug sales literally line up to pay for the privilege, the dealers sometimes don't have the forthright menace of violent felons. In the movies, there are a lot of drug-dealer villains, but the characters usually have to slap their girlfriends around or kill a lot of cops to heighten the dramatic point of their bad-guyness. While life has provided art with plenty of rough stuff to imitate, some people have argued that it need not be so bloody; that the violence generated by the drug trade would disappear upon legalization. In other words, we can't eliminate the drug business, but we might try improving it. The usual analogy offered is that of Prohibition, which shifted the liquor industry from an aspect of hospitality to an engine of organized crime. But for history to repeat itself in this case would be more wishful than anything else; after the repeal of Prohibition, the Mob not only moved on but grew even richer, larger, and more destructive. In SNEU, it seemed that the illegality of narcotics was precisely what drew the sellers:

most players had rap sheets for robbery or theft before settling on the more lucrative and "less illegal" world of drug sales, and many remained committed to a diversified life of crime. The perps were perps before they became dealers, and the question they asked—and answered—was not whether to commit a crime, but what kind of crime to commit. Amid all the heavy weather of the issues, it was surprisingly easy to make out the bad guys.

And if I had any doubts, the dealers were good enough to spell it out for me. Heroin is stamped with a brand name on the little wax-paper envelopes in which the drug is packaged. This practice gives a glimpse not only of a corporate structure, when the same brands appear in different locations, but also of a corporate imagination, showing what they believe their product should mean to their market. Some convey the blandly generic aspiration of quality that you might find on brands of corn flakes or detergent: First Class, President, Original, Amazing, and Amazed, though the last was more distinctive, as it was illustrated with a picture of a baby gazing at his enormous penis. I liked the politeness of Thank You, the impoliteness of Fuck You, and the surliness of No Joke, because it suggested a certain lack of self-esteem. Others invoked a racier allure, but the gimmick is so hackneyed in regular ads that the genuinely illicit thrills of No Limit, Poison Ivy, or Knockout invoke the mock-illicit thrill of ads for perfume or fat-free ice cream. Topical references are common, from the flat-out copyright infringement of DKNY or Ford, to movie tag-lines like Show Me the Money. But the best brand names are the literal ones, which announce without apology the bad things to come: 911, 25 to Life, Undertaker. There is the suicidal candor to Lethal Injection and Virus, a forthright finality to OD. There is a truth in advertising here that few products can match.

· · ·

EACH OF US PUT TOGETHER A LITTLE KIT, OF BETTER THINGS and extra things, like handcuffs, knives, Leatherman tools, a smaller, more powerful flashlight than standard issue, antibacterial soap, latex gloves, and batting gloves, whose thin leather allowed for a better search. I had several sets of binoculars from my father—he was a collector of potentially useful devices, like telescopes and barometers—and we went through them all. *You got eyes?* Yeah, I got eyes. They would get beat up on the street and dropped in the van, and one eye would lose focus, and then both, but even so, it seemed an honorable end to them. They were large and unwieldy, however, and since I couldn't move in plainclothes as well as Sammy or Orville could, the additional tip of the binocular case would have made me look like I was on safari. But when subtlety is not an option, banality can be, and so I'd dawdle over to an OP in uniform with the binoculars in a Dunkin' Donuts bag, so that my presence did not draw any great interest. We made do with what we had.

We also made do with each other. I could talk to Alicia about books. I went back with Stix to our first days on the Job. Anyone could get along with Sammy. Orville and I usually wanted to push things, to stay out longer and take more bodies. Tony and I were hungry for guns, for mix-it-up adventures like hitting the Hole. Sgt. Carroll and I were determined to move up in the game, to get search warrants. Our idiosyncrasies also were duly noted. Orville and Tony didn't like dogs, Alicia didn't take attitude, Stix had a dread of roaches, and Sammy drove like Grandma Moses. I wasn't big on heights. In a sneaker-conscious environment, I had ratty old white canvas high-tops, the like of which most of us hadn't seen since childhood. I ate big sloppy sandwiches that I had to hold with both hands, usually with gobs of hot sauce. I stuffed my old paperwork into the bottom of my locker, which Tony regarded with horror. I tended to show up for work at the last minute, or a minute or two later.

Though we were a tight group, we didn't go out together. Everyone was married or had a steady girlfriend, with plenty of friends outside of the Job, and to keep each other company for fifty or sixty hours a week was enough. If the four-to-twelve shift went out for a beer, a couple of times over the summer Orville and Sammy might stop by for one, and Tony, Sgt. Carroll, and I for a few more, but Stix and Alicia wouldn't go at all. But that was the extent of it. Other cops were close, off duty and on, like the Bike team, with Sgt. Steve O'Hagan, Scott "Smacky" Mackay, Tommy "Stretch" Dolan, George "Chicky" Mendez, Steve "Sprinkles" Vergeli, Andy Bielawski, and later, Joey Castaldo and Joe Barongi. And they went out often, for a beer or to go golfing, even sometimes for vacations. As cops, they were at least as good as we were, at least at first, in part because the players somehow couldn't take a cop on a bike seriously—in the summer, they wore polo shirts and shorts, and in general there was something innocent and playful and time-killing about a guy on a bike. It seemed less like a vehicle than a toy, as if they patrolled on pogo sticks. But when they hit a set, they could move in like the cavalry.

So could we. One morning as we drove to get breakfast, we passed a player as he hit off three or four junkies in a park, on One-Four-Six and College, plain as day, one after the other, with a deft, practiced hand like a black-jack dealer over a green felt table: *Hit me!* It was so near and so clear that it set off an animal instinct in us—*Fetch!*—and when we swerved in and jumped out, it seemed like we dropped on them from above. The junkies tried to run and the player tried to fight and the drugs sailed up into the air, but in a moment, we had it all wrapped up. A day's work was done in half a minute, with a solid catch: six or seven bundles of dope, a few bodies, a dealer who glared at us, muttering threats. It wasn't the French Connection, but it was good, quick work. We hadn't seen that spot before, and we didn't again, and that was a fine feeling, since it was across the street from Mother Teresa's convent. Cops make collars, DAs make cases, the bad guys go away, and the neighborhood gets better. That's how it's supposed to work.

When we brought them in to the precinct, a few of us felt another pang, nearly as deep: "Couldn't this have waited until we ate?" Aren't the dealers like mosquitoes, and in the South Bronx it's an endless, sweltering summer, with plenty of rain? None of us had any regrets, but we did wonder whether we might have swatted them just as well on a full stomach as an empty one. After a few days, when other cops looked at the spot, intrigued by our stories of easy pickings, one of them yelled at us, only half-joking, "What the hell did you guys do! You killed the spot!" It was as if we'd not only caught the biggest fish, but drained the pond afterward. In a narrow view of things, a cop who steadily delivers a couple of misdemeanors will never have a problem with the bosses about productivity. Cops used to call the practice of picking off an apple with a care for the cart "angeling," and in Pat Brown's day, gangsters supplied cops with "friendly collars" for gambling raids, so the brass could claim success and move on. On patrol, where you spend your time putting out fires and preventing them, in kitchens and on street corners, you could be a great cop with little "activity" to show for it, and so angeling in some form had its ass-covering value. But in a specialized unit like SNEU, the point was to make collars that meant something. Of course, that wasn't entirely up to us.

Once, we took a dealer for trespass. We knew him and had watched him run his spot, stepping into a building to direct junkie traffic to another player in the lobby. He had left when we hit the set, but we picked him up a few blocks away, and though he had no contraband, he also claimed that he hadn't been inside the building. As I said, the trespass collar is the Swiss Army knife of the beat cop, but a device with so many uses can sometimes be misapplied. In response, the Bronx DA developed a protocol for trespass arrests, an affidavit that required you to fill in blanks about what you asked and what was answered, where the person did reside, what explanation was offered for their presence, and what you did to check the story. The purpose was to lock in the elements of the crime and to screen out shaky arrests by cops who were too literal-minded—"If you live on the third floor, what are you doing on the eighth?" But for certain ADAs, the form seemed to inspire an equally senseless rigidity of interpretation. For my collar that day, the ADA inquired, "Did you ask him if he knew anyone in the building, if he was visiting anyone?"

"No, I didn't. He denied being there."

"Well, why couldn't he be visiting people there?"

"He was. He was visiting lots of people, to sell them drugs."

"Then why didn't you charge him with sale?"

"We didn't have enough to go on. All we had was the trespass."

"For trespass, you have to ask him if he has a reason to be there."

"No, I don't. I have to find out why he's there. Not even that—if he doesn't live there, he has to tell me why he's there. If he lies to me, I don't have to help him come up with another story."

"On the affidavit, you have to fill out—"

"The affidavit isn't the law. It's a handy way to spell out a charge. It's a useful tool, unlike yourself." Actually, I only thought the last bit, I didn't say it.

"I'd better get my supervisor."

"Okey-doke."

But the exchange I had with the supervisor was even more weirdly circular. She tried to undermine the case in ways I'd never imagined.

"Where was he in the building?"

"He went into the lobby."

"Did you arrest him there?"

"No, when we hit the set, he was gone. We took him a block or two away."

"So you never actually saw him *inside* the building."

"I saw him go through the front door."

"Right, but you didn't see him inside?"

"The door leads to 'inside,' it's where they keep it, inside the building."

"You didn't see him—"

"Maybe you should talk to my supervisor."

Sgt. Carroll had the pleasure of the rest of the conversation, which continued in the science-fiction vein: "You're right, we saw him *go* inside, but not *while* he was inside. He could have vaporized."

Once it was conceded that the door did not lead to another dimension, the line of argument shifted. As I watched Sgt. Carroll, his sense of humor did not leave him altogether, but it took him to places he did not expect to go. We had been together in the OP, and his conversation picked up where mine left off: "He went in and out a lot, all afternoon."

He pursed his lips, nodding.

"Maybe ten seconds here, half a minute there."

There was an ill-concealed sarcasm in his voice, as he conceded, "You're right, it wasn't very long at all."

There was another pause, after which I knew the talk would not go on for long.

"I see. Are you telling me that someone has to be in a building for a certain amount of time before they're trespassing? Can you tell me, as a matter of law, how much time we need? Two minutes? Ten? I'd like to be able to clock it, if that's what we need, and to let the other cops know."

Of course, the trespass "time limit" was pure fabrication—the law says to trespass is to unlawfully "enter or remain" in a premises—but the charges were nonetheless dropped. The collar was a misdemeanor, and it was hard to think of anything that could matter less to any of us—perp, cops, ADA—but the indifference did rankle. Alicia asked me, "And you care about this because . . . ?" The answer was partly and simply having a stiff neck, but I also knew that if I didn't fight for my cases, no one else would, and not caring was an easy habit to fall into. When they taught us boxing or judo takedowns in the Academy, they told us, "As you practice, you will play," meaning that if you dog it now in the gym, you're more likely to come up short in the street. And physical and verbal self-defense are not so far removed in mind-set, deriving from an ability to think on your feet and act as you are trained.

"Ya gotta ah-tic-ya-late," we were told, and if you were asked why you stopped someone, you can't say "because they looked funny," unless you can spell out the funniness, the heavy clothing in warm weather, the way they circled the block, their nervous reaction to your arrival. What might begin as pure instinct has to stand as hard argument. The skill of articulation lay in balance of detail and clarity: if you left too much out, it could seem evasive or dishonest, but if you supplied an overabundance of information, the story might be simply incoherent. Anyone would rather handle a simple situation than a complicated one—there is a turn-of-the-century story of a patrolman dragging a dead horse from Kosciusko Street over to Smith Street, so his report would have fewer spelling errors—and in SNEU, the language of each complaint for an observation sale was virtually identical: "At T/P/O Perp #1 did exchange small objects for US Currency from Perps #2 & #3." Perp #2 and Perp #3 might have acted in concert with Perp #1, to exchange small objects for US Currency with Perps #4, #5, and #6, and you would also list what money and drugs were recovered from each, but the language was the same because the situation was the same. No matter if the set was as simple as a cheese-line, or it worked with the many-sided misdirection of the Statue of Liberty play in a football scrimmage, the essential act was a hand-to-hand transaction. The entire criminal-justice system functions as an editorial process, as a story is refined, supported, and checked from the complainant to the cop, to the sergeant and maybe the lieutenant, and then to the ADA, and then to the judge, and sometimes to a jury.

For all that, in the Bronx, they rarely indicted for an observation sale, unless there were four or five buyers, with stash and cash recovered from the dealer as well. If you caught two buyers and the dealer, but he had no drugs, you didn't have a case. Or if you missed the buyers and just grabbed the seller, they only charged misdemeanor possession, even if he had felony weight several times over. They did prosecute with vigor if the perp had prior felony convictions, but that suggested that the perp's past rather than your efforts mattered. My sister-in-law, Beth Brennan, was an ADA in Manhattan, and she was amazed to hear it, and cops who came from other boroughs often found themselves in bewildered confrontations with Bronx ADAs: "I saw the one guy hand the other guy drugs, I saw him take the money, I got them both, what do you mean you're dropping it?" The labor of articulation seemed futile when your word meant so little.

In response, most cops tried to speak up for each other, on duty and off. There were rackets for Sgt. O'Hagan, who had two autistic kids, and Sgt. Kelly, who had triplets with cerebral palsy. There was a funeral for Sgt. Poplaski's boy Frankie, who had a heart condition. There was another funeral for Sgt. Walker Fitzgerald, from the Four-Two. Walker had always been a cool-headed and lighthearted leader in the field, and had looked out for me in his precinct when I was there with a collar. He laughed more than most cops do, but he also was a rising star on the Job, graduating first in his class and gliding through promotional tests. One night in Queens, he was in a car accident, and when he pulled over, a block away, he was jumped and killed. Sordid speculations found their way into the press: Hadn't he been coming from a strip club? Hadn't he "fled from the scene of an accident"? What was he doing in that neighborhood? For cops, the presumption of innocence is a rarity, not a right, and Walker would never get to tell his side of the story. I thought of other questions: wasn't he a murder victim, and a police officer, and a young man with a bright future? The Mayor and the Police Commissioner didn't go to the wake, which was held at the same funeral home where my father's was. I shook his brother Eddie's hand at the casket, where he stood in his dress uniform with an honor guard from his own precinct, Midtown South. He had a fixed smile and a faraway look.

Some days I laughed at how easy it could be: once, we wrapped up a set with five collars, when there were six of us on the team. I didn't take a collar, though I wanted one. As the rest of the team processed, I went up to the second floor of the Four-O and watched the project across the street, at 215 Alexander Avenue. I saw a crackhead pop in and out of the building, and I slipped out after him. I loped down the street, cut into the lot next to St. Jerome's, and grabbed him. I walked him back to the precinct and put him with the rest of the prisoners. "Now we got six," I said. On other days, you were reminded how hard it might go, like when Tony and I took a guy the size of both of us and put him over the hood of a car, and I thought, *Shit, I thought crack's supposed to make you skinny.* As we tried to connect two sets of cuffs behind his back, the perp only then seemed to realize that he was being arrested, and he lifted us up like boats on a tide. Tony and I looked at each other, knowing that we had seconds before he would toss us aside, and locked the cuffs tight. For months, we hit a dope spot run by a guy named Lamont, taking bundles of heroin weekly and in one nice grab, over a thousand dollars in cash. Though we were little more than an aggravation to him—he was always released, usually without bail—the aggravation did mount, and after I collared him the second time, he told me, "You're making this personal, you're costing me. You watch your back out there, something might happen." Lamont had a few bullet holes in him and I didn't doubt he gave better than he got. At the time, I thought his threat meant that he'd say he was paying me, or I was robbing him, but later I realized he intended something else.

One under, two under, three under. Orville once watched a dealer as the guy bounced a spaldeen off a wall, hitting people off as he whiled away the afternoon. When Orville grabbed him, he searched him all over without finding the stash until he squeezed the pink rubber ball, and a slit opened up to reveal the drugs inside. Richie Hyde from Crime saw four junkies in a car, looking out as one of them hid something under the hood. He stopped the car and went through the engine block without finding anything, until one of the junkies admitted what he had done: he had a container of clean urine warming below the fan belt, so they could provide body-temperature drug-free specimens for their parole officer. One day with Bike, we did a car stop. I checked under the seat and felt something heavy in a brown paper bag. I pulled it out and looked inside, but it was a different kind of weapon than the one I expected. "Ugh," I said, "Look at this," and handed it over to one of the other guys. He reached inside and pulled out a dildo, crusty and stained, heavy as a lead pipe. We all looked at him, horrified. "Why don't you head in and wash your hands?"

We ran, fell, and got up again. Once, I chased a guy on a bicycle, and because he had to turn as he saw me I gained on him, and I could see him pump down on the pedals with all his dead weight, but I gained even as he started to pick up speed, and I knew he was thinking, *If he catches me when I'm on wheels, it's time to give it up.* . . . As he rounded the corner I closed in to a few feet away, until I hit an oil slick and my feet flew out from under me. My radio, nightstick, and ass bounced in three different directions over the pavement. It was a good spill, I knew, because the crowd winced instead of laughing. Of course, my partners laughed. Our entertainment didn't depend on seeing each other trip, but it helped. I watched from an OP as they prepared to hit the lobby of 175 Alex, creeping along the wall in the dark, toward the railed stairs and the locked front door, which meant they would have to leap over on cue as someone left the building. When I gave the signal, it was like watching a herd of wildebeest charge across a river, losing the unfit to the current and the crocs.

We didn't develop a herd mentality as much as a hive mentality, instantly known to each other by temperament and task, but a droning, indistinguishable whole to an outside observer. That's probably what it sounded like, too, if you heard us argue over which diner to go to for breakfast:

"We can't go there, I saw five roaches. Let's go to the other place."

"By the clinic? That place is full of junkies, the Number Two special comes with methadone."

"Well, I'm not going where you want, I heard a cop got a bloody Band-Aid in his BLT."

"It was an honest mistake. What do you think the 'B' stands for in BLT?"

Whenever I got a minute with a perp, taking him to the bathroom or for a drink of water, I tried to talk. I'd say, "You don't have to talk to me, but don't lie to me, either. You can save us both some time." Some cops say that you can get anyone to talk, and I'd at least agree that if you can get them to say anything, you can get them to give a little more. But if the perp had been through the system a few times, we couldn't threaten credibly with long prison sentences, and we were also limited in how much time we could devote to each collar. Moreover, the detective from the Squad who interrogates a suspect is looking for any kind of useful admission—if a robbery suspect says, "I was there, but I didn't do anything," he might have effectively owned up to the crime. A detective may only need a moment of cooperation to get what he needs, the utterance of a self-defeating half-truth, and as such the range of persuasive methods is wide. You can threaten the perp with the flames of hell, or promise him candy; you can offer friendship or cash; you can lie about having fingerprints or the confession of accomplices, or whatever pledges or threats it takes to reach that moment of capitulation. You're not even looking for a one-night stand, you're looking for the quickest of quickies, standing up, with your clothes on, and you have no intention of staying friends later. At SNEU, we were looking for a more serious relationship; we didn't need confessions, we needed collaborators, and for the perp to stop and realize, a day or two later, "Wait a second, there was no hidden camera in that crack vial!" would not have done us any good.

Still, there was need of persuasion, even if what you were after was a straightforward, businesslike bargain instead of a heat-of-passion surrender. You had to make the perp concentrate on the moment, and then on the future, and how you could work together to change them. You wheedle, enlighten, repeat. I've heard the sum of these techniques referred to as "jerkology." When I first tried to flip Maria, who was collared for selling heroin, the first ten minutes brought nothing. She was a hard-core junkie, an operator with such mileage on her that the first word that came to me when I saw her was "survivor," though it should have been the last. She didn't look just dirty but dusty, as if she'd been left in the attic, and she had ulcerated limbs as if someone had taken bites out of them. On being questioned about whether she knew anyone who had guns or was doing robberies, she offered a bored denial, and when she was asked about the heroin spot where she worked, she just shook her head. I knew she had done state time, and I knew a bit about the spot she worked—the brands, the players, the hours. Debriefings are like poker, even though it's clear that you're the better player, with the better hand. It's also unlike poker, in that if you play well, you both win.

"Maria, there's only one way you can make this go away, right? It's through us, right? Talking, helping us out? It's not through your boss, JJ. We know him, too. Today, he was hanging out on the corner while you were running your ass ragged, taking money, handing out bags of dope. And you're in cuffs, while he's home, watching *Oprah*. Yeah, Maria, it's four o'clock already! You moved a couple hundred decks this morning for JJ—ten bucks each, that's a couple grand. How much did he pay you, fifty bucks? Or did he just throw a couple of bags your way? Is he gonna send a lawyer down for you, is he gonna water your plants while you're away?"

But she didn't reply. I asked her about prison, and she said she didn't like it much. She still owed time for parole, and if she was convicted, she'd have to do that time before she started what she earned today. She knew that, she told me, but she told me nothing else. My mistake with Maria was to keep pitching appeals to her freedom. She was an addict, whose life was a closed circuit of having it and needing it, and nothing I could say would affect her truly solitary confinement. But she'd been talking, and I wanted to keep her talking. I asked if she had kids. She flinched, and asked for another cigarette. She nodded.

I changed the subject back to her dealing that day, describing customers, lookouts, and so on, authoritative blather to lead her to believe we had her down. Then I asked her what her kids' names were. As she said them— "Fernando and Lucy . . ."—it was as if she were watching them sleep. She breathed deeply, and softly began, "JJ keeps it in the corner building, on the second floor, the first door on the right. He brings enough for the day, from a stash house in the middle of the block." At that moment, I felt like I had jerkologically arrived.

. . .

SUMMER PASSED. A NEWS STORY BROKE ABOUT A HAITIAN man who claimed to have been sodomized by a cop with a plunger in a precinct in Brooklyn. A lot of cops didn't believe it because they couldn't imagine it; in their worst, what-if-he-killed-my-mother nightmares, they could picture killing someone but not—*ever*—that. I didn't recall ever having seen a plunger in the precinct, but the rumor was that the Job had henceforth banned them. I remember talking to a friend, a veteran homicide detective, and we lowered our voices to say we suspected the accusation was true. Autumn passed. On a Sunday in November, we had to come in for an overtime shift for "CPR" training at Fordham University, short for "Courtesy, Professionalism, and Respect." We heard lectures and were sent in groups to classrooms, where we met with people from the neighborhood, all of whom were eminently decent and respectable except for a teenager so snot-nosed and rotten that we suspected he was a plant: "I hate cops! They *stoo*-pid!" We had to say our names and how much time we had on, and Stix and I, who had less than three years, decided to amplify things a bit—"PO Cataldo, PSA-7, six years on the Job," "PO Conlon, PSA-7, I got, oh, six and a half years on"—as if to bolster our credibility, though we had no intention of doing anything but sitting there and shutting up. When we returned to the auditorium, an announcement was made: PO Edward Fitzgerald, brother of the late Sgt. Walker Fitzgerald, had committed suicide hours after a family memorial service.

As it got colder, we visited Housing management offices for keys to vacant apartments, so we could set up OPs protected from the weather. We slipped into buildings, leaped out of vans. Old people and working people thanked us on the sly, while the perps shouted that we were crackers and faggots. If a lookout took off on foot from us, leaving his bike, we made sure it found its way to a needy child in a nearby neighborhood—"Hey, kid, want a bike?"—and community relations thus moved forward on both fronts. We called it the "Bicycle Relocation Program. We saw dope called Stingray, Passion, and Independence Day. I look at my memo book and see that I collared Benita H, three blue slabs right front pocket; Miguel V, eight glassines, Samuel T, nineteen black-top vials. I don't remember Benita or Miguel, but I remember Samuel, because he fought Orville and me in the lobby of 3050 Park Avenue. My note says "MOS injured," for Member of the Service, but I couldn't remember at first who it was—it was Orville, who got conked in the head. After you catch your breath, you get up and keep going.

And then Sgt. Carroll did just that. After we had worked together for six or seven months, he was promoted to lieutenant. For the ranks of sergeant, lieutenant, and captain, there is a civil-service test, and the grade, along with experience and several lesser factors, provides you with a list number. The Job promotes people in groups, moving down the list. Sgt. Carroll hoped that his promotion would be delayed, at least until after the holidays, so that he would keep his old schedule, rather than show up in a new place, where he would be just the man to fill in on the midnight for Christmas Eve. I also like to think that he liked us. But before Christmas came, he was gone.

Again, we were reshuffled back to patrol, sometimes together, mostly not. Sgt. O'Hagan grabbed us when he could, to work with Bike. We filled in for random footposts, sectors and conditions cars, and my memo book is filled with now-meaningless headings for assigned radio numbers, meal times, posts, and jobs. The notes from jobs are hardly more vivid: "Cabbie slash," and "Abusive, threatening one week, unknown if taking meds," and "It's my brother's jacket." Another one came to me, but only after some thought: "Known perp, asked c/v for $ . . . grabbed all $20 . . . shows crowbar. C/V . . . says fuck it . . . perp turns, tries to stab, block with crowbar, clean thru right hand. Unknown flight." One four-to-twelve, I worked with a cop named Steve Carroll, and we had seventeen jobs, all of them ridiculous. The last came over as an EDP, called in by a man who said his wife was on drugs. The apartment had the blasting-radiator project heat that forces many people to keep their windows open through the winter, and on one wall there was a poster with a poem in Spanish entitled "My Son," illustrated with a drawing of a toddler pulling on his foreskin. An amiable man greeted us and showed us a drowsy woman watching TV, a baby sleeping peacefully in the bedroom, and another, younger woman, in shorty-shorts, cleaning the kitchen. "Who's she?" I asked Steve. "Um, let's call her the au pair," he said, as he tried to write it up, though none of them spoke English. Because the job was an EDP, the sergeant and his driver arrived, and an ambulance with two EMTs, but they didn't speak Spanish either, and so another set of cops were called to translate. I wondered how many hundreds of dollars per minute it cost the City. The woman on the couch casually admitted that she did smoke crack, but that had been hours before, and she'd been lounging around ever since. All of them lived there—husband, wife, girlfriend, kid—and happily, too, as far as she was concerned, because the "au pair" pitched in around the house when the wife was on the pipe. The husband felt there was no particular emergency but he wanted to send her away, preferably to the hospital but to jail if necessary, because he wanted the apartment. One of the cops remembered that he had been locked up before, when he claimed his wife had a gun to expedite her move. The wife agreed to go to the hospital, and the eight public servants went home. On Christmas Eve, I walked my old beat in the Village.

We had been pretty good that year, we felt, and hoped that Santa would bring us a nice, new boss. I don't know how much influence we had in the selection; certainly, we were a productive unit, and our commanding officer, Deputy Inspector Cavanagh, wanted to make sure we so remained. Rumor of who we wanted would have reached upward, but it hardly would have been the weightiest concern. And so when we heard that we were getting Sgt. Tommy Carrano, it was a relief. Carrano was the least bossy of bosses, acting as if his sergeant stripes were a kind of accident, like a birthmark, that let him sign our paperwork and give us days off. If we wanted to take a break, it was fine, and if we wanted to work, it was fine, too, and since we were a driven group, we wanted to work most of the time anyway. Sgt. Carrano was as regular a guy as you could ask for: he played on the precinct hockey team and in a rock band at home, and since SNEU was something in between a contact sport and a pick-up jam session, he fit right in.

We got used to having a good time again. We lumbered after perps through snowbanks and down icy sidewalks. We picked new spots. Stix caught a guy on a bike after a six-block foot pursuit. Carrano tackled a dealer with a cast on his arm and mashed it; fortunately, it was a prop, a fake for concealing the stash. For a while, we diverted ourselves by giving *Cosmopolitan* quizzes to each other, and then to the perps:

"If you could be any kind of animal, what would it be?"

"Now use three adjectives to describe it."

"What's your favorite color, and why?"

"If you were in the desert, would you rather take a quick shower or a long bath?"

"Bear in mind, the desert question is a sex question."

"Shut up! Don't ruin it!"

We oohed and ahhed like psychiatrists as they told us they liked tigers because they were tough or green because it was like money. I think the animal question was how you see yourself, and the color question was more or less the same thing, and the desert question was how you liked to have sex. As we filled up the van, the old perps quizzed the new perps, and giggled with us at the answers: "So, you like black panthers, 'cause they're all mysterious, huh? Yeah, right!" As we dropped them off at Central Booking, we'd call out, "Thank you for being arrested by PSA-7 SNEU. Is there anything you'd recommend for next time?" Most of them laughed, and some said that though we were the nicest cops who'd ever collared them, they hoped we didn't catch them again.

But Sgt. Carrano had put in for a transfer to a unit in midtown, so he could commute in on the train. Though his move could take months, we knew his was a short-term posting, and as it happened, we had him for six weeks. We were beginning to feel a little orphaned, and to chafe at the precariousness of the arrangement. We had been lucky with bosses, but who knew how long that would hold? Not surprisingly, the best bosses, like Clark and O'Hagan, already had their own teams and wouldn't leave them. Most of the bosses who had steady tours, like days or four-to-twelves, were used to the schedule and had arranged their lives around it, whether they were going back to school, working a second job, or taking care of the kids while the wife worked in the day. We were glad to hear that Sgt. Pat Kelly was thinking about taking over the unit. Kelly was on the midnights, and he was genuinely beloved there. There was a rumor that the fix was in, that Sgt. Spinelli from Admin had even called Kelly's wife, Vicki, to sell him on the change, and that her reaction was favorable. That almost sounded like a dirty trick, calling the wife, but I was glad Spinelli did it. The midnight guys began to curse at us when we saw them, which was a good sign. We had a feeling it would work out just right.

SIX

Everyone always asks, "Is it like how it is on TV?" There are more cop shows than any other kind, and more are set in New York than in any other place: *Car 54, Where Are You?* and *Naked City, Kojak* and *Barney Miller, Law & Order* and *NYPD Blue.* To watch a cop show with a cop can be a joyless experience, as they scold like Sunday school teachers at each departure from the facts as they know them. But most people seem eager to know the degree of realism in these shows, which always seemed to me beside the point, as my colleagues Batman, Superman, and Spider-Man would likely agree. In the national dream life of movies and television, the good guys and bad guys do battle in our heads, much as they did in our childhood reveries. And while gangsters might learn how to be gangsters by watching *The Godfather,* there are tests designed specifically to screen out Academy candidates who've grown up on too much cops-and-robbers TV. But I didn't want to be a cop when I was a kid; my disappointments had nothing to do with expectations shaped by Hollywood. When I watch a police drama, I like what they get wrong as much as what they get right, especially if the story is drawn from the headlines or history. I watch them for what I can use. The best movies are like the kind of daydreams you have during a long roll call, of rescues and revelations that are unlikely to happen on this tour of duty, but that aren't out of the question. You have to remember as much as you have to imagine: this could be the day that could change you.

On October 7, 1961, Roger Maris, Sonny Grosso, and Eddie Egan each had a day that would change him. Maris hit a home run in the ninth inning to win Game Three of the World Series for the Yankees, and Egan and Grosso, two detectives in the Narcotics Division, were so elated that they went out on the town, despite having worked for the past twenty-seven hours. They went to the Copacabana, where Egan had an eye for the coat-check girl, but their attentions were soon distracted by a large party across the room. Egan and Grosso recognized several of them as Mob-connected dope dealers and gamblers, although the center of their attentions, the big shot, was a new face. They watched him for a while from inside the club, and then from outside, and then they followed him as he stopped in Little Italy, where he switched cars, until finally, at six in the morning, he crossed the bridge to Brooklyn. As the sun rose, he went into a little luncheonette and opened it up for business. How did this guy from a greasy spoon on the wrong side of the river get to be the man to see at the Copa?

That is how the French Connection case began, perhaps the most celebrated investigation in NYPD history, as related by a fine book and a great movie. Egan and Grosso were classic cop partners: Egan, known as "Bullets" or "Popeye," was an Irish street kid, outgoing, hard-charging, skirt-chasing, strongly built with a bit of a belly, ruddy and fair. He never knew his father and his mother died young. Before he joined the NYPD, he was in the Marines, and he might have made the Yankees if an injury hadn't ended his baseball career. Sonny Grosso was known as "Cloudy" because he kept an eye on the down side. He was disciplined and reserved, a black belt, tall and thin, with dark hair, dark eyes, and olive skin. His father died young, too, but he became the teenage man of the house for his mother and three sisters, with a courtly manner and old-fashioned beliefs. Sonny hated drugs because he could see how they were changing his old neighborhood, in East Harlem; Popeye hated them after four junkies beat his six-year-old niece to a pulp after she walked in on them robbing the piggy-bank in her bedroom. Both hit the NYPD running, and Popeye got his shield a year after he joined. They teamed up in Narcotics in 1959.

When Sonny and Popeye made the man from the luncheonette as Patsy Fuca, they were excited. Fuca was the nephew of Angelo Tuminaro, who had been a major Mafia heroin dealer since the 1930s and a fugitive since 1960, when he skipped bail before the federal drug trial that sent mob boss Vito Genovese to prison for the rest of his life. A task force of NYPD detectives and federal agents was assembled. Sonny and Popeye set up surveillance from the X-ray room of the hospital across the street from the luncheonette, where they became familiar to Fuca as the medical technicians who stopped by for coffee. They obtained wiretaps on the phones there and at Fuca's house, where they pieced together his aspiration to take over his uncle's role as the New York Mafia's conduit for Marseilles heroin. They also realized that Fuca was aware of surveillance in the area, so Sonny arranged for Vice to raid a nearby numbers joint as a diversion. When Fuca's wife ordered curtains for their house, Sonny and Popeye intercepted the delivery van and donned UPS costumes, so they could get a look inside. Popeye got a girlfriend a job in a bar that Fuca frequented. There were a lot of those funny little things you notice when you get inside someone's life, but mostly, there was waiting. October passed, and then November, and then December. New York was running out of dope. Any junkie could tell you there was a "panic" on the street. Sonny and Popeye had a pretty good grip on what was happening, lacking only the Frenchmen and the heroin.

On December 21, in France, Jacques Angelvin, the debonair host of a TV show called *Paris Club,* announced that he was taking a trip to the United States. Angelvin was short on cash and unsteady in his prospects, and I picture him as a cross between a poor man's Johnny Carson and a poor man's Hugh Hefner. Through the nightclubs, he came to know a Corsican gangster named François Scaglia, a pimp, kidnapper, and drug dealer with underworld interests throughout the Mediterranean. Scaglia offered Angelvin ten thousand dollars to take a car with him on his trip, a 1960 Buick Invicta, which had 112 pounds of nearly pure heroin concealed in the rocker panels, on the sides of the chassis below the doors. Angelvin probably didn't know precisely what his errand was—he once took the car out for a spin in Paris, to Scaglia's horror—but he knew that his employer was not in the grocery business. Scaglia and another veteran heroin broker named Jean Jehan, a striking figure in his mid-sixties who stood six-foot-four and favored homburgs and white spats, would meet him in New York and manage the exchange with Fuca.

The movie *The French Connection* is perversely gripping in its depiction of the grueling dullness of a surveillance. In Narcotics today, there are all kinds of sophisticated technologies for collecting information, while undercovers and informants penetrate deeply into criminal organizations—sometimes it almost seems unfair. But the French Connection was a SNEU case: aside from the two wiretaps, it was all shoe leather and peeking around corners. There were hours and hours of tails: standing on sidewalks in nine-degree weather, pretending to make a phone call or window-shop while Frog #1 had coffee or Frog #2 tried to pick up a waitress after his fifth cognac. The cops stamped their feet and choked down dirty-water hot dogs and cold coffee in styrofoam cups, hoping they wouldn't get the runs the moment before the briefcase was exchanged for the car keys. It wasn't even like a ten-day poker game, it was a ten-day poker hand, raising and staying and raising again. The Frogs enjoyed the city, walking for miles and then doubling back; getting in cars, driving, stopping, switching; trying to spot the cops, or shake them, or simply exhaust them. The scene in the movie where Popeye and one of the Frogs do an elaborate dance in the subway, stepping on the train, then off, then on, until the Frog is on and Popeye is off, and he tips his hat as the train pulls away—that happened. The famous pursuit of the elevated train didn't—Sonny and Popeye had to beat a train to the next stop, but the train was underground. Sonny and Popeye did seize the Invicta, and Sonny noticed on the shipping declaration that the car was to be 112 pounds lighter on the return trip to France—an economy on Angelvin's part, through which he hoped to save thirty-three dollars. But they didn't give the car back with the dope, of course—it had already been removed—and the ending of the case is slower, stranger, and more compelling than the screen version.

After nearly four months of surveillance, there was a certain amount of tension in the task force. Popeye got in a fistfight with a federal agent. Though all involved were determined to succeed, of course, several would not have been unhappy to see the cocksure Popeye fail. When they finally made their move, taking Scaglia, Angelvin, and another Frenchman—Jehan escaped—then executing a search warrant at Fuca's father's house, where twelve pounds of heroin, several machine guns, and a grenade were recovered, it looked like a success. But the numbers didn't add up, and Sonny and Popeye continued to look until they found a steamer trunk in the basement of 1171 Bryant Avenue, in the Bronx, where Fuca's brother Anthony lived. It was labeled A. FUCA, #5C, and it contained eighty-eight pounds of heroin. The problem was that Anthony had been arrested with his brother and father, and he hadn't made bail. They could voucher the drugs, but the collar might not stick—the Manhattan DA had passed on the case, in fact, though Brooklyn prosecuted—and they wanted a body to go with it, whether it was An-

thony Fuca or anyone else. The first phase, on Fuca alone, had taken three exhaustive months, and the still more intensive second phase, on Fuca and the
Frenchmen, had taken another ten days. And then Sonny and Popeye had to
sit in the basement of 1171 Bryant for almost another month. They got a little
punchy. Because they couldn't tell anyone who they were or why they were
there, a variety of people drew their own, nearly lethal conclusions. Days and
weeks passed, as Popeye, Sonny, and the others sat quiet in the dark, shotguns on their laps. After a time, one man became convinced that the red light
on the furnace was a man smoking a cigarette; on another occasion, when the
superintendent karate-chopped a wooden plank, he was very nearly shot.
There was a painter working on the building who became obsessed with the
sinister men in the basement—he didn't believe their story that they were on
a burglary stakeout; he didn't believe they were cops at all, and they didn't
take great pains to correct him. But his constant calls to the authorities
brought visits from beat cops, the Department of Sanitation, and even a raid
from the 41st Precinct Squad, which had near-disastrous results. Finally, they
arranged for Anthony Fuca's bail to be lowered, and he was released. On
Saturday, February 19, Sonny was the best man at a wedding, wearing
a tuxedo at St. Patrick's Cathedral, when he got a call from Popeye: *Get
back, this is it.* Sonny skipped the reception and came back to collar Fuca in
black tie.

A great investigation became a legendary one: 112 pounds of heroin
seemed like a diamond as big as the Ritz. In the NYPD at the time, there were
only 200 cops assigned to the Narcotics Division, and there were sixty federal
drug agents assigned to New York. The size of the pot, relative to the scale of
the game, broke the bank in a way that has subsequently been impossible to
duplicate. Popeye and Sonny essentially confiscated one month's supply of
heroin for the entire country. That one collar could almost make you believe,
not altogether foolishly, that we could stop crime as we were getting to know
it. The movie gets so much right: the feel of police work, the easy camaraderie and the well-stacked chips on the shoulder; the deep moral passion of
it and the pure joy of the game. I get a charge from imagining the nightlife
of a hot-shot cop in New York in 1961, when you'd put on your porkpie hat
and go out to the Copa for a couple of rye and gingers. What couldn't be
done? *And the Yankees win! And the Yankees win!* The case that began with a
home run ended with two, in Brooklyn and the Bronx, and inspired the best
cop movie ever, which reverberated back in the real world by helping push

the French government into shutting down the Connection. Popeye and Sonny aimed high, pushed hard, and won bigger than they'd ever imagined, but there were times—maybe most of the time—when it looked like it was heading straight down the drain. Always, always, there was the edge of doubt: Do we move in, and blow it? Do we wait, and miss it? If we pull back, can we pick them up again? How long will the Feds give us to let this play out? How long will our boss? The wiretaps will expire, and then the search warrants, and maybe the next time, the judge will say, "You guys again? I heard it before, forget about it." And the Feds will roll their eyes the next time the cops come up with something, and the PD will yawn the next time Narco has a caper, and Sonny and Popeye—well, if someone wanted to make a movie about them, it would be more along the lines of the Keystone Kops. Almost forty years later, Sonny told me that when he and Popeye chased the subway, screeching and dodging through midtown traffic, trying to beat the shuttle from Grand Central to Times Square, his dismay grew acute. "Whaddaya think?" he asked. Popeye smiled as he looked over at him and said, "I think Paul Newman's gonna play me and Ben Gazzara's gonna play you."

. . .

WE DIDN'T THINK AS BIG AS POPEYE, BUT WHEN SGT. PAT Kelly took over SNEU, we couldn't be small anymore. We were never especially petty, but on the team, there were frequent external aggravations, such as doing without vehicles or being sent out on footposts, and occasional internal ones, like griping over who was quick to grab a collar, or who was slow to help with yours. As it was often intense work, and we could be intense people, the frustrations could grow beyond their proper proportions, and a lesson in perspective had its value. Pat Kelly, or PK, was ours, and he didn't need words to teach it.

PK was in his mid-thirties, amiable and unassuming. He was a little softer around the middle and thinner on top than he might have liked, but when he described himself as "the fat, bald guy" he made it sound like a good thing to be. He had almost fifteen years on the Job, and he became a detective before he made sergeant. He was shot once, in the leg, during a pursuit. He was an extremely capable cop whose management style was extremely low-key. He'd say, "You guys know what you're doing," but he didn't have to repeat himself if he made some alteration to our plans. He called you "laddo," as if he were old and you were young.

PK had been working midnights, a tour with some heavy activity on the early end, followed by hours of down time. You finish at almost eight in the morning. I got the feeling he spent many hours looking at the night sky, thinking about things. PK and his wife, Vicki, had four little boys—Paulie, Dominic, Sean, and Brendan—and the first three were triplets with cerebral palsy, in varying degrees of severity. Paulie was in a wheelchair, Dominic was in braces, and Sean was on crutches. Together, they had undergone dozens of operations, progressing steadily but painfully, until the previous September, when Paulie had died suddenly from a respiratory infection. After years of daily struggles that would have been beyond the endurance of most of us, PK suffered a loss that was past what we could begin to understand. You wouldn't have known it to look at him.

PK made it impossible to be small about things. He never came in without a smile on his face, never complained about any of his problems, never hesitated to help another cop. Amid the martinets and bureaucrats scattered through the upper ranks, it was easy to forget that PK was our boss, but only because our admiration for him was so deeply felt that rank was immaterial. The less he asked of us, the more we offered. SNEU had always been a cliquish group, but now we became positively cultish. Because of his family situation, PK needed to change his tours frequently or take days off. When that happened, the desk would put us in uniform and send us out to footposts—often, it seemed, with a certain glee. But we would all change our tours to work with him, regardless of the instability it brought to our own lives, and we would rush the desk to try and get off when he wasn't there. People began to call us "the Manson family."

Everything got better with PK, even the food. We started going to breakfast at a diner called Stacy's, or the Locust, in Port Morris, the industrial spit of land on the bottom of the Bronx, east of the Bruckner. There was some consternation about bumping up the average expense of breakfast from around four dollars to six, but the consensus came to favor two bucks as the price of freedom from methadone and roaches. Stacy and her brother John, who ran the place, always saved newspapers for us and remembered what we liked. They opened up at five in the morning and closed twelve hours later, but if we came by when the door was locked and all the seats were up on the tables, they took us in and fed us. Often, I sat at the counter to read the papers while the rest of the guys took tables, until Tony noticed that my seat offered a better view of Stacy, and the rest of them jammed around the counter. We ate better and so we felt better, all around.

We chased people through alleys, hopped fences, and ran along rooftops, more sure in our paces. We watched, rolled in, and packed them up. We saw cops at the Four-O as much as we saw those in our own command. And there, we saw the new classes of cops look at us with curiosity and admiration, as they shined their shoes and readied for roll-call inspections, while we walked past in our street clothes and goatees, acknowledging the desk with brief nods. We were serious about work, about SNEU and PK; otherwise, we cracked each other up, all the time.

We also made some progress with our vehicle problem. Every other week, we worked ten-to-sixes, which began at nine-thirty in the morning, although the Warrant team didn't finish with the vans until eleven or noon, or sometimes later. We could catch up on paperwork, get something to eat, or hang around and bullshit, each of which had its attractions but none of which required half a day. Moreover, the sight of a bunch of cops doing nothing was an aggravation to the desk officer. If we didn't sign the Interrupted Patrol Log, we could get in trouble, and if the duty captain looked in to see we'd been there for hours, he could get in trouble. As some DOs seemed to think that whatever cops did in the street was merely the crude raw material that was made useful and true by the art of administration, several of them developed a distaste for us that they did not conceal. If enough time passed without hope of a vehicle, we would set up nearby on foot, but it was less safe and less effective, as it required stopping to walk every prisoner back to the house. And so we started to use my car.

Most cops don't use their cars on patrol because they couldn't afford to total them—in the event of an accident, the insurance situation would be a mess—or out of a prima donna belief that police cars should be supplied by the police department. But PK told me that there was a form you could fill out to get approval to use your own car on duty. I had a 1980 Oldsmobile Omega, blue as a whale but not quite as big, which hearkened back to other family vehicles, generally large and near-derelict, with names like the Gray Ghost and the African Queen. Patrol cars have four-digit numbers—"9786, can you eighty-five 9222 at One-Four-Nine and Third?"—and in Housing, the term "Triple-O" meant "out of operation." My car was christened Nine Triple-O. The interior of the roof was covered with mock-velvet cloth, affixed to the frame with a foam adhesive that had long since dried out; when I drove, the cloth billowed and the foam flaked, swirling around the car like snow in a paperweight. Alicia wouldn't ride in it. After a while, I yanked out the cloth and scraped off the foam, so the interior was bare, rusted metal. Alicia still wouldn't ride in it.

Triple-O was a great car to have, because it fit in the neighborhood, and because I frankly didn't care what happened to it. One night, when Tony and I transported prisoners in the van up to the Five-Two, there was a vehicle pursuit that went on for over an hour. The car went from local streets to highways, from the Bronx to Westchester, and then to the Bronx streets again, speeding past us with its caravan of cars in tow. There were more than a few reasons why we couldn't join in: we had perps; the van was unmarked—it didn't even have a working horn, let alone a red light; we were on overtime; and there were plenty of cops involved. But a vehicle pursuit is just too much fun to miss altogether, and we kept close, as if our faces were pressed against the glass. Once the car passed, Tony said, "I bet I know where he goes!" We took off in a different direction and parked by a corner, where the pursuit flew by, and then he picked two or three more streets, anticipating precisely where the chase led. If we had Triple-O, I thought, we could have rammed the hell out of it, and the car would have gotten an Inspector's Funeral. Alas, it runs to this day, though without glory.

For all our burgeoning confidence, we didn't forget how the street could outmatch us at any moment. Once, we worked a set on One-Five-Six Street, and I had to pick up a guy in the middle of the block, between Courtlandt and Morris. I stepped out from the corner and walked toward him, approaching within about thirty feet before he made me. He was a big man, well over six-foot-four, and he was built like a sack of clams, thick all over and bottom-heavy. He moved like one, too, dragging one leg behind him and propping up his bulk with a cane. When he saw me, he froze, and I could see him think, which I expected, and then I saw the result of his thought, which I did not. We're trained to say, "Police! Don't move!" and it was as if he took the injunction to mean "Move slowly!"—he practically made a three-point turn to reverse his course, and I just started laughing. I could have caught him if I was wearing cement shoes. He had over a hundred pounds on me, not to mention his cane, so I didn't go in lightly, in spite of everything. I stepped up and put him in a headlock with one arm as I tried to control the flailing cane with the other. I wound up for a roundhouse punch but it seemed to go wide—I felt it connect, though it had no effect on his bucking and heaving. And it was then that I saw that I had help from PK, who was taking him down from the other side, and we put him on the street and cuffed him. When we caught our breath, I noticed the red welt that began to rise from PK's temple.

"Did that asshole whack you with his cane?" I asked.

"Um, no, actually, it was you."

"Oh. Sorry."

"It's all right, laddo."

"I guess this would be a bad time to ask for next weekend off. . . ."

In retrospect, I can think of a lot of bosses who deserved a wallop in the head, and I regret all the more that I wasted a free shot on PK.

. . .

AS EVERYTHING WAS GOING SO WELL, THE NEXT CHANGE IN the unit didn't appear, at first, to be such a stroke of fortune; on this Job, it always seemed that your opportunities to move arose when you were content to stay, but when you were in a hurry to leave, all the doors were closed. The Job had begun to rotate SNEU cops through Narcotics, and Sgt. Spinelli told me that I was being sent there in appreciation of my work, which was nice to hear, though it was also true that Stix, Tony, and Orville had pointedly announced that they had no interest in going. I don't know whether the idea was to train cops from SNEU, or share intelligence, or just make it more likely for us to recognize one another in the street. There were three teams for each module, with a sergeant for each team and a lieutenant for each module, and three modules for each precinct, plus a school team, which totaled some ninety cops in Narcotics for the Four-O, in addition to the SNEU teams from Housing and the precinct—more than half as many in one precinct as there had been for the whole city during the French Connection case. We bumped into Narcotics teams often, and they always had the right to play through. If nothing else, having friends there would make the reminder of our second-class status less pointed and more polite.

And when I found out that the assignment would only be for thirty days, there was little doubt that it was the right thing to do. Traditionally, there had been two ways to get a detective shield, which is purely appointive: you might make a great collar—The Door, they called it—and the chief or the Commissioner will whisper, "Where do you want to go, kid?" as the flash-bulbs pop at the press conference. More often, you would work for eighteen months in what was classified as an investigative assignment. In the past, most cops would work their way up in a precinct, from a beat to a team like Anti-Crime, and then go upstairs to the Squad, where you'd work for eighteen months as a "white shield" before promotion to gold. But after the merge, Housing didn't have their own detectives anymore, and the Squads stopped taking white shields. There was also Applicant Investigations, which interviewed recruits and was more of a clerical position, and Internal Affairs, which—to put it mildly—was not what I wanted to do. Most cops grudgingly respected the need for IA, but it had only recently been separated from Inspections, which primarily investigates smaller, procedural violations, and the impression remained that they'd swarm all over a precinct looking for thugs and grafters and leave with a raft of complaints for wearing white socks and signing out in blue ink instead of black. Finally, there was Narcotics, which expanded considerably in the late 1990s, and offered work as an investigator or as an undercover. For women and minorities, especially, undercover work offered a fast track to the shield, as you needed only two years of experience to go there, whereas you usually needed at least five years for a "career path" transfer. Since then, Warrants has also expanded, and the Squads have reopened to cops, but at the time, Narcotics was the only way to a detective shield, and I found myself with the rare opportunity to be able to test a new assignment before signing on.

The shift from making drug collars in the Four-O to making drug collars in the Four-O, was not, as you might expect, such a radical one. There was a scattering of connections: Bea Moore and Hector Nolasco were from PSA-7; John Reilly's best friend, Angelo Ricci, was also from 7; Eddie Engel knew Mike Shea, from my neighborhood; Jack Keane was a friend of my brother Steve's; and Rob Richardson knew PK from PSA-8, in the north Bronx. Cops are often cautious around each other, as you never knew if the new kid was going to be a pain in the office or a liability in the street, but almost as soon as I arrived, it was as if there was a great choral mutter of "This guy's all right." It had come over "the wire," as the grapevine used to be called, and I checked out OK. The rest of the crew, Vicky and Jenny, Carlos, Nefti and EB, Marty, Adam, Abe and Dex, Janet and George, were all good cops and a pleasure to be around. I was assigned to Sgt. DeNaro, but I also went out with Sgts. Turner and O'Brien, all solid bosses who reported to Lt. Zerbo. The name sounded like a villain in a James Bond movie—"*Ahh, pleased to meet you, Mr. Bond,*" "*The pleasure is yours, Lt. Zerbo*"—and he was only slightly less intimidating. He had almost thirty years on the Job, but he was still the first one to charge through the door on a search warrant. When I walked into the office, he yelled, "Jesus! What the fuck did they stick me with another Housing guy for?" So much for Courtesy, Professionalism, and Respect.

But I knew the sets we worked, the players and the brands, the layouts of the buildings and the streets, and it was good to know that I could move up to the next level without anyone even much noticing how new I was. Teams went out for B&B (Buy and Bust) twice a week, hitting eight or ten sets, with catch cars tailing the undercovers to pick up the sellers immediately after each buy, and "ghosts," who followed the undercovers on foot, at a distance, reporting their progress and watching their backs. It was a rapid and systematic way of working: hit or miss, you moved on to the next set in fifteen minutes. While SNEU stuck to crack and heroin, Narcotics scooped up everything: marijuana, methadone, pills. They were more methodical and less discriminating, and their cases stuck—the evidence included marked money, drugs vouchered by the undercover, as well as his or her firsthand testimony. The undercovers were miked for the boss to hear, and he or she directed the field team over the radios; unless you drove the boss, you received your information secondhand. That never presented any tactical impediment, but the remove sometimes made me feel less involved in the action, and the division of labor between investigators and undercovers was not the case with SNEU. The rest of the week, the investigators mostly worked on "kites," or complaints about drug sales phoned in to 911 or the Mayor's Hotline that couldn't be handled by patrol. If someone called to say drugs were sold in an apartment, cops from a squad car couldn't just walk in to take a look. Investigators would observe the location, and undercovers or informants would be sent to make buy attempts, and a report called a DD5, the standard detective's memo, would be typed up after each effort. The kite would be closed after arrests were made, or after it was found that they weren't selling, at least not to strangers. A good percentage of kites were nonsense, called in out of boredom or spite, or against neighbors who were noisy, messy addicts but not dealers. I had no kites assigned to me, so I went out with a B&B team for most days.

In SNEU, we would spend hours on a set: a peek first, and then a surreptitious trip to the OP, walking over from several blocks away, and then the patient wait for buyers or sellers or both. Often, we recovered larger stashes, spending time searching the vicinity of the sale for where the drugs were concealed, whereas Narcotics had their case when they had their collar—the pre-recorded ten-dollar bill, the two slabs of crack—and they moved faster.

In SNEU, you were more invested in your collar, so to speak, whether in watching or catching or both; the arresting officer in Narcotics—who was always an investigator—would simply be the one who collected the body, after the transaction by the undercover and at the direction of the boss. If someone else on the team made the physical apprehension, the relation between cop and criminal might be only on paper. But Narcotics was also serious and professional in ways that we were not. The Job was committed to their work: they had money to spend to buy drugs and guns and to hire informants; they were supplied with equipment, transmitters and recorders and surveillance devices; they didn't have to use their own cars. For them, word might come in, late in the day, that everyone had to suit up for a case takedown; for us, the news flash was more likely that we had to get in the bag to write tickets. As a temp in Narcotics, I got a month closer to my shield, and I got a glimpse of the next step. It was a good place to go, and I was in no rush to get there.

When I got back, the guys asked me, "How was it?"

I brushed them aside: "Listen, I'd like to tell you guys, I really would, but this is need-to-know stuff, and why sugarcoat it? You people do not need to know."

. . .

BUT THE URGE TO MOVE ON, OR AT LEAST MOVE UP, WAS IN all of us. While I was away, an informant had presented herself at the precinct, announcing that she wanted to work. She had known a cop named Paul Callahan from PSA-7, who had since moved on to Narcotics. Callahan seemed to have more informants than Kennedys have cousins, and most of them were a bit on the odd side; more than once, some shady figure would creep out of an alley and whisper, "Pssst! Tell Paul to call me!" We joked about them all living together in the Callahan Compound, making dinner, buying each other Christmas presents, and taking trips to Great Adventure. This particular CI, or "Confidential Informant," was a crackhead who didn't like the way one dealer had treated her, so she decided she'd turn him in "for the mood of it." When she came into the precinct one day, someone called out, "Conlon, your girlfriend's here," and she said, "He don't want this twisted ass." Actually, she was working for Tony, and he didn't want her twisted ass either, but the name stuck, and so Operation Twisted Ass was born.

Operation Twisted Ass was, among other things, a lesson in why Operation Hindenburg ended up the way it did. Twisted Ass was officially registered as an informant, for one, and Callahan could attest to her credibility. She didn't have a complete name for her dealer, but she did know that he lived with his girlfriend in a project on Park Avenue. With the address and apartment number, we could run it through the Housing Authority, and confirm, at least, that the tenant of record was a woman of the right age and race, and we could get a blueprint of the floor to ascertain that the layout was as described—there would be no after-the-fact corrections along the lines of, "Come to think about it, it was apartment #14G, not H." We took our time, sending her back to describe the door in detail, its markings and position. We knew that the subject had a tattoo that said "Shadow," and that he was sitting on a gun and a lot of crack.

The moment before you execute a search warrant is heavy with anticipation, a cross between opening a present and defusing a bomb. We hit the apartment at dawn, with the Emergency Services Unit taking the door. ESU is our SWAT team, with responsibilities that include shooting wild dogs with tranquilizer darts and rescuing people trapped in elevators. "When a cop needs a cop," the saying goes, "he calls ESU." They take a door with a ram or a kind of jack, which pops it out from the frame, and then charge in with ballistic shields, helmets, heavy vests, and shotguns. It makes an impression. The man with the shadow tattoo was roused by the noise and got out of bed to greet them. Once ESU cleared the apartment, I guarded him in the hallway where he stood, blinking sleepily in his underwear, as Tony and PK searched the place. They found sixty slabs of crack, some money, rounds of ammunition, a fake Rolex, and a big cake of crack on a dinner plate, ready to be cut. When they wrapped it in plastic to take it down to the precinct, it looked like leftovers from a picnic. Shadow didn't talk to us, but we had made it through the door, we felt, in more ways than one.

We continued to work on Lamont's heroin set, around 305 East 153rd Street, which dominated the dope in Melrose Houses. They were affiliated with two brothers, known as Satan and Loochi—short for Lucifer—who controlled most of the narcotics in those projects. Lately, we had heard a lot of machine-gun fire at night, and one evening, someone had targeted us with a red laser pointer, which could have been a kid playing or someone aiming a gun. I'd heard Lamont had withdrawn from the street-level hand-to-hands, so we'd hadn't collared him recently. Moreover, since his grandmother lived in the building, we couldn't even pick him up for trespass. We had to content ourselves with hacking away at the edges of the operation, but there was plenty to do there, regardless.

One night we picked up a dealer after five or six sales. A second player had worked with him, in the lobby, but he'd escaped. It was a decent grab, though a little low on stash. Since they had access to several apartments on lower floors, we had limited expectations of finding much in a public area, but we searched anyway. I worked my way up to the third floor and found an unlocked janitor's closet. It was full of trash, and a mouse dove down through a crack in the wall, which sent me back a couple of steps. There was also a plastic garbage bag full of clothing. Homeless people often have caches of possessions hidden in such places, but when I opened it, the clothes were for a teenager, smaller and cleaner than was likely for a street person. I didn't have gloves, and as I felt through the top few garments, I half-hoped to find nothing, which would give me reason to stop the search. But when I pulled out a pair of overalls, two .38 caliber bullets dropped out and bounced on the floor like dice. I thought, Damn. Now I'm gonna hafta spend half an hour groping through mouse shit. When I put the bag down on the floor, it made a clank.

I dumped out the clothes and found a submachine gun, a MAC-11. I went over the air: "PK, come on up to the third floor, the slop sink."

"You got someone?"

"I got something."

"Ten-four."

PK and the other guys gathered around, with the near-reverent hush that falls on cops around such hardware: *Look at this, look at this. It could have been aimed at us.*

PK said, "All right, I guess we'd better go through the rest of the building."

I said, "Hold on a minute, let's finish off this one first."

PK paused and leaned into the closet. "You're right, laddo. There's another one."

On the floor was another gun, a silver Smith & Wesson 9-millimeter with a black grip.

"Okay, then, I guess we ought to put on gloves."

In another closet, we recovered a long-barreled Colt .45, which wouldn't have looked out of place in the hand of Wyatt Earp. We picked up a box with 120 decks of heroin (worth twelve hundred dollars, and probably less than one day's supply), boxes of ammunition, and then a plastic bag containing almost 100 rounds for an AK-47, copper-jacketed and each over two inches long, coming to a long, sharp, conical point like a dunce cap. The AK-47—the one that got away—would send these bullets out at over 1,200 feet per second, passing through my vest with barely a pause. We packed it all up and went in to the Four-O, where my Narcotics team was in with collars as well. They gathered around to see our arsenal, all the more amazed that it had been collected from somewhere open to anyone who bothered to look.

We had opened up another door.

• • •

WE HAD OFTEN WORKED WITH OTHER COPS, SUCH AS BIKE, when we were short of people or vehicles, or when a set was especially busy. Sometimes a beat cop would hook up with us, if he was looking for a collar. PK's reputation was well known, and we were earning ours as well, as a team that made things happen. There was a growing list of people who wanted to join us, though we were more or less content to keep things as they were. One exception was that of John Timpanaro, who was working six-to-twos so he could finish college at St. John's in Queens, and he took to jumping in with us on our four-to-twelve weeks. He fit in, not so much because he was like us, but because he was unlike anyone we'd ever met.

John was boisterous and buoyant, a natural on patrol who would always stop for a pick-up basketball game with local kids. He was Italian—*Hunnid percent, half Sicilian, half Na-bolly-tahn*—and while he could talk like Tony Soprano, he planned to go to graduate school. He was an athlete, talented and disciplined at once: he had been a competitive bodybuilder, wrestler, and skier. His blond hair and blue eyes made him look more like a lifeguard in Malibu than a Bronx cop, and his nickname on his old post was "Baywatch." John had made some great collars, including a fugitive from a bank robbery who had been featured on *America's Most Wanted*. I thought of him as a shit-magnet, with the perverse admiration cops have for people with a talent for bumping into bad guys. Several bosses had picked him to be their regular driver, and he'd had to plead to be allowed to work alone, to go out and collar and learn the business of police work. When he finished college, he was ready to concentrate harder on the Job, willing to work the long and changing hours that come with dedication to collars. He was a serious cop, but his effect on us was like laughing gas.

"Look at him," Tony said. "He's so damn cute!"

If there was a joke behind his jokes, it was that he loved the world and it loved him back, madly, and he sometimes wasn't sure if either he or the world was kidding. He offered sexual favors to PK and he'd tell Alicia that he was in love with her husband, with whom he played on the precinct basketball team: "With all due respect, Alicia, if you don't want Big Ed anymore, I gotta have him. He's gotta be hung like a butternut squash." When we were in the van and he'd see a girl on the street, he'd say, "That's it, no fooling around anymore—out come the guns." And then he'd roll up his sleeve and hang an arm out, flexing a biceps. "The poor girl, she doesn't stand a chance. . . ." He could make his pectorals jump independently, as if he had exploding breast implants. "Look at this, I'm on fire here!" was his refrain. He was always on fire: if he went out to a club, he was on fire; if he walked down Webster Avenue, he was on fire; if he stood alone in a phone booth, he was on fire. We took to calling him "GQ."

It's not as if we didn't have a good time before John began to jump in with SNEU, but I remember the jokes from that time better; they may not have been any funnier, or funny at all, but they stick with me like songs. There was a rumor that another cop we knew was trying to get off the Job with a psychiatric disability. He had stayed home, AWOL, and when the bosses called, his girlfriend claimed that he couldn't talk because he was curled up on the floor in a fetal position: "He can't come to the phone, he's in a ball." That became our catchphrase for the casual psychosis of work, the strange reactions to stranger demands, and summed up everything:

"You wanna get something to eat?"

"Sorry, I didn't hear you, I'm in a ball."

"Hey, OV, when you stopped that guy, did he have anything on him?"

"Nah, I didn't get around to it, I was in a ball."

"What did you do last weekend?"

"Nothing, really, I was in a ball."

We didn't joke like Bike, who busted on each others' mothers and wives, but there was an ethnic tinge to the mix-it-up. Our affection and respect for each other—so we kept telling ourselves—gave us permission to treat each other to torrents of abuse on the most personal level, and because we were a mixed group—Puerto Rican, Short-a-Rican, Jamaican, black, Italian, and Irish—our conversations were a gorgeous mosaic of insult. The frame of reference veered between the ghetto and the trailer park, regardless of which of our ancestral islands was reputed to have produced car thieves, spliff fiends, mafiosi, or drunken terrorists. Stix seemed to get it coming and going, as an Italian with what might be called a Roman nose—

"This nose, in my family, it goes a long way back."

"It goes a long way forward, too."

"I'm saying there's a lot of history there."

"Geography, too."

And as a guy from upstate, he also got the white-trash jokes, the parking tickets for your house, rebel flag on the pick-up, not having sex with your sister until you're engaged kind of thing. Stix got all of that, which suited me, the other white guy in the unit—just fine. Moreover, I was not above stirring it up a little myself:

"Hey, Stix, what's this in your memo book: '98 to 52 Pct with eight PRs'?"

"What's the matter, what do you think it means?"

"Eight PRs—why do you have to say you took eight Puerto Ricans to the 52?"

"It means 'prisoners.'"

"Hey, Tony, Sammy, Alicia, listen to this—Alicia, you only have to half-listen—does PR mean Puerto Rican or prisoner?"

"Listen, you people—"

"'You people!' Did you hear him? Whaddaya mean, 'you people'—why don't you come right out and say it!"

With the memory of PK's loss of a child so fresh, the fact that we were having such fun took on a kind of moral dimension. No one would have been so bold as to compare what we offered to what he had lost, but when we made him laugh we were proud of ourselves. And we looked to make him proud, too. We looked forward to coming in to work, and at the start of the tour, you'd hear talk around the office that was not typical of the civil service, as we'd let slip what we'd done on our own, off duty:

"Driving in, I saw Luther out on One-Five-Three, they're pumping there."

"Yeah, I saw 'em. Also, on One-Five-Seven and Elton, the usual crew."

"The fat kid?"

"Nah, it was a new chick."

"'Cause I saw the fat kid over on Melrose, but he wasn't holding, I don't think, I watched him for a while. . . ."

While there were still plenty of drugs in the Four-O, it was getting crowded with cops, and we decided to expand our horizons. Two partners who had the Four-Six conditions car, Chris Hickson and Rob Dressler, said they had a guy who wanted to work for us, a street guy, a junkie. We took a ride up to the neighborhood and liked what we saw. The Four-Six was north and west of us, in a neighborhood called University Heights, which extended from west of Webster Avenue to the Harlem River, above the Cross Bronx Expressway and below Fordham Road. Unlike the rest of the Bronx, which was a flat, glacial plain, the terrain was hilly and the streets broke from the grid, angling and curving over the lay of the land. But if the neighborhood caught a break during the Ice Age, recent history had been less kind. Homicides were twice that of the adjacent precincts to the north and east. For dope fiends, and hence for drug cops, the Four-Six was God's country. In the four or five blocks around the intersection of Tremont and University avenues, there were more than a dozen dope spots, and almost as many for crack. Washington Heights, across the river in Manhattan, had been the center of the East Coast cocaine trade from the mid-eighties onward; when the NYPD cracked down in force, some of the traffic had moved across the river to the Bronx. They got a lot of Jersey junkies, who crossed the bridge, at first, for fun. Charlie had been one of them.

Charlie was tall and lanky, with long hair and a scraggly beard like a hippie Jesus. He had been on the street for two years, and he made his living— such as it was—as a steerer, an intermediary between the suburban addicts and the dealers who were wary of white people. They had no worries about Charlie; they knew him, for one thing, and there was no mistaking him for anything but what he was. He slept in the dirt and he stank like a corpse. I asked him, "How often do you get high?"

He told me that he shot eight to ten bags of dope a day, but added, "I haven't been high in years." It was a medicine, like insulin, that kept him from getting sick, and the pleasure it had once offered was a distant and mocking memory.

When he wasn't at the extremes of stupefaction or desperation, Charlie's intelligence and decency were plain to see, and sad to consider. He was quick to learn and eager to please, and he came to look forward to seeing us, as much for the company as the cash. Charlie had been locked up plenty of times before, and even though he thought a lot of them were bullshit collars by bullshit guys—"C'mon, all I had was a needle and some empties!"—he nonetheless looked up to cops. His father was on the Job, a lieutenant in a small city in another state. At the moment, they weren't talking, though Charlie called home now and then and talked to his mother. She kept some hope for him, and would not close the door, figuratively at least. He'd mention his mother with love in his voice, and his father with respect, but he usually wouldn't talk about them for long.

For the past year or so, he'd lived on a wooded median strip above the Cross Bronx Expressway, a hundred feet in from the street, with a few other, more transient addicts who'd set up an encampment, with blankets on cardboard, and heaped and battered possessions—a radio, paperback books, a winter jacket—that surrounded their little hideaway like flotsam from a shipwreck. Farther away, at the stone ledge over the highway, was their shooting gallery, with beer bottles and empty glassines littered over the bare rock, and I wondered sometimes whether it was the cliff's edge that drew them there, or the sight of traffic, the thousands of people going heedlessly home, as if it was a daily and natural thing, because they could. You knew that you were close to the camp—"Charlie's Gardens," as we called it—mostly because of the smell, which was like nothing I'd ever encountered before. It was a rotten-meat smell and a sour chemical smell, pungent and pervasive, and it held in the ground, even after a heavy rain, as if the earth had not just been polluted but defiled for the ages. I know that it was my imagination, but I thought I could smell the place on my sneakers, even after I left there, the first time, and when I got back to the precinct, I threw them out and went home in my uniform boots.

I told Charlie that street sets were fine, but that we didn't really need anyone to help us find them. We were happy to hear whatever he had to tell us, but what we wanted was to find apartments where they sold, to get search warrants. Charlie said that he knew a teenage kid named Justin who sold crack, mostly, in white-top vials, with a sideline of five-dollar half-bags of dope. Justin lived in the apartment down the hall, but his mother wouldn't let him sell there—it was his girlfriend's place that he dealt from, as her family had no such objections. Charlie thought the dope was garbage, and so he didn't go there, except in emergencies. He was an authority on the subject, and it seemed that the vintages and blends of heroin were as distinctive as those of wine—there was purity, of course, but there seemed also to be varied qualities to the cut—and when someone wanted to introduce a new brand, they tested it out for free on Charlie, as the junkie's junkie. Charlie wasn't into crack, really, but he was a Renaissance addict, and he'd be happy to go there, too.

Justin lived in a project, but the Housing Authority had leased it to a private company, with whom we had to confer for lobby keys and tenant information. In general, we were cautious about speaking with civilians about the particulars of an investigation, as you never knew whether the janitor or secretary or administrator had a son or girlfriend or cousin who might wind up in the crosshairs, still less who might broadcast the information in the coffee room, or even be on the payroll of the bad guys outright. But at this company, we had an "in," a woman named Yvonne, who had enthusiastically helped Dressler and Hickson with identifying drug dealers, who not by coincidence happened to be problem tenants. Whenever we went there, in fact, the problem was not access but exit, as Yvonne was a cop buff in general and fond of me in particular. When that became apparent, Timpanaro, especially, was happy to intervene. "No, Eddie doesn't have a girlfriend," he volunteered. "And to be frank with you, Yvonne, I don't want to tell tales out of school, but I think he's a little lonely, looking for a good woman to help him settle down." Whenever we needed something from the office, I took to waiting in the car. John would bring her out to see me.

Such were the unexpected hazards of my first warrant for SNEU. I had to make excuses for my romantic availability, and I had to not throw up when I went looking for my informant. I learned the actual investigative preparations for a warrant, the computer checks for kites and collars in the building through the NYPD "NITRO" computer system; the background checks on the tenants—one arrest, on a previous warrant, for possession with intent to sell; the tenant research through the phone company or Con Ed; the "claim" of the apartment through the Drug Enforcement Coordination System, or DECS, which is a central registry for people and places that are the subjects of city, state, and federal investigations, to make sure we don't step on each other. I had to do reconnaissance on the building, so that I'd see that it was as described, in layout and detail, and count the number and kind of locks on the door. I also had to get Charlie in there to buy drugs, preferably three times within a ten-day time frame, and to find out if there were children, old people, dogs, guns, fortifications, or traps in the apartment, not to mention where the drugs were. When it was done, I had to bring him in to the DA to write up an affidavit, which would be sworn before a judge.

Under ordinary circumstances, it was a fair amount of work as well as risk—you had to meet the Confidential Informant (CI) often, and you never knew who might notice—but several particular problems presented themselves with Charlie. As a stone junkie, he had a shelf-life of only a few hours before he would go into withdrawal and its attendant sweats and nausea. We'd have to take care of business in the course of the morning—if they were busy at court, and told us to come back after lunch, we were done for. And in sending him after the white-tops, I seemed to have turned him into a crackhead.

"Didja get in there?"

"Ohyeahyeahyeahyeah, oh, boy yeah,"

That disturbed me—it wasn't as if Charlie's life wasn't in the toilet anyway, but he didn't need me to help him flush. When we went to court, I told him to clean himself up before we went in, and though I was impressed with the results, the grimaces of the ADA and the judge suggested that, at best, his hygiene was only relatively improved. That may have worked in our favor, however, as they moved us through with some haste, and Charlie performed admirably, testifying in crisp detail of the times and takes of each visit. I gave him twenty bucks and took my warrant back to the precinct.

Again, we met in the muster room for the "tac" plan, plotting out the times and contingencies, listing the assignments for who would watch the windows, freeze the lobby, and wait in a car to race to the hospital, if necessary. Though the drill was becoming a little more familiar, the exhilaration—the tension and the hope—did not fade. We had a captain from the Borough with us, and, of course, Yvonne, who would secure the apartment after we finished; ESU would take the door, and EMS would wait outside, on call. The particular configuration of the building required that we approach it from behind, slipping down an alley to scale a wall, then cutting in through the back door. We ran upstairs and I pointed out the door for ESU, then stepped back as they hit it with the ram. In retrospect, I have to give the Housing Authority credit for the sturdiness of the door, although I was not grateful at the moment: they hit it, and hit it, and hit it, and then set up the jack. Time does not pass quickly when you wait like that, but I could have sworn it was several minutes before we stepped over the threshold.

It looked right, as we rushed inside, the kitchen to the right, the living room, the bedrooms on the left, and there were three people in handcuffs, face-down on the floor. But I felt a spike of dismay as I looked down on them, a middle-aged husband and wife, and a young girl, thirteen or fourteen years old, it seemed, slim and pony-tailed; it was the right place, maybe, but it was the wrong time, as there was no sign of Justin. I bent down to the girl to look closer, to say that it was all right, we would look around and move on, when I saw that it was a guy. I asked him his name and he said, "Justin." I beamed at PK and gave him the thumbs-up: *Laddo!*

There were three more people in the apartment, and foil-wrapped packets of cocaine, and dozens of pre-cut foil squares to package more; we got some weed, and a ledger of transactions, crudely scrawled columns of accounts for guys named Mikey and Murder. Where the white-top crack was, I had no idea. The apartment was big and messy, and it would take a long time to search thoroughly. I found a big garbage bag full of stuffed animals, at least fifty of them. I looked at the teddies and duckies and tore one open before putting it aside, out of embarrassment. Yvonne was thrilled with the action, and she stepped in and seized a bunny, tearing off its head like a wolverine: "We gotta look here! It could be anywhere!" She disemboweled several little creatures before she was gently reminded that only police officers could search, and the remnants of the menagerie survived. It wasn't spectacular, but it was solid, and the captain shook our hands. We'd done it, he said, smiling, and he added, "Again."

At the precinct, I figured I had the best shot at the father. The mother's English was chancy and Justin was cockily—and correctly—betting that his age would allow him to walk on the charges; when I interrogated him, he listened as if I were a telemarketer offering a new, low-cost long-distance plan. The father offered weepy protests of all-encompassing household innocence, but when I told him an undercover had bought from his apartment, he changed tack, claiming Justin sold drugs, but he couldn't stop him. His daughter liked Justin, but he was so afraid! He also had other children, younger ones. He wasn't well, you know, he had his blood pressure to think about. I didn't begin the interview with a very high opinion of him, but at the end, I thought that if he were a roach, I would have stepped on him. And he was a roach. I said something like this to him, only a little louder:

"You let this five-foot-three, hundred-pound, sixteen-year-old fuck with a smirk and a ponytail bang your underage daughter? You let him broadcast to every junkie and crackhead around to come to your house to get happy? This is the choice you've made, as a father? This is what you're telling me? And you're not going to tell me where he gets it, or where it is, because you're scared of him? And you have other kids? Guess what, shithead, I'm gonna make sure they don't grow up with you. I'm gonna take your kids away."

He held his head in his hands and blubbered: "They already took my kids away!"

Since his face was still downcast, I looked over to Tony, still furious but holding back a laugh: *Oh, well, never mind then. Wait, no, I'll double-take them away!* Tony took him back to the cells, and when he returned, he said, "Shit, I would have confessed."

Some weeks later, I browsed through the inch-thick stack of paperwork for the eviction proceedings. Yvonne had sent it to me, as I would have to testify about the arrest. Idly, I looked back at the earlier criminal history of the family—they'd been locked up after another warrant, in an apartment around the corner. I read about how an undercover had been steered there, and the father had sold him heroin. A Narcotics team had done the warrant, and they'd recovered a respectable stash of dope. I sat up as I read where they'd found it, and thought maybe Yvonne wasn't such as lunatic after all: the drugs had been hidden inside a stuffed animal.

. . .

WHEN YOU SIGN UP AN INFORMANT, YOU OFFER A NEW LEAF, a new life, an appeal to the better angels in their nature. When an informant signs, however, he sees it as a deal with the devil, and though he'll take his cash or freedom for now, he knows that one day he'll have to pack for the warm weather. The informant is constantly renegotiating the contract in his head, considering his options and opportunities. I don't remember what I knew about Melvin Jones when he called the house when I was young—"Daaaah! It's your informant!"—but obviously I knew what he did. I don't remember many calls afterward. Maybe my father had decided that work and home should maintain their distance, or maybe their business would conclude soon after. My mother remembers Melvin's South Carolina courtliness and manners: "How are you, Miz Betty, is everything all right? I'm glad to hear that! Is Mister John available?" Melvin had worked as an informant for my father since the mid-fifties, supplementing his on-the-book work as a truck driver, and presumably supplanting his off-the-book activities as a thief.

In their respective capacities, both Melvin and my father were assigned to Thefts from Interstate Shipment, which centered on the movement of freight on the West Side, from the docks to the streets and the rails. It was the landscape of *On the Waterfront*, the Hudson piers and the walk-up tenements of Hell's Kitchen, of water towers and pigeon coops and fire escapes hung with laundry. Even in the fifties, the old Irish laborers and gangsters watched as the city became more modern and corporate, and generally less interested in their abilities and their demands. Honest work became less physical, and the dishonest kind became more vicious and less local, as the airports began to compete with the docks, and the ships found new ports in Jersey. Marlon Brando's *I coulda binna contenda* speech spoke for any number of guys who saw their best chances pass, whether at an odd, introspective moment or after long conversations with a radical priest. Brando's character, Terry Malloy, wanted to be a boxer but wound up as union muscle; as he realized how the gangsters betrayed him, he struggled to convince himself that his break from them wasn't a betrayal as well. He couldn't think of himself as an informant, a role which no culture respects but the Irish particularly despised, from the traitor-ridden centuries of revolt against England, and even farther back, to Spy Wednesday, when Judas collected his silver from the Pharisees, for passing along a tip. I don't know if Melvin Jones suffered any torments of conscience when he changed sides on the waterfront, but he knew what the costs might be, should the shift in his allegiances become known.

Melvin Jones had first been arrested by another agent, who was nearly ninety when I spoke to him. The agent pressed me not to use his name, lest his old enemies come to seek him out, professing humility with a razor beneath the hat brim. But when the agent moved to another assignment, Melvin stayed to work for my father. When Melvin saw merchandise diverted from the ships or the trucks, or heard of plans to do so, he let my father know. My father made collars and Melvin made money. When I read through some of those cases, I was surprised at how penny-ante many of them were, especially at first—a case of pet food here, two boxes of ladies' coats there. The complete arrest reports were not made available to me, but I wasn't desperate to learn the details. Had the ladies' coats traveled to the city from Buffalo or Albany instead of Newark or Paris or China, their disappearance would have been a matter for the local precinct instead of the FBI.

At the same time, I knew that my father much preferred the work to his previous assignment in Communist surveillance, if only because it was more fun to play cops and robbers than spy-versus-spy. He told me how they set up a reverse sting at a pawn shop, buying stolen property to identify the thieves. Once, when he had to make an arrest, he found himself without a partner and without a gun—details which didn't seem worth interrupting the story for, at the time—and he followed the man down the block to stop him. Though my father was six-foot-two and averaged around two hundred and fifty pounds, he said that his perp towered over him. He stuck his fist in the pocket of his trench coat and extended a finger: *FBI! Get your hands up or I'll put one right in your back!* He saw the man tense up, deciding, before he obeyed. As the two walked back to the pawn shop, passersby stopped to give their opinions:

"What did he do wrong!"

"What's the matter with you, let him go!"

"We're watching you, there better not be any police brutality!"

I'm sure my father was tempted to take his hand out of his pocket and wave his finger at them, but such satisfactions are better postponed. It's also the part of the story you leave out of the official reports.

After the ships stopped coming in to the West Side docks, there was less work for Melvin, and for my father, too, at least in Hell's Kitchen. Melvin's only other arrest was for getting picked up in a stolen car, in the late 1960s, in Washington Heights. Because Melvin was not the most successful criminal, I'd suspect that the long stretch without arrests meant that he stayed out of trouble generally, and he stuck to driving and whatever else he picked up on the side. It was in the 1970s when he and my father had occasion to speak again at length.

On September 17, 1974, a thirty-year-old Yonkers police officer named Harold Woods stopped by a supermarket on his way to work for the midnight shift. He picked up a pack of cigarettes and quart of milk, and as he walked up to the checkout line he saw that the clerk looked afraid. "Are you okay?" he asked. "I'm a cop. Is there a problem?" And then one of the two men who were robbing the store stepped out and shot him in the face. Woods died five days later. He had a wife and three children.

Not long after, Melvin overheard a conversation in a bar in Harlem, where a man said that he had "wasted this dude upstate." I don't know if Melvin read the papers or otherwise knew of the killing, but he'd been in the business long enough to know there would be a reward. Did Melvin know a first name, full name, nickname, or an address? Or did agents or cops pay a visit to the bartender, and urge him to rack his memory for further details about the man who sat in that stool, that night? The case was further complicated because it was split between three different jurisdictions: a federal informant gave up New York City perps for a Yonkers homicide. With NYPD detectives and Yonkers cops, my father cruised the streets of Harlem, hunting the men. After a four-day stakeout, they picked up one perp in Harlem, at his girlfriend's apartment, and the other was arrested weeks later, in New Orleans. Both men were convicted and sentenced to death, though the sentences were later commuted to life in prison.

Of all my father's cases, I am proudest of his role in the Woods homicide. I spoke with the detective lieutenant from Harlem, Herman Kluge, and he told me that without my father, this case might well have remained unsolved. Robbery-homicides can be among the most difficult to break: the perps were not local, there was no relationship between them and their victims, and eye-witness testimony is often of little value. The perps were prepared to kill but had not apparently planned to, in that Woods's arrival was by chance. It was by chance, too, that Melvin came upon the information, but it became rele-vant because my father had built a relationship for nearly two decades. There was trust there, at least enough of it, and there was ten thousand dollars. As the saying goes: How does a fish get caught? *He opens his mouth. . . .*

Melvin took the cash and bought a social club in the Bronx, at 1822 Carter Avenue, a block east of Webster and Tremont. My mother told me that my fa-ther had to fight for Melvin's reward money, but it didn't buy happiness for him. In a later set of police reports, I read that Melvin had all kinds of prob-lems. Though he was selling marijuana and taking bets at the club, he owed a lot of money. He owed money to the landlord, he owed money to his part-ner, he owed money to a certain Vito Ambrosiano, from whom he leased the cigarette machine, juke box, and pool table. Without intending any offense to Mr. Ambrosiano, the vending machine business in New York City at that point in history was not considered entirely reputable. Melvin even owed money to his bummy barback, Shorty. The police had occasional reason to visit: in June of 1977, Melvin was at the club when he was hit in the head with a bottle and robbed of a shotgun, a radio, and five bottles of whiskey. Not long afterward, he had a dispute with an employee, during which he was again struck in the head with a blunt object. There was a report that a man named Johnny Eagles was interested in taking over the club: Johnny Eagles drove a white Lincoln Continental and had gambling arrests going back to 1946, and he'd menaced a cop with a gun in 1974. For all his problems, Melvin was untroubled on the afternoon of January 18, 1978, because he didn't even look up from his game of solitaire when someone walked up be-hind him and shot him once in the back of the head with a .38.

Melvin was fifty-eight years old, clean-shaven, with dark skin and "full teeth." He was six feet and one inch tall and weighed two hundred and fif-teen pounds. He wore a brown turtleneck, gray trousers, black dress socks, and brown construction boots. His widow, Beverly, could provide no rele-vant information. Shorty claimed to have left the club at noon. Johnny Eagles was never found, though I don't know how hard they looked. The Four-Six probably saw fifty or sixty homicides that year, and twice as many shootings, and thousands of robberies, burglaries, and other felonies. I haven't read enough homicide files from the 1970s to know whether the effort made for Melvin was casual, typical, or exhaustive. Several reports describe neighborhood canvasses for Eagles's white Lincoln Continental, all with negative results. They are the kind of thing you bang out, just to have something in the file. No mention is made of Melvin's public testimony in the Woods case, and reprisal by associates of the imprisoned cop-killers doesn't appear to have been considered as a theory. There were people who would have killed him, on principle, had they discovered how he came across the windfall that bought him the club.

Melvin was executed as he played cards, unaware of what was about to happen, which is generally not the style of stick-up man or even a jealous husband, who usually wants a word with the victim before the trigger is pulled. Melvin could have known the other man in the club as a customer or friend, and thought he didn't need to watch his back more carefully than his cards. Then again, maybe the jukebox was playing and he didn't hear anyone enter. You can't even rule out robbery, because you don't know what was missing if you didn't know what was there before. Melvin was broke all the time anyway, and he could have lost the last cash in the register, playing solitaire against himself.

My father would retire a little over a year after Melvin was killed, and he had moved to another assignment, doing liaison work with Scotland Yard. I'm sure that my father said a prayer for Melvin, though my mother doesn't recall that he was especially saddened or surprised by the news. She doesn't recall him making any particular effort to see what happened in the investigation, or to offer assistance. As far as my informants went, I'd have taken more trouble with Charlie than George the hit man, but I don't know if I'd have done much beyond telling the case detective what they'd done for me. My father would have had sympathy for Melvin's good intentions but no illusions about his bad habits. Melvin was a human being who offered service in the course of justice, no matter if that service was unwilling at the beginning and accidental at the end. Did he help himself along the way, or did he hurt anyone else? We all have our vocations, and we all have our mysteries. Not all of us find religion over the wandering years, but sooner or later, everybody gets to meet God.

• • •

AT THE BEST OF TIMES, YOU FELT THAT YOU COULD GO ON forever, with bigger cases and better collars, and the Job would ask only how they could help. You'd think, "Who could touch us? Who would want to?"

And then you'd catch yourself, because you knew the answer: Just about anybody, any time. In June, John asked PK about joining us as a permanent member of the team. PK asked us what we thought, and after we all agreed, he worked out the post change in Admin. The next day, we received word that SNEU would cease operations, as such, for the indefinite future.

That spring, it was believed that four serial rapists were at large in the Bronx. The first had strangled one victim on the roof of the project called Twin Parks, in the Four-Six, a vast maze of a building where Larry Davis had lived. Davis was a psychopath who made his living robbing drug dealers, and he was wanted for four murders when he shot six cops who had come to arrest him. Davis's acquittal on six counts of attempted murder—and three out of four of the other killings—helped make famous the term "Bronx Jury." Two other men, one Hispanic, one West Indian, according to their descriptions, were believed to have committed attacks on middle-aged women in the Five-Two, breaking into their apartments through fire escapes. The last was not least: the perpetrator of Citywide Rape Pattern #6 had raped and robbed fifty-one women, at gunpoint, over several years, from upper Manhattan to lower Westchester but mostly in the Bronx. Our Anti-Crime team had already been shifted to steady midnights because of it, and then further redeployed by assigning several of them on foot in uniform. They still made some collars, but their productivity did, of course, decline; the inspector who ran the Borough then summoned Sgt. Clark to his office and informed him that he wanted ten felonies per month, per cop, which would have been impossible without any restrictions whatsoever. Clark quit, and the rest of the team followed. The rapists didn't. In June, a Task Force of more than a hundred cops was dedicated to the condition, for Street Crime–style saturation of target areas throughout the borough. Each command was asked for a team of cops, and we were volunteered.

We would work from nine-thirty at night until six in the morning. One team had Monday and Tuesday off, the other Wednesday and Thursday. PK, Tony, Orville, and Sammy were on one team, and Alicia, John, and I were on the other. I was fuming; I was out the day the teams were decided, and I saw it as the short end of the stick, day-wise and PK-wise. It effectively meant that I only had one full day off—Wednesday—as you'd work through dawn on Tuesday and have to come back for Thursday evening. I had just started to date a girl—not Yvonne, thank you—and had hopes of seeing her more often than for an occasional breakfast. It was the full flush of summer, and it was the custom of my countrymen to find outdoor places near water on weekends, which would not be possible for me. I partnered with John, and I explained that it was nothing personal, but that he could expect me to be in a bad mood for the rest of my career.

"I gotta tell you, pal, I'm glad to have you here," I told him, "but I think you're an idiot for staying. This is a raw deal. You just got in, no one would hold it against you if you waited. We'll get back to the regular shit sometime, and you can join SNEU again then."

"Nah, I can't. I've wanted to work with PK and you guys for a while, and I can't back out on the first day, at the first bump in the road. Let's see what we can make of it, it might be all right."

DNA had been recovered from many of the victims, but the wanted poster showed a masked man; we knew his genetic code but he could pass us in the street without notice. We would get him, but only when we got him. Sometimes it appeared that the rapist had followed women home from a bar or a club; in other cases, the point of interception appeared to be accidental. There were targets of opportunity as well as victims picked out of crowds; there were older ones, younger ones, taller and shorter ones, of differing physical builds, and he had attacked two and even three women at a time. He wore a mask and carried a gun, and he took money and jewelry. One night, John and I were assigned to a quiet neighborhood of single-family houses, and we drove until we found the site of one attack, a vacant lot. We got out of the car and walked through it, staggering through the shoulder-high weeds and ankle-twisting nests of briars, the angry greenery of the city ground returned to seed. The earth was rocky and divoted, and I was thinking that it would have been hard to find a less hospitable place, when I remembered that the rape had taken place in February. Had she cried for help, no one would have heard. I wondered if the misery of the surroundings was part of the pleasure he took, or if his concentration was such that he wouldn't notice if he was inside a burning building. Another crime scene was as public as this one was isolated, behind a housing project along Westchester Avenue, a major street with the elevated train tracks overhead. This assault was in the summer, on a Friday around midnight: the three young women were leaving the building for a party, and he forced them outside, through the back door. The project was one of several around a courtyard with benches; a playground was a few yards to the side; there would have been people outside, in the summer, and it was brightly lit. He herded them to a patch of lawn behind the building, where a fenced-in rock ledge separated the grounds from Westchester Avenue below. Above them, the trains passed, and beneath them, the buses, cabs, and cars rolled along; twenty feet away, there were hundreds of neighbors who talked, watched television, and slept. The three women were raped and robbed beside a vast, oblivious audience; had they screamed, they might have escaped, or summoned aid in droves, or died.

Though I wasn't glad to be there, the neighborhood was delighted to see us. In the streets, there was a gratitude I'd never experienced before in such forthright manner and volume. Passersby practically applauded when they saw us, and even those we stopped to question often thanked us and wished us luck in the hunt. After each, we had to fill out forms called "250s," or "Stop and Frisk," which were designed to cast a wide net around just such pattern crimes, to see if any names turned up with a telling familiarity. Each night began with a roll call for the gathered forces of Street Crime, Narcotics, Special Victims, and patrol, and in the beginning, various chiefs and inspectors gave speeches about the urgency of our mission, and how they believed in us. They gave us new cars and let us ride.

We drove and watched. A week passed, and then another. One night, John and I had a post in the Four-Three, in Soundview, where there had been a concentration of attacks. Just after midnight, we did a vertical in a housing project, checking the roof, the stairwell, and the terraces. On one floor, we found a padlocked terrace with a broken window, narrow and shoulder-level, a foot high by two feet wide. We looked in, and saw a sleeping derelict. We extracted him, ordering him out at gunpoint through the window, each of us taking an arm once he was halfway out, then handcuffed him, searched him, and tried to get him to admit if there was anyone else still on the terrace. Satisfied that his answers were as good as we would get, I went through the window to see if there was anything—specifically, a ski mask, a gun, or jewelry—to connect him with the crimes. The pane had been shattered, and the frame was edged with shards of glass like shark's teeth. I clambered in as well as I could, with John holding up my legs, wheelbarrowing me in to the ominous dark. There was nothing there, beyond a soggy couch littered with pizza boxes and crack vials, and I crawled back out. We took the man in for trespassing, but mostly to talk.

On the street, John started with him: "You know what we're taking you in for! You know what you did! Where's the ski mask?"

I turned away so neither he nor John could read my face. This guy was no more the rapist than he was Josef Mengele or Judge Crater. There were bluffs, and there were bluffs: *Give me three cards, and I'll raise you fifty.* "Sorry sir, this is the craps table." The man mumbled sleepily in denial.

John charged ahead, undaunted: "You know who he is, don't you, guy? Give it up!"

And then the perp looked away uneasily, stammering, "Well, you know . . . I don't know if, I don't want to say, you know . . ." My pulse quickened. This would be an interesting conversation. We called for a car and took him in.

The man knew what we wanted; everyone in the neighborhood did. We talked at length and at leisure, to put him at ease and build up some trust. He sort of had a wife and he did have kids, and they lived with his mother in a nearby project. He lived there, too, now and then, when he wasn't on a crack binge, but that happened as often as he could afford. He thought he knew the man, after an odd exchange some time before, which had stayed with him. He was peddling some stereo equipment he had come by—we didn't ask— when an acquaintance from the neighborhood struck up a conversation, the key parts of which went as follows:

"That ain't makin' money."

"Don't I know."

"What I do, is I rob bitches and then I fuck 'em."

"Oh—that ain't me, man."

Even at the time, he said, the remark disturbed him powerfully, and later he came to believe that the man was the rapist. When I inquired why he hadn't told the cops before—there was a twenty-thousand-dollar reward for his capture—he said that no one had asked him. Moreover, he had another problem, in that he couldn't remember the man's name. After strenuous recollection, he could only say that he had a funny first name, and a common last name.

"How do you mean funny, African-funny? Muslim-funny?"

"Nah, not like that—it was a little funny, though."

As far as he could recall, the guy had been locked up before, but not for rape or anything noteworthy. He thought that he sold drugs, and when I pressed him for the brand, he thought it might have been red-tops. We were reaching, I knew, and I knew that for most people—let alone a mind as ill-used as his—the strain to recall could break down the boundary between memory and fantasy. But from a fragment such as "red-top crack vials," there would be a string of perps on the NITRO database; from an address, there would be several systems that would provide names of robbers and rapists. He did remember where the man's mother lived, and from that slender fact alone, an investigation could begin.

We talked for a long time, and when a detective from Special Victims arrived, we told him what we knew before leaving them alone for another interview. Special Victims had doubtless received vast amounts of that kind of low-grade but tantalizing information. The detective was intrigued, but if he had any deeper feelings, he did not betray them. He'd look into it, he said, and if it panned out, he'd let us know. I was excited by it, and so was the crackhead, and what struck me was that we all cared a great deal about it, and in almost the same way. This man was a criminal, too—a nuisance from afar, a tragedy up close, to the wife and children who lived with his mother—but in relation to the rapist, he was a concerned member of the community. John and I imagined our gold shields, and maybe our collar imagined enough crack to fill a pipe the size of the Holland Tunnel, but, ambitions aside, we both wanted the man gone: we wanted the mothers and sisters and daughters of this troubled neighborhood to walk the streets unafraid. It was us—all of us, the cops and the street—against him. I gave the crackhead my beeper and work numbers, and I took down the address where he lived when he was not lost to the pipe. I told him that I would not only make sure he got the reward, if it led to an arrest, but I would put twenty dollars in his hand the minute he came up with the name. We were both determined to continue our partnership. Weeks later, I even wrote to him, but by that time, we had already returned to PSA-7 SNEU. I thought sometimes about going to look for him again, but my resolve thinned as other responsibilities piled up, and time went on.

When the rapist was caught, the following April, I read that his name was Isaac Jones—funny first name, common last—and I wonder about it to this day. Was there anything to the story? How thorough was the detective in running down the names? Did the crackhead get the right building? Did Jones give another address in his prior arrests, to spare his mother aggravation from the Housing Authority? Jones was caught when his girlfriend tried to pawn jewelry that the store owner recognized from a police flyer. She admitted that she knew it was stolen but said she had no idea about the rapes. Jones was from Soundview, the neighborhood in question. He was sentenced to many lifetimes in prison, and I don't know if he had committed other robberies and rapes between that summer and the next April, but much would have been different, for all of the cops in the city, had our chance meeting led quickly to an arrest.

Back at PSA-7, Deputy Inspector Cavanagh said to me, as I brought him a bottle of single-malt scotch, "You know, when they told the Inspector that they want him to give up his best guys, he actually understood it to mean that we should give up our best guys. What am I supposed to do without a SNEU team?" He gave me a hapless shrug. Our return was as abrupt as our departure had been, as joyous as our exit had been dismal. The scotch didn't count as a bribe, I figured, since it was after the fact, but if it had occurred to me that it could have gotten us our weekends back, I'd have given him a truckload of it. We were back in business.

. . .

AUGUST WAS A GOOD MONTH FOR US. WE HOPPED BACK AND forth between the Four-O and the Four-Six, picking up bodies a dozen at a time. Our numbers crept up, to twenty and thirty and forty collars, a third of them felonies. Thirty would have been respectable, and forty excellent, and more than that would have raised questions as to why we hadn't been doing better all along. We wondered what we should shoot for, heading as we were toward a record-breaking month, and PK said, "Well, Roger Maris's record was sixty-one." And why not? Weren't we the Boys of Summer?

The farther we reached, the more we grasped. We started taking bikes out, which let even Stix and John cruise around with a degree of anonymity. To beat the lookouts on well-guarded sets, we'd hail livery cabs to roll up on them, popping out from feet away on startled dealers. Once, we grabbed a junkie who was driving a dry-cleaning truck, which we borrowed for the rest of the afternoon—if my car, Triple-O, was low-profile, the truck was perfect cover. PK asked over the radio, "What's up with the green van? When did we get that?"

There was a pause before someone responded, "Uh, what van, boss?"

"Ten-four."

There was no mistaking what we did for anything vast or grand; our collars and cases didn't lead us to Mexican generals or offshore bank accounts, let alone the French Connection. We were little scrappers who worked some rough ground, and sometimes left it a little more level than when we'd begun. But we sometimes found a place in the larger scheme of things: a joint NYPD and federal task force called "HIDTA," for High Intensity Drug Trafficking Area, was working on a case against our friends Lamont, Satan, and Loochi. Various detectives and agents would call, or come by with pictures, and we'd fill them in on background, associates, and the like. We worked most often with Mike Donnelly, who had been a detective in the Four-Seven and had known Uncle Eddie: "Sure, heavyset guy, worked midnights, always reading?" Some of the Feds had Southern or Midwestern accents, and it was fun to take them through the projects, looking for perps, walking them through the pissed-on and bullet-pocked halls and the stairwells, pointing out the stash spots in the cable boxes, fire extinguishers, and trash disposal chutes. You could see the looks on their faces: *This is what you guys do, every day? Here?* Some of them didn't seem all that comfortable. We were the Indian scouts for their cavalry, sniffing the air and saying, *No perp-hunt today, HIDTA-sabe, heap big rain come. SNEU go to Stacy's, eat meat loaf special. Yum-yum!*

Every day, Satan and Loochi's crew might commit a hundred felonies. When we caught them, they'd sneer and laugh at us, bragging that street-smart guys like them could run circles around clueless country boys such as ourselves, and we'd say, "You got a point there. Lemme know if those cuffs are too tight." In a funny way, we had a similar view of the Feds: If we had the savvy, why did they have all the success? We locked them up, over and over; but HIDTA locked them up just once; when they took their case down, Luther, Lamont, Satan, Loochi, and a dozen others pled to sentences of fif-teen and twenty years to life. It wasn't that we thought we were the best team, so why weren't we winning; it was more like we were a great team, so why weren't we really in the game?

In the Four-O, we worked sometimes with Hector Berdecia. He was the gang officer, a newly created position, and I'd check in with him and share information. Hector had been a cop when the CO of the Four-O, Capt. Shor-tell, had been a sergeant; as Shortell rose in rank and moved through com-mands, he took Hector with him. Good cops make their bosses look good, and Hector was a one-man beauty school. He made things happen: when-ever a cop collared some semi-derelict or little wiseguy who decided he wanted to talk his way out of a problem by offering up where his best friend had the crack or his uncle hid the gun, Hector stepped in. Hector was gener-ous with credit, and that helped his various joint operations go smoothly. While we paid informants out of pocket and drove Triple-O, Hector had fed-eral grant money and a car from the DEA.

Hector's talent for diplomacy only took him so far, sometimes. He once told me, furious, about how a Narcotics team stole one of his warrants—my old team, in fact. After they'd done the entry and a large amount of heroin was recovered, their captain announced they were taking the collars. Nar-cotics did their own search-warrant entries, which we preferred to ESU; they did "dynamic" entries, taking the door, then rushing in to prevent the drugs from going down the toilet. ESU's was a defensive entry, methodically clearing each room from behind ballistic shields, one by one, for maximum safety. From the street to the door, they were a highly visible and relatively slow-moving deployment, and I sometimes wondered if we'd do any worse with a marching column of bagpipers from the Emerald Society. Then again, ESU would take the door, cuff the perps, and go home, whereas we were in competition with Narcotics, working the same territory, for the same purpose. Hector could have called Capt. Shortell to square things away, but one of the reasons for their long partnership, I'm guessing, was that he didn't call him at home too often to complain.

That was always the dilemma: you could reach out for help to Narcotics or HIDTA, who had the experience and resources to develop a case properly, but you risked losing control altogether. Maybe the whole team could go out with them once or twice, for a warrant or a canvass, and maybe one or two of us could work with them for a longer period, through the course of the investigation. But it would be in effect a "ride-along," as the back-seat tour of patrol arranged for reporters and community leaders is called. And though there is far greater cooperation now, within the NYPD and between agencies, the division of credit isn't always the model of congeniality. One collar goes to one cop, regardless of how many others watched, chased, fought, or otherwise worked to get it, and every boss on the Job knew the difference between going to Compstat with a formidable array of arrest statistics as opposed to a lovely album of thank-you notes.

And so when PK told me that SNEU guidelines required that informants be handed over to Narcotics, after one search warrant, I dutifully made a call to the Four-Six Narcotics module about Charlie, while plotting sabotage all the while. Before the rape detail, I had gingerly broached the matter of hygiene with him, one night before I was to pick him up in Triple-O: "Don't take this the wrong way, Charlie, but you gotta clean yourself up when I get you tomorrow. You're a little ripe."

"Nah, it's all right. I know it, I know where I live."

And to my surprise, when I met him the next morning, he'd bathed and found clean clothes. In general, his range varied from stinking a little less than usual to stinking a lot more, and in my car, I averaged around two spray cans of Lysol per week. To be fair, there were several weeks when a foul odor seemed to hang about the car, which John blamed on the cream in my coffee that spilled on the mats, curdling in the summer heat. That theory was demolished when Sammy found a doggie bag from a long-forgotten dinner in the back seat, and the very act of dislodging it unleashed such a rancid cloud that I had to race around for blocks with all the windows open before it could be dispelled. But when I'd arranged for Charlie to come to the precinct to talk with two cops from Narcotics, no such sanitary preparations were undertaken; he was at his outer range, stink-wise, and the interview was brief.

"Well," said PK, "Narcotics had been notified, so I guess we're in the clear."

The Four-Six was a great hunting ground, not least because it was the first place where we began to lock up white people in any numbers. PK called them "strays," and they wandered around like lost dogs. Everywhere we had previously worked had white populations that were virtually microscopic. There was a slight overrepresentation of white arrests, of lost-in-time locals and the suburban addicts who commuted for a fix, but that part of the South Bronx was generally off-limits to white strangers. It was a double-reverse racism, as the dealers refused to collaborate in white suicide, while growing rich on the suffering of their like-colored neighbors. In the Four-Six, however, there was a spillover of the old white Heights trade; the dealers welcomed them, and so did we.

For us, there is a house brand of bullshit that black cops have to take when they lock up black people, and another brand for when they lock up white people, and the same for white cops locking up white, black, or brown, and so too for Hispanic cops—not to mention what female cops go through, when accused of harboring hidden agendas. If you lock up someone who looks like you, you're a race-traitor; if you lock up someone who doesn't, you're a racist. In the end, the color of your skin doesn't matter but the thickness of it does. Sometimes, we gave out scrips not by color but by counterpart on the team; there were no blacks or Hispanics, but instances of a "Male Orville, blue shirt and jeans, Yankee cap, south on Elton," or "Male Sammy, that's a male Sammy, north on University toward Tremont."

We enjoyed the contingent of white faces—for what you might call diversity grounds, in part, but also because so often they were so easy, from the street to the station house. Many even came when you called them. The strays seemed to have less of a lower-middle ground of "functional addiction" than black and Hispanic addicts, whether because their survival skills weren't there, or their families cut them off faster; there was no slippery slope of decline but a sheer drop-off, and the whites we collared either looked entirely normal and healthy at first glance, or like poster children for Skid Row. For many people, being arrested is an aggravation on the order of getting a flat tire—you see them put on a pair of handcuffs like you'd put on a pair of socks. For others, it is a trauma comparable to a death in the family. Many whites fell into the latter category, and it was a pleasure to collar them: they were so obedient and polite, they'd fill out their own paperwork if you asked. We'd get excited by the sight of a white face on the street, thinking an easy pinch was on the horizon. "Fifty bucks says it's a nun, in plainclothes," I'd say, spoiling the fun. I could do this because, as I'd tell my partners in a grave whisper: *I know white people. I know what makes them tick.*

Even better, it set off a competition between Stix and John and me, for who could lock up more Irish and Italians, respectively. The competition came to be known as Wopstat, as I called it, though they seemed to feel it was Mickstat. When we'd stop two white guys, they would stare at us, perplexed, as we asked for their names and listened as if it were a lottery drawing:

"McCarthy."

"Shit!" I'd say, as Stix and John high-fived each other. "Hold on a second, you—what's your name?"

"Russo."

"Yes!"

"All right, one and one, let's get back in the van."

Once, we locked up a Cuban guy, or rather, a Cuban who, under interrogation, admitted to some remote Irish and Italian ancestry, a grandfather who was half-and-half, which confused him to no end at the precinct:

"Whose collar is the Italian guy?"

"Hey, Irish, step out, we gotta print ya."

"Seamus—yeah, you, tell me your address."

"Hold on a second, Vito, you can make that phone call in a minute."

Mickstat and Wopstat each picked up a number through our informants in the Four-Six. Charlie had a "partner" named Tommy, another homeless guy who knew of our arrangement and hoped to work for us as well. Tommy was also in his late thirties, shorter and darker and generally less imposing than Charlie, who had a kind of wild hillbilly look from his life outdoors. Tommy had also lately migrated from the Heights after it was locked down. Like Charlie, Tommy steered white junkies to the dealers, but he made more money panhandling during rush hour, by the side of the entrance ramp that led from the Major Deegan to the Cross Bronx Expressway, when the traffic moved ten feet a minute. He told me he had a severe circulatory problem with his legs, which manifested itself in a rather showy limp, and as he stood at the roadside with a sign that said, "Homeless, Hungry, AIDS," he was a pitiful sight.

Tommy once confided in me, "Don't take this the wrong way, but Charlie got real down when you guys weren't around for a while. It's like he missed you. Me, this life—I mean, it's not like I wanted to do this when I grew up, but I always been a street kid. Not Charlie. He goes a little crazy sometimes, he'll rip off stashes from dealers, you know, not rob 'em–rob 'em, but peep out where they hide the shit and sneak back and take it later. Here, you do that if you want to die. Charlie was like a small-town guy—high school jock, lots of girls, nice car, all that shit. For Christ's sake, his old man's a cop! Anyway, you guys mean a lot to him."

Charlie and Tommy had moved from the median strip to beneath one of the great stone arches of a bridge that led to Manhattan. The hideaway was at the crest of a ridge that rose north from Yankee Stadium, on a wooded slope between the Harlem River and the neighborhoods of Highbridge and University Heights. You had to climb an eight-foot fence and then scramble across the loose and rocky soil of the hill, cutting over and then climbing back up like a ski slope. At the fence, there were signs of primitive religion: for weeks, the body of a three-foot-long snake was threaded through the steel mesh like a garland; for days, it was joined by a chicken carcass, plump as a pom-pom, with greasy white feathers, and neatly decapitated. Under the bridge, their encampment had a stone-age simplicity, with its humble and soiled basics of bedding, food, and fire; you could picture a cave painting of primeval Charlie and Tommy in animal skins, bringing down a mastodon with flint-tipped syringes. But what brought us to the woods was scarcely more complex than what kept them there; in our way, we were hunter-gatherers, too.

Charlie bought drugs. We gave him money. We didn't give him money for drugs, but that's where it went. In the sixties and seventies, it was said to be common for cops in Narcotics to give their informants drugs directly, throwing them a bag or two from a seizure. Though the practice was plainly illegal and fraught with risk, morally, I didn't see the problem. The payment in cash instead of drugs was a necessary legality, but, in human terms, nothing more: if Charlie didn't stick a needle in his arm ten times a day, I wouldn't be talking to him. If he wanted to get well—and I hoped he would—I would help him. Until then, I would take advantage of what he knew to do my job. For me, there was a concrete benefit in the relationship, but I wasn't sure whether the same held true for Charlie. He and Tommy both told us about young dealers who sometimes beat and robbed them for fun. Before, he wouldn't have pressed charges out of fear of both cops and crooks; ironically, our new availability made the idea of reporting a crime still less attractive, should it expose our relationship. He liked us, and he trusted us, but he needed the dealers.

All of us collected old clothes to give them, and John even gave Charlie a Walkman radio he had lying around. He had always been deferential to me, out of respect for the badge and recognition that I was in my way his employer, and he became increasingly grateful. There were moments of equality and familiarity between us, as if we'd met at a bar or a ball game, but they always had an undercurrent of the pathetic; we were the same age, from similar backgrounds, but not even everyone on the team could bring themselves to shake his hand. Once, when I drove him to court to get a search warrant, he changed the radio till he found a song he liked (Supertramp's "Breakfast in America": *Could we have kippers for breakfast, Mummy dear, Mummy dear . . .*) which annoyed me at first—Hey, it's my car, and that band sucks!—when I realized how long it had been since he'd looked for a song on the radio, and what it meant to him. It was in the casual and conversational—the remarks on how he liked my leather jacket, because it's hard to find a plain one, without zippers or buckles or a fancy cut, or how he used to drive a Mustang, years ago—that the gap between us yawned. I reminded him of his life before drugs, with its glories, such as 1980 Oldsmobiles and sleeping indoors. It occurred to me that these visits, when I sought him out for information or to take him to court, had something of the affectionate but awkward quality of a divorced dad picking up his kid every other weekend. The streets had custody of him, but I had visitation rights. And while our relationship may have consoled and inspired him for a few hours a week, my job was not to reform him and his heart was not in reform.

For me, the most routinely nerve-wracking part of work occurred during brief periods of time with Charlie. There were a lot of confrontations that I remember with some dread, but they were haphazard and scattered, and they struck with the randomness of fate. I trusted my partners, my ability, and my luck. But with Charlie, there were built-in moments of potentially lethal exposure, every time we met, stepping into the precinct or out of court. I might stop by the bridge on the way to work to ask who was on the street, and where the stash was hidden. When we'd head up to the Four-Six, we might see Charlie on the street; passing by, we might honk the horn and yell at another car—"Can't you drive?"—to get his attention without acknowledging it, and meet in the woods. If we ran into other forest junkies, we'd play tough-guy cops: "You got anything on you? I toss you and find something, you're under. Go ahead, now, move." They were glad to be clear of us, and they wouldn't have any stories about the nice guys who came to talk to Charlie. We were more careful than he was, until the day when he left the precinct through the front door, in his hurry and indifference. The precinct was some two miles from his turf, but he passed a woman he knew from the street, a crackhead, and he thought she recognized him. It didn't matter if she hated dealers and loved cops, or loved Charlie: it was information she could use, and that glimpse of him was like finding a ten-dollar bill on the sidewalk. Maybe a twenty! If she was out of money, she could say to a player, *Listen, I got something to tell you, but you gotta front me.* . . . For days, Charlie was in a panic, and his panic, like his elation, sorrow, ambivalence, and every other emotion, was treated with the same medication. He shook more, he smelled worse, and his extended sentences were not prizes of clarity and grammar. But the shock may have served a purpose: he told me that he'd talked with his mother, and he was ready to go into rehab.

"That's great, Charlie. When do you want to go?"

"Soon, today maybe. No, tomorrow."

"You want a ride home?"

He thought a minute. "Nah, I think I'll take the bus, get my head together. I could use the bus fare, though, if it wouldn't be a problem."

"You got it. Tomorrow morning, you want to go for one last warrant?"

There were two places where we were working on warrants. At one, the dealer lived in a first-floor apartment on University and sold from the lobby. If he ran out, he'd go back in to re-up, or if an established customer—say, Charlie—went there early enough, he could knock on his door and get done. After one buy, however, Charlie hadn't managed to catch him in more sales from the apartment. We worked a lot at adjoining buildings on Nelson Avenue, a block over from University, which sold four different brands of dope—Checkmate, Shotgun, Brainstorm, and Fugitive—as well as cocaine and crack. Charlie had got done in an apartment there the day before, and he made two more buys in quick succession. The next morning, we went in for the warrant.

With Charlie, we obtained "sight warrants," the weakest of the three types of information used to establish probable cause. Generally speaking, the Bronx DA wanted three "looks" within a ten-day period if there were only drugs present, and they preferred additional corroboration, such as an identified subject with a criminal history, the complaints of neighbors, or other arrests in the building for the same kind of narcotics. Another approach is through "controlled buys," in which an informant is sent in with marked money, and the drugs purchased are field-tested and vouchered, a method that improves the quality of evidence a step beyond the say-so. In most instances, two buys were required for a judge to issue a warrant. Finally, through the firsthand testimony of undercovers, whether buys or observations, one visit was sufficient. A variety of other factors had their weight, such as the cops' familiarity with the target location, and the past credibility of the informant. Where one judge or DA saw a bright line of probable cause that we crossed twice over, another saw shadows and doubt. But you never know what's on the other side of the door until you look, do you?

Judges varied in their thoroughness. Some simply looked over the affidavit prepared by the ADA, which recounted the details of each transaction, and asked the cop and the informant if it was accurate; others grilled each of us for an extended period. With the warrant on Nelson, it was the former style, and we moved quickly—all of us motivated, perhaps, by Charlie's deterioration and its attendant odor. In the rush, I didn't do the recon the night before. The building was Perp Central, and difficult to enter without being made; in such instances, you might visit in uniform, in a marked car, to suggest a general visit rather than a specific purpose. Another trick was for the informant to mark the door in some subtle way, or draw graffiti on the frame; with Charlie, especially in his state, it was not possible to expect him to hold on to a pen for couple of hours. In any case, we got the warrant without having seen the door.

When I did see the door, the next night, it was as if it had been slammed in my face. It was where it was supposed to be, on the second floor, the second apartment to the right of the stairs, but instead of being marked 2D, say, it was marked 24. In housing projects and in many other buildings, the floor is numbered and the apartment is lettered, but it is hardly a universal system. The apartments in this building were badly marked, and the most visible door marking on the floor had simply an A. What I suspect had happened was that Charlie had seen the A, assumed it was 2A, and counted over to 2D. He had also said the door was brown, while to me, the paint looked not-so-brownish, though in a certain light, maybe, you could . . . no, it was lime green. The paint was fresh, so the color difference could be accounted for, but the warrant said we could knock down the door marked 2D, and there was no such apartment in the building. Legally, that stopped things flat. Further, it meant our claim of the apartment through the Drug Enforcement Coordinating System (DECS) was meaningless—naturally, no one else had a case in a nonexistent apartment—and indeed, the real address had already been claimed by Narcotics, who had done a warrant several months earlier. I talked to the case officer, who said they didn't get anything out of it at the time, but he was glad to hear it would be worth starting up again.

When I told PK, I made a couple of half-assed arguments, thinking aloud as much as talking with him, trying to come up with a way to pull it off. That kind of perseverance is a good thing, sometimes. I didn't let little things like walls get in my way when I wanted to get somewhere. When Mike Donnelly came to the precinct, Tony told him, "Eddie doesn't take 'No' for an answer. He's the most determined one on the team, when it comes to it." I was proud of that, but John tended to remark on the flip side of the characteristic: "You're *gabbados*. It means thickheaded, you don't listen." With PK, I had to listen; we all did, mostly because of his very lack of argument. He didn't give orders, because he didn't have to; we knew that he did every good thing that he could for us, and every tough break was equally shared. He smiled a little and listened, and said, "It's a shame, laddo. We'll all have to be more careful next time." When my hot air cooled a little, he said, "OK, so let's go out."

· · ·

BECAUSE IT WAS PLAIN THAT I HADN'T QUITE REACHED THE peak of the learning curve, it was interesting to see how much I had mastered, or at least what now came with thoughtless habit: the attitude on a stop, the thoroughness of a search, or phrasing the question, "When was the last time you were locked up?" instead of "Were you ever arrested?" John had certainly been a capable cop before he joined SNEU, but there were aspects of work than only came with practice, like what to look for in an OP, or guarding your speech around perps. As the van filled up, you put the perps in the back seat and turned up the stereo, but not so high that you couldn't hear your radio. You had hours to kill, sitting there in the van, driving, sitting again, and so naturally you talked to your partner. But you didn't talk about work—you didn't want them to pick up useful details about how we operated, where the OP was, or whether someone told us about the dealer, which could lead them to guess who might have, correctly or not—and you didn't talk about your personal life, either. You couldn't say your wife's name, or complain about the commute this morning, because it might tell them where you lived. Although few perps would make serious use of that information, many would take advantage of stray personal details in the short term, calling from the cells, "How's your wife? You know, Jenny, your wife?" And so you have to bullshit about nothing in particular: TV, girls, cars, the joke of the day, the more stupid the better. It had a morally uplifting effect on the perps, I thought, as they shifted in their cuffs in the back seat, listening to two cops argue for hours over who farted. They had to wonder: *These are the guys that caught me?*

Other lessons were common cop lessons, hardly unique to SNEU. One day, John and Stix were on bikes when we worked One-Five-Seven and Elton, and Stix got a flat. He went back to the precinct to fix it, while John stayed out to catch bodies alone. The OP gave out a body, and John went after him. This was a body indeed: two hundred and seventy-five pounds of it, stacked up six feet and three inches, which found work in the evenings guarding the door of a strip joint. John came in aggressively and put him on the wall, but when the bouncer saw that John was alone, he stepped out and faced off. John's eye was drawn to his right fist, which both held the dope and sought to meet his face. John put him down in the street: his radio slipped out of reach, while the perp threw the dope down a sewer. A crowd drew near, neither to help nor to harm, and John and the perp locked into each other, the perp swinging for John's face, while John massaged the perp's head against the curb. John was able to reach his radio, yelling for backup; the perp was cuffed, and ESU retrieved the dope from the sewer.

In the cells, the perp fumed, in disbelief that he hadn't been able to take him: "I woulda kicked that guy's ass if he wasn't on steroids."

"Yeah, you had your chance. Look who's spitting tough juice now," John responded.

Far more unnerving to John was an early appearance in Grand Jury. A Grand Jury is composed of sixteen to twenty-three people, impaneled for several weeks to vote on indictments in felony cases. Defense counsel is not present, and the standard of proof is the same as it is for an arrest; for the most part, they mechanically affirm mechanical accounts of collars, and it is dull work. Testimony for observation sales generally begins with the cop in the OP saying he saw the buyer and seller make an exchange, and ends with the apprehending officer saying he made an arrest based on directions from the OP. Sometimes, a juror might ask a question like, "Were you using binoculars?" One panel that I appeared before several times had a man who asked that for each case—he'd found a good thing to say, and he stuck with it. More often, they said nothing, and the tedium of the panel was usually so pronounced that I expected someone to ask one day, "Yes, Officer, I have a question. What's a five-letter word for 'bedspread'?"

The DA asks, you answer; you should know what's coming, and so should they. It goes like this:

"Good morning, Officer."

"Good morning."

"Would you please state your name, rank, and command for the record?"

"Police Officer Edward Conlon, shield number nine-eight-seven-six, Police Service Area Seven, Housing Bureau."

"Officer, I'd like to direct your attention to events which occurred on or about August 15, 1998, at approximately two-fifteen in the afternoon, at the corner of One Hundred and Fifty-seventh Street and Elton Avenue, in the county of the Bronx. What, if anything, did you do then?"

"I was working as a New York City police officer, in the Street Narcotics Enforcement Unit of PSA-Seven, in an observation post. I observed the defendant for a period of one hour, during which he made exchanges of small objects for United States currency with numerous individuals."

"All right, Officer, and then what happened?"

"I transmitted the information to the field team on point-to-point radio."

"Thank you, Officer. If no one has any questions, you can go."

Grand Jury is easy, but it is still public speaking, which makes me a little nervous. I was slightly more nervous, during the first case that I had with John, as the ADA ambushed me with all kinds of odd questions—not only rudely co-opting the binocular question from the poor man in the back, but following up with a pop quiz: What was their power of magnification? There had been no preparation for the testimony, which is not unusual for such a formulaic appearance, but it is received wisdom among trial lawyers that you do not ask a question to which you do not know the answer. This was somewhere between a game show and a fraternity hazing. As it happened, I knew the specifications of the binoculars, but then he asked me, "How did you recognize the voice of Officer Timpanaro over the radio?"

It stumped me. What the hell did it mean? Were we supposed to be trained in voice-recognition techniques? Was he after something metaphysical: Does another person ever *really* know someone else? Is there something particular about Timpanaro and broadcasting: *Sir, as you are well aware, Officer Timpanaro is one of the most beloved entertainers of our generation.* I think I said, "Umm, because I work with him?"

John followed me, and returned several minutes later, pale and stunned, looking like Frank Costello before the Senate Subcommittee on Organized Crime, stammering denials to Bobby Kennedy. When the binocular question came, I think he even took the Fifth. He expected to go in and say, "Based on a radio transmission by Officer Conlon, I arrested the defendant. I took ten glassines of heroin from his right pants pocket, a hundred dollars from his left." God Bless America, and Good Night. Boy, was he was pissed at me. And it was only the memory of him telling Yvonne not to give up, to keep on trying to win my heart, that gave me the courage to laugh in his face. And then we went back out.

Out was always good. It was summer in the Bronx: new songs from San Juan and old ones from Santo Domingo blared from the bodegas and the gypsy cabs; the "icey-man" made his rounds with his little white cart that said HELADO, filling a cup with shavings from a sweating block of ice, then squirting it with mango, coco, or cherry syrup; laundry hung from the lines strung across the alleys, as if to proclaim, "Our drawers are clean. Are yours?" There were some women you wished wore more clothes, and some you wished wore fewer, and others who had it just right.

We cowboyed it a little bit. When we drove to the Four-Six, PK once blanched to see John and Stix skitching on the back of a bus—on bikes, holding on to the back bumper for a tow uphill. I found that if I worked alone in my car, no one looked at me twice in the neighborhood. I chased a guy over the bridge into Manhattan, if "chase" is the word for a pursuit that coursed along at three miles an hour. The man had a mastiff in the back seat, a dog that was almost as big as I was. When the rest of the team got there, I had the perp in cuffs. Tony and OV would have preferred to stop a man with a live shark in the back, and the rest of the team was in no hurry to become pet food either. The dog seemed friendly enough, though, and we were stuck with it, so I got in the passenger seat and told the perp to drive back to the Four-Six, adding, "If this dog bites me, I'm gonna shoot you both." The dog laid his chin on my shoulder during the ride. We rushed the perp out with a Desk Appearance Ticket, so he could go home with his pet.

Cops don't do this kind of work alone, or at least they shouldn't. I did, sometimes, even off-duty, checking out spots on the way home from a night in the city, especially if I was well dressed. At midnight, a solo stray in jacket and tie would attract notice in the neighborhood, but he'd be made as a Wall Street junkie readying for a binge. I'd rub my eyes bloodshot, and stagger a little. In truth, I was more concerned about being stopped by a cop than a perp. But I could walk into a building we were looking at for a warrant, see the layout of the hallway, the marks on the door, and then look at the roof, to see where the windows faced, over which airshaft and alley, and whether there was a fire escape. Orville or Sammy might be able to look while we were working, but no secondhand report would give me the detail and certainty I'd have if I saw it myself. One night, I went out with a few friends, one of whom had the use of the company limousine. At the end of the evening, the car drove uptown, dropping people off, and as there were no other Bronx residents in our party, I was left as the last passenger. The driver had an English accent, "Where can I take you, sir?" *Home, James, by way of Junkie Town.* . . .

One night, Stix and I walked up University, checking things out. It had looked a little slow, and when the same black van with tinted windows makes too many trips up the street, whatever's out won't stay out long. PK and the rest of the team followed from a distance. "See what turns up," said PK. We were both scruffy-looking, skinny white guys, looking around for drug dealers; there were two possible explanations for our stroll through the neighborhood, and we decided to see if the players would fall for the other one. Slipping into a lobby, we stuck our radios down the fronts of our pants; we had big, loose shirts on, which covered vests and guns. Stix was breezily confident, enjoying it as the practical joke it was—in a certain sense, working undercover is the ultimate practical joke—whereas I was nervous as an understudy thrust onstage for opening night. What were my lines? What was my motivation? Why was my dressing room so small? Still, I thought that the combination of nerve and neurosis could work on our side, and we stepped out.

No one was out for Marlboro or Audi, or for Turbo or Checkmate or Brainstorm. The West Hell Cartel no longer used 1669 and 1675, and the rest of the street looked clean of players. Up the block, by the bodega on Tremont, there was a crew on the corner, easy to make. We walked up and stopped, walked again and stopped to consult each other: they would see us coming, desperate and lost. We waited under the bodega awning, in the light, nattering audibly as out-of-town dope nerds: "No, you ask!"

"No, you! It's your turn!"

"I asked last time!"

And a guy from the crowd sauntered over: "What you want?"

"Heroin," said Stix brightly. "We want to get some heroin. You got any?" *Look, Ma, I finished all my vegetables. Can I have some heroin now, please?* It was slightly surreal, but also perfect. Stix didn't play ghetto, because he couldn't—"*Got D, yo? Anybody holding the D?*"—would have come out of his mouth like Charlton Heston reciting from the collected works of Snoop Dogg.

He stared at us, taking it in. He was not, by the look of him, any deep thinker: *Could we be cops? Has the NYPD sunk so low? Don't they teach them anything?*

"I don't know, maybe," he said. "How much you want?"

He was on the fence, and I spoke up: "We want a bundle."

If he doubted we were worth the trouble for a ten-dollar bag, a hundred-dollar bundle might tip the balance. He went back to the crew at the corner and consulted with them before returning.

"Give me the money first."

"No."

"Lemme have the money, I'll get it for you. You gotta front it."

I think we had twelve dollars between us. I spoke up again, heatedly: "Forget about it, let's go down the street for Miracle or Macho, we don't need this shit, fuck this! This guy don't want our money, somebody else does." We walked up the street, and got about fifty yards before the dealer called us back.

"C'mon, I got ya."

Waving us to follow, he stepped into the building. 1815 University has a narrow, iron-gated courtyard, with the lobby door recessed in the back. We followed into the dim corridor and inside the building. We didn't look back at the crew, milling at the gate, with whom the player had consulted after each step. Again, the player asked for money, and again, we refused, and he walked upstairs, promising to return. I weighed my options, which seemed to be to take the drugs and then blast him with mace, or to take the drugs and punch him in the head. Stix and I looked at each other, in quiet unease. I forget if we giggled. Another player drifted in from the street.

And then the team rushed in. They took the player and put him against the wall, and I tapped Stix and we grabbed the wall, whispering to OV to search us. The first player was nowhere to be found. Three of us left the building in cuffs, and when we were out, Stix and I were loud in our protests: "What happened? We were half a minute from a collar! Why'd you come in?"

PK told us, "The rest of the crew was coming in after you. They were gonna rob you." I thought, So? A robbery collar would have been all the better!—which, in retrospect, was a fearsome indicator of our level of enthusiasm that summer. The next night, we gave it another try—this time, Stix and I even took out our shoelaces, as if they'd been removed after a night in the cells, and wrote up arrest paperwork for ourselves. I made mine for an Italian guy, of course, and Stix's perp was Irish, though had the dealer looked closely, it would have said I lived at 12 Junkie Lane. A player on a bike circled around us, intrigued, disinclined to do us but all the while peppering us with questions like "Where's your car parked?" He even touched my shoulder to see if I had on a vest, though he felt the wrong spot. "Nah, nah, nah . . ." he said, "I don't know nothin' about dope around here. . . ."

We'd get him next time.

After the warrant that we didn't execute, I wondered whether I'd see Charlie again, to tell him what had happened. He seemed to be coming closer to a move, a change in his life. Though he'd yessed me a little on the door markings, I could hardly beat him up over it—it was my responsibility, for one, but also he'd been trying to come to terms with the idea that his suicide on the installment plan might be fast-forwarded by a .38 behind the ear. I found Tommy first, and he said Charlie was in a bad way. He also told me about another inside spot, as well as the players on the street that day. When I handed Tommy some money, he held up his hands and said, "C'mon, Eddie, you don't have to, it's okay." I said, "It's all right, you guys work, you take risks for us, you should get paid." He took the money, but he shook his head.

"Don't take this the wrong way, but I feel a little funny, since you guys pay out of your own pockets. Do you know how much we make out here, pan-handling, during rush hour?"

"No, how much?"

"About a dollar a minute."

"Oh."

I didn't take my money back, but I saw his point: Charlie and Tommy made more money than us. I should have realized that earlier, as the math was not complicated—we took home less than a hundred dollars a day, while their habits were at least that. I tried not to dwell on the fact that, economi-cally, a New York City police officer was a notch down from a bum.

When I did find Charlie, he said he was sorry about the warrant. He had an abased and abstracted look, as if his career as a junkie hadn't been going all that well, and the informant's life might not be quite the thing, either: maybe it was time to clean up and go into rehab. But the next time he called home, to tell his mother that this time, this time was finally it, that he was ready to go into the hospital and start living again, his father answered the phone and told him that his mother had died, days ago, and hung up. The funeral was already over.

By the end of August, we had sixty-five collars. We got twenty-two in two days, hitting One-Five-Seven and Elton, for blue-top vials of crack, China White, and Eazy Money, and Bike worked with us on one of those days as well, taking a dozen collars more. It killed the spot. OV watched from the projects, I watched from the senior citizens building, giving out bodies as they moved west to Melrose, east to Third, north to One-Six-One, south to One-Four-Nine. We caught them in vans, cars, bikes, and on foot:

"Is he a hit?"

"He's a hit."

"Good, I got another one for ya. . . ."

At the end of our Roger Maris month, PK wrote in the margins of our collar book, "Roger who?"

Narcotics was picking people up in great numbers. By that time, Inspector Mullen was at Bronx Narcotics. I told him about our month, and he said to bring everyone up for a talk. We packed into the van and rode up to his office, then gathered around his desk as if it were a campfire. "I need people," he said, and we leaned in to hear more. We said we all wanted to work together, as a team. He said that at first, he'd probably have to mix us up with veteran detectives until we knew what we were doing. We looked at one another and murmured assent. It was like all your best friends from high school getting a scholarship to the same college. We were going to be OK.

In early September, it was PK's son Paulie's first anniversary. The team bought PK a mass card. I handed it to him at the end of the day, and he smiled and nodded, and walked quickly to his car.

SEVEN

I t was Inspector Mullen who told me about the glass toilet. One of the airport squads uses it for drug mules, forcing them to sit until the cocaine or heroin-filled condoms they've swallowed on distant shores reappear here, at the journey's end. The device so fascinated me that I was afraid to ask him for details about how it worked—was there a safety or a trigger-lock on the flusher, to prevent destruction of evidence?—because my interest was so avid that I thought it might disturb him. But I also didn't want to know more about the glass toilet because the way I imagined it, it had become the perfect symbol of police work, and I didn't want facts to spoil my fantasy. You picked people from crowds, took them aside, and waited to see what came out. Every cop was a bowl keeper, in his way, in possession of tools and techniques for the inspection of what people had deep inside them; each tour of duty was a reminder that innocence and guilt can leave an equally foul odor. You realized that to work beside the bowl could be awful enough, but it was better than being on it, or in it. It made you appreciate that a good life is full of decorous separations, from its own parts and from other people, so that its intimate functions, moments of weakness, occasions of sin, could pass on and be forgotten.

I'd become used to a kind of double life, or at least two jobs, apart from each other and largely out of sight. I thought of the arrangement in terms of privacy rather than secrecy, though the edges blurred, and it had been that way from the beginning, when my family and most of my friends had no idea that I was about to go into the Academy. Like many cops, I was reluctant to tell strangers or new acquaintances what I did, and was irked when non-cop friends would preemptively announce it, to a girl in a bar or whoever else, because it brought out strange reactions in people. Most were enthusiastic in some manner, but sometimes you got the feeling that if they'd met a comedian, they'd demand to hear something funny. You also met gun nuts and other ostensible supporters, who were disappointed that my mastery of firearms didn't extend far beyond the ability to make mine go *Bang!* A lot of people asked me if I'd ever killed anyone, and a few asked, "Do you see much corruption?" I wondered if those people asked newlyweds if they'd cheated on each other yet. And those were the ones who liked the police.

At a Christmas party, I was pointed out to someone's date, who tried to corner me on the subject of parking tickets, a perennial conversational hazard for off-duty cops. My usual tactic of measured agreement—Yes, some cops are petty, but sometimes it's because the sergeant ordered them to be, and Yes, of course you should fight the ticket if you didn't deserve it—did nothing to deter his harangue.

"You know, in alternate-side parking in Manhattan, there's just no place to put your car sometimes, and—"

"You're right, it's a shame."

"Yeah, but what you do is—"

"I don't write tickets, and I don't work in Manhattan."

"But *still,* what you have to do about the parking below 59th Street, is—"

I ducked him and he followed me, and again, until I turned and barked at him: "Listen, guy, what do you do for a for a living?"

"I'm a chef."

"Fine, next time I get a bad meal at a restaurant, I'll call you at home on your day off."

The fact of the matter is that most cops lead double lives of some kind, of high contrast if not outright contradiction. At the most ordinary level, there are the cops who commute daily between suburban order and ghetto mayhem, or who at least have a home that is some kind of refuge from the streets. That was how it was for my father, who spent nine-to-five with the bad guys, nights and weekends with the wife and kids. Conversely, the steadiness and definition of the Job, with its rules, traditions, and diffuse base of blue-collar Catholicism, provided a workaday counterbalance to many cops' off-duty worlds, whether they were twice-divorced loners at the bar or in other straits of familial chaos. In some way, that was the situation of Pat Brown, as a crooked cop and a man-about-town. Just about the only exception I can think of was Uncle Eddie, in Harbor, who spent his days hanging out with cops on a boat, and then went home to hang out on his boat, often with cops. Sometimes it must have felt like it wasn't like working at all; at others, it must have seemed that he spent his whole life on overtime. But for most cops, there is a split of some kind, a distance if not a discord, between public and private, their passions and pastimes.

I was no different. As a cop, I worked out of love and for the money, as I had when I was a freelance writer, always hoping that there was enough of each not to force a choice between the two. I hadn't done much writing since. And so when I was asked to write a magazine piece about being a cop, and then a few more, I was glad for the opportunity to pick it up again, but I was insistent that it be published under another name. I was still new, and while I didn't want to lay claim to any larger experience than I'd earned, I also didn't want to be dismissed as a rookie, or worse, someone who'd gone on the Job as a stunt or for a story. I didn't want to speak for other cops, but rather to portray the Job as I'd known it and let that speak for itself. When I described some adventure or encounter on patrol, my partners' roles were related in a narrowly factual manner; I didn't want cops to have to second-guess me, to wonder if they were under a kind of surveillance. No one in any occupation likes the idea that they are being observed unawares, and cops have a particular aversion to it, as they are used to conflict on the streets and criticism in the press. With your partners, at least, you should be able to depend on a measure of reflexive support.

The fact of the matter is that all cops exist in a state of mild infraction. Their memo books aren't up to date, or they don't have the new insert for Spanish Phrases or Domestic Disputes, or their shoes aren't shined, or their socks are white, or they stopped to eat or cash a check without putting it over the air, or they signed out a little early, or they left their hat in the car when they went to a job. It was only recently that I learned that you can get a Command Discipline for reading the newspaper in a patrol car, an offense for which I'd be serving life without parole if I'd been caught each time I'd committed it. No one is completely by-the-book, because our book is the *Patrol Guide,* which not only maps out every turn in the bureaucratic labyrinth but is self-described as "flexible," which could be read cynically to mean that even if you followed every step, you could still get jammed up if things didn't work out, because you could have done it differently. Everyone knows this, from cop to commissioner, and if you work hard and in good faith, in compliance with the basics, the best you can hope for is that the trouble you get in won't be too frequent or too deep. You were probably breaking some kind of rule just by showing up, it seemed, and this general understanding that the less said the better is yet another basis for the "blue wall of silence."

I was careful, but not paranoid. I wasn't a CIA agent or a Soviet spy, but a more-or-less-contented witness to the daily travails of big-city police work. I had permission to write from the Deputy Commissioner of Public Information, Marilyn Mode, and the commanding officer of that office, Inspector Michael Collins. Mode and Collins both read the first piece, but only Collins the later ones. My initial fear that they would see the articles as a public-relations opportunity—"Give us something on bicycle summonses, the Mayor's all over it this week"—was baseless, though Inspector Collins did point out several typos. Outside of work, it was a fairly open secret, and I was almost casual in my confidence that the two worlds wouldn't meet. I gave copies of the pieces to cop friends from before I went on the Job, like Mike Shea and Brian McCabe, though I'd caution them not to mention my real name or where I worked if they showed them to other cops. I was supposed to fill out an "off-duty employment" form, but that had to be signed by the commanding officer of the precinct, which was a little close to home.

And home was where the first breach took place. John, who lived with his family some sixty miles outside of the city, had begun to stay over at the Vanity Court apartment one or two nights a week by the end of the summer. I never quite understood how cops like John—or PK, who lived seventy miles away—could manage three or sometimes four hours a day commuting to and from work, where they might spend another eight hours in a car. It seemed contradictory to the whole point of being a New Yorker. But after John had been staying there a few weeks, it seemed polite to explain why the floor was littered with manuscript. It may have been the least of the peculiarities of the place, with its perpetual back-alley twilight, the mysterious leaks and smells, the sounds of roosters and neighbors crowing from all sides; and the fact that he didn't question it may have reflected generally lowered expectations. But I told him, and as a hidden diversion he thought it was reasonably interesting, and for successive mornings after the revelation, he showily brought copies of the magazine pieces with him into the bathroom. *Ya gotta have a story, don't ya?* It wasn't a glass toilet, but it was there that John became familiar with the idea of one, as our innermost workings ran parallel courses, body and mind.

· · ·

THE FRENCH CONNECTION HAD TWO SEQUELS, ONE A DISAP-pointment, one a disgrace. In the movie, Popeye goes to France. In life, no one knows where the drugs went. In 1971, *The French Connection* won the Academy Award, and in 1972, at the height of the Knapp Commission scandals, it was discovered that much of the heroin had been replaced with pancake flour. It had not been a good year for the NYPD. Throughout the nation, there was general upheaval in attitudes and beliefs, and the blind faith with which many supported public institutions was replaced with an equally blind contempt. The Knapp Commission was set in motion by an expose of police corruption in *The New York Times* based primarily on testimony by two cops, David Durk and Frank Serpico. Serpico became *Serpico,* the book and the movie, where the old expression of "good cop, bad cop"—which referred to an interrogation technique, rather than integrity—was reframed as good cop . . . and everyone else. It was a time when history repeated itself, and reversed itself, moving from farce to tragedy to something in between; the shifts in fortune were dizzying, as bit players made it big and the great figures were brought down, and cops negotiated between movie deals and indictments.

Frank Serpico has many admirers and many detractors, but there was no disagreement that he was a very strange man. A chief told me he remembers him with his pet mouse scrambling around his coat collar. Peter Maas, the author of *Serpico,* was infatuated with the idea of the hippie cop in his velour bell-bottoms, leather jerkin, and huge gold Winnie-the-Pooh medallion, with his love of opera and one-night stands. The enthusiasm sometimes takes on an Austin Powers tone, such as when he notes that Serpico's amorous attentions were divided between "a carefree airline stewardess who looks as if she just walked in off the Southern California beach where she was raised on sun and surfing," "a somewhat tense, twenty-six-year-old, blond, hundred-dollar call girl with stupendous breasts," and a "volatile black model." *Yeah, baby!* Next to the poor stiffs who went home every night to their cookie-cutter houses to eat meat loaf with the same old frau, Serpico's superiority is depicted in nearly evolutionary terms.

Serpico was moody, intense, and self-absorbed; from childhood, his admiration for cops ran so deep that he traded a bike for a Cub Scout shirt because it looked like a police uniform, and he'd explain to other kids that he couldn't talk because he was "on a case." Like many who come on the Job with fervid, romantic expectations of police work, he was disappointed with the rule-bound, time-killing nature of patrol, and the tone of cynical self-preservation that prevails when cops talk among themselves. And yet his resistance to cutting corners was hardly absolute: he didn't "coop," which meant to hide somewhere, to sleep or hang out with other cops . . . except when it was really cold. On his post, he accepted free meals . . . until he noticed that cops tended to get leftovers, and so he decided to pay . . . part of the check. That was why the commonplace, small-time "gifts" could spoil cops' relations with the neighborhood, even if there was no great crime being committed—a merchant might well be delighted to offer the local beat cop a free haircut, shoeshine, or lunch, but word of his good nature would spread, and the sector cars might stop by, and the sergeant, and so on, so that the small gesture became a larger burden, resentfully proffered and with greater expectations of payback.

But the long-anticipated thrills were there, too, at Serpico's precinct in Bedford-Stuyvesant: he caught burglars and delivered babies. He shot the balls off a rapist. One collar, after a brutal gang rape, showed that Serpico had both real ability and awful judgment—after catching one perp, he brought him back to the Squad, where a detective beat the man, demanding the names of his accomplices. The perp clammed up, and when Serpico brought him to court the next morning, he stopped, uncuffed the perp, and took him out for breakfast. It's not a technique recommended in the *Patrol Guide,* but Serpico got the names. Where Maas sees the episode as maverick and humane, I see a cup of coffee in the eyes and a perp who'll send you postcards from Florida. Another episode that made me cringe told of how, off-duty, Serpico would dress in shabby clothes and wander alone through the ghetto, hoping to be jumped. He was.

After a few years, he was rewarded with a transfer to Vice, as a plain-clothesman, because a new department regulation had mandated assignment there before promotion to the Detective Division. The idea was to circulate as many honest cops as possible through the traditionally rotten detail, to flush it clean. The old characters like Pat Brown would make way for the new generation of Serpicos. At the time, the NYPD made 10,000 arrests for gambling every year; the DAs barely prosecuted them, and the judges barely sentenced them. Though Vice was a charade, Serpico had been assured that the age of the grafter was over, by bosses who were certainly honest themselves, and presumably better informed about the Department as a whole. Serpico accepted the transfer, though he shared his ambivalence with his new friend David Durk, whom he met at a criminal-investigation class.

When Serpico met Durk, it was like meeting Bobby Kennedy and Leonard Bernstein at once. Durk was well connected and well read, living with his wife and child in an Upper West Side apartment that was a salon of like-minded people. Serpico would go to dinner parties there and sit in silence, but he could talk long into the night with Durk. In *Target Blue,* in which Robert Daley tells of his year as a deputy commissioner in 1972, he describes the instant bond between the two, who were in most ways as unlike each other as they were from the rest of the rank-and-file: "There were cops who took gambling graft and cops who didn't. There were those who thought gambling graft amusing, or unimportant, or exaggerated, or negligible, or deplorable; and there were those like Durk and Serpico . . . who were fanatically opposed." They had earnest debates over how to show your badge to a city bus driver, so that you wouldn't "blow your cover," and even whether to do so to the motorcycle mechanic who was ripping off Serpico. (When Durk did, Serpico was furious.)

Though Durk was older than Serpico, he had less time on the Job—in 1966, when they met, he had three years on, to Serpico's six. David Durk was Jewish, a doctor's son who grew up in Manhattan and graduated from Amherst. He was brashly confident and a genuine intellectual, idealistic and dedicated to reform. In the Academy, when the recruits were asked why they had become cops, the first answers were the typical ones—because my father was, for the pension, because the Fire Department wasn't hiring—and Durk made a fiery speech about justice and public service. The next cop asked responded, "What he said." At his midtown precinct, when the desk officer told him to mop the floor, Durk would protest, quoting articles from scholarly journals on effective time-management. Unlike most reformers, however, Durk also enjoyed the daily, hands-on oddity of patrol; he actually liked cops, and saw them as people who, for the most part, wanted to work harder and more honestly than the system permitted. He saw them as the victims of graft as much as its beneficiaries—for example, cops were forbidden to carry lunch with them, but many had posts which were too far from the precinct to eat what they brought from home. On what cops made, the cost of a daily meal in midtown might have been as much as their rent. Durk also had a good perspective on the matter—that a free lunch was often just a free lunch—but he took mischievous pleasure in persuading cops not to go along. In one case, a steak house that gave cops free meals even advertised that it had "free parking" for its customers, who double-parked and blocked hydrants. Durk needled the other cops into enforcement, asking if they liked being ordered around by waiters in exchange for a piece of cheap meat, which they probably spit on anyway. He wrote anonymous letters of complaint to Headquarters, which gave them a pretext for action. The parking problem around the restaurant stopped, and Durk noticed the new pride that the cops took in their work.

That kind of success inspired Durk to believe that things could be changed, in small ways and large, and that he was just the guy to do it. In a chance encounter, he upbraided some hecklers at a speech in the park, and his eloquent explanation of the First Amendment was overheard by Jay Kriegel, a young volunteer for John Lindsay's mayoral campaign who became one of Lindsay's inner circle of advisors. Kriegel stopped to talk to Durk, and in conversation it emerged that he, too, was an Amherst graduate, and a friendship was struck. Durk, while still a rookie, wrote much of a Lindsay policy paper on crime and policing, and opened up a critical line of access to City Hall. When the head of the Department of Investigation—which monitored all city agencies, though in practice it left the police alone—needed a police captain assigned, Durk chose the man, who in turn brought in Durk to work for him.

Six months into his new assignment in plainclothes, in Brooklyn, Serpico was passed an envelope with three hundred dollars in cash. There was no doubt in his mind who could solve the problem. There was no doubt in Durk's mind, either. He took Serpico to his boss at the Department of Investigation, which marked the first of many disappointments and betrayals. The captain's horror at learning of the corruption was matched only by the idea that he might have to do something about it; he told Serpico to forget about it, or he could wind up "face down in the East River." From then on, Serpico became resentful toward Durk as well, though the latter shared his frustration and worked relentlessly to help him. Serpico kept his distance from the other cops, but his arrests complicated arrangements with the gamblers, and the strain increased. The canard that gambling money was "soft" or "clean" was again brought home when Serpico collared a three-hundred-pound mafioso. When Serpico returned to the cells, he found the perp sitting outside, talking happily among the cops, who brought him coffee and saw to his comforts. Serpico exploded; he had checked his record, which showed that the man was a cop killer. The arrest also brought out the vagaries of corruption in the NYPD, which was no more one big happy family than the City was. Paying for police protection was like paying for rain insurance in the desert; it worked most of the time, except for when it didn't. Gamblers could pay the precinct, but then the Division could hit them; they could pay off the Division, but then the Borough could hit them; they could pay off the Borough, but then Headquarters could hit them; and even when everyone was paid off—or was supposed to be—they remained vulnerable to any honest cop.

Together and apart, Durk and Serpico searched for an audience; though Durk's access was extraordinary, his results were lacking. Serpico was transferred to the Bronx, assured by a high-ranking police contact that it was as "clean as a hound's tooth." In the Bronx, however, things were no better. Serpico was persuaded that Headquarters understood and was grateful for his work; for the present, he should sit tight. They would be in touch. They weren't. For hours, Jay Kriegel listened to Serpico and Durk in rapt attention, taking notes, asking questions, and assuring them of an immediate response from the Mayor. Mayor Lindsay's relations with the NYPD had always been poor, however, and Kriegel, too, had disappointing news: the summer was approaching, and so was riot season, and the Mayor didn't feel that he could further alienate the police. Returning to the Department of Investigation, the commissioner first offered Durk some primitive surveillance equipment, but his aversion to Serpico was so pronounced—again, the Winnie-the-Pooh medallion, but also a hardening attitude of sarcastic disconnection—that he shortly demanded its return, calling Serpico a "psycho."

Serpico grew more combative in his dealings with the honest bosses, adding conditions and demands for his participation: he wouldn't wear a wire, and he didn't want to testify. He didn't want to "get" them as much as change "It"—the worst possible outcome was for the Job to shitcan a couple of cops, declare victory, and move on. Durk was instrumental in this demand for systemic change, in his affection for street cops, and in his belief that they were pawns on the chessboard, the injured parties as much as the injuring. But while this kind of big-picture thinking galvanized Durk, it seemed to overwhelm Serpico, provoking an angry and erratic absolutism. His frustration was more than understandable, after a year of empty promises, but his was a self-defeating position: if you have facts, you have a case; if you have ideas, you have an editorial.

When the Bronx DA, Burton Roberts, indicted eight plainclothesmen, Serpico was largely left out of it. A gruff and flamboyant character, Roberts had been an honest and hardworking prosecutor for a long time, and he found Serpico insufferable as a person and awful as a witness—vast amounts of energy were expended in persuading him to shave his beard. When Serpico's cooperation was finally induced by promising the kind of case he'd hoped for—stretching across the five boroughs, throughout the Department—it went no further than a handful of convictions, though Roberts blamed Serpico's recalcitrance for the limited results. Regardless of who was at fault, Serpico was neither promoted nor protected for his efforts. The gold detective's shield never materialized. Leaks of the investigation made him an outcast, the victim of threats, subtle and otherwise—"I oughta cut your tongue out," said one cop, playing with a switchblade—and when he was transferred, it was to a plainclothes division in Harlem, where his reputation preceded him. On many nights, Durk had to persuade him not to quit.

In Harlem, however, Serpico found an unexpected friend in his commanding officer, Inspector Paul Delise, known as "St. Paul." Delise offered to work as his partner, and together they hit the streets, breaking through doors and chasing people over rooftops. Delise pressed his superiors for assistance in rooting out corruption, but the response was meager. In his own way, Delise provides an oblique counterpoint to Serpico—not to mention *Serpico*—and the sweeping judgments made about the NYPD, which was that the whole system was rotten, perhaps most of all the bosses, who failed to listen, or failed to act, or failed to eradicate corruption in any way. Delise was able to report his suspicions only as such, virtually without details, though in fact he was a highly experienced commander who spent his days on the streets with a veteran plainclothesman who was literally obsessed with corruption. Certainly, there was a lack of will to root it out, but Delise did show that even when there was plenty of will, the way was not always so clear.

Meanwhile, as Serpico suffered, Durk prospered. Though his cases at the DOI were mostly penny-ante—twenty-dollar bribes to building inspectors, stolen gallons of paint—the rest of his waking hours, and many in which he might have been sleeping, were devoted to whatever cause he happened upon, Serpico not least among them. An old partner told him about a building manager who was terrorizing tenants out of his apartment house; when the DOI passed on the information, Durk leaked it to *The New York Times*, whose front-page story prompted an indictment. A friend's cleaning woman forwarded him a tip about narcotics in Harlem, which led to the seizure of two kilos of heroin. He won a Department of Justice grant to tour colleges for a year, making speeches to recruit young people to become police officers. At the height of anti–Vietnam War sentiment, cops were viewed by many as "worse than Dow Chemical"—the manufacturer of napalm—but Durk loved to challenge the complacent and superficial militants of his audience: "If you see social progress as a mass movement with you as the director, this job is not for you. But if individuals count, become a cop." Durk sold the Job as a domestic version of the Peace Corps, where "altruism mixes with fun." He was profiled in *Life* magazine and appeared on talk shows, including *The Tonight Show* with Johnny Carson. Of himself, he wrote, "Modesty is not a flower that grows in my garden."

Though Durk had been in contact with David Burnham, the police reporter for the *Times,* for several years, the relationship was not always firm or fond. Burnham was unwilling to merely take dictation from Durk, while Durk was afraid that Burnham just didn't get it. Burnham wrote a front-page story on cooping, which made a surprisingly big splash, that Durk thought flat-out ridiculous: *Civil Servants Doze Off After Midnight! Stop the presses!* Not only did it pay a great deal of attention to a trivial issue, but in the fall-out, Durk felt there was a strong odor of upper-class disdain for the working stiffs. And the story that mattered, that he'd been trying to tell for years now, was about the big shots who were napping, not the little guys.

On February 12, 1970, David Durk, Frank Serpico, Paul Delise, and three other, still-anonymous cops sat down at *The New York Times* with David Burnham. A three-part story led with the headline POLICE GRAFT SAID TO RUN INTO MILLIONS. Lindsay formed a commission, headed by a former federal prosecutor named Whitman Knapp. Commissioner Howard Leary, a dull, pliable man who had been brought in from Philadelphia—and returned there most weekends—didn't resign, but rather simply left the office and didn't come back. He didn't make an announcement or even leave a note; he took a cruise, and after some days, a puzzled City Hall announced his resignation, with gratitude for his service.

Nine months after the *Times* story broke, in February 1971, Serpico was shot in the face during a drug bust. He had been transferred to Narcotics but otherwise left to languish, and the shield which had been dangled in front of him had never been awarded. He had to keep testifying in the trials of the Bronx plainclothesmen, but he skipped appearances, forgot what he'd said, or contradicted himself. His part in the trials was public, and he had few friends; he had even broken off with Durk. When he was shot, there was widespread dread that a cop had done it, and he received several notes from fellow officers wishing him ill. Months later, the new Commissioner reluctantly gave him his long-sought gold shield. Serpico didn't want it anymore. He got a disability pension and a movie deal, and then he left the country. *Serpico is living in Switzerland,* we are told, as the screen fades to black.

Durk was close to a deal for a movie about himself and Serpico, starring Robert Redford and Paul Newman. Their story might have joined *Butch Cassidy and the Sundance Kid* and *The Sting* as a classic buddy movie of the 1970s. But Serpico pulled back, afraid that he might be treated as a "lame-brained Italian sidekick," a fear that was inflamed by Peter Maas, whose own version was adapted for the screen. It probably didn't help that when Paul Newman bragged about how he charmed his way out of speeding tickets with autographs, Durk called him "a poltroon." Durk had to settle for a supporting role in *Serpico* as a Yalie twit in seersucker named "Bob Blair." He's not even a Jew anymore.

Serpico is not a buddy movie. It is the opposite of a buddy movie, a virtual sermon against buddies in general and cop buddies in particular. Almost no one is honest, and the honest cops offer only a mirage of fraternity, a false hope that working together will be better than working alone. Though its treatment of real-life cops varies in accuracy—the movie is fair to Inspector Delise, unfair to Durk, and profoundly unfair to the cops who worked with Serpico when he was shot—the overall effect is one of dismal distrust. *The French Connection* has a lonely maverick hero, too, but Serpico describes a tragedy so extreme it precludes a sequel. There's no place to go, and no point in trying. And that's what rings false about *Serpico* to many cops, in New York and elsewhere, even more than the implicit rebuke of our fathers being on the wrong side of history. Police work is a buddy movie, and there are always sequels, because you don't do it alone, and it goes on, with or without you.

. . .

AS PARTNERS, CHARLIE AND TOMMY WERE NOT FARING SO well. I had begun to think about signing up Tommy, in the event that I was obliged to surrender Charlie to Narcotics. But with Charlie, I had a nearly ideal informant relationship, in terms of comfort and control: he was loyal as a dog from the pound, and he presented no risk beyond drug-addled inaccuracy. We were not up against kingpins or cartels, and I was not concerned that he would lead us into ambush or otherwise betray us. Charlie wanted drugs now, and freedom from drugs at some point, and I figured prominently in both ambitions. But Tommy remained an unknown commodity, to a degree, and even his sly confidences—that Charlie had stolen a dealer's stash, or was on a worse binge than usual—had a slightly unsavory quality, as if he was reaching for leverage rather than expressing concern. One day I went to see them and found Charlie truly jubilant, the only time I'd ever seen him in that state, whereas Tommy hung back, sheepishly. "I got great news," Charlie announced. "A real miracle!" Both had been tested for AIDS, he explained, and both were negative. I didn't expect Tommy to take an eraser to the bottom third of his HOMELESS, HUNGRY, AIDS sign, but I wondered why he'd told me he had the disease. Maybe he'd just assumed he had it, I thought, having dedicated the last decade and a half of his life to the risk of infection. But the next time I saw Charlie, he said that Tommy had just made the whole thing up.

Tommy had other problems, too, Charlie told me, chief among them that he was a "complete psychopath." Charlie was furious, and surprisingly afraid, wiping his hand through his greasy hair and looking around as he explained the latest complication: "Whenever I panhandle on the ramp, I make decent money. Sometimes I work with Tommy, and sometimes I do it alone, but when I do, he tells me I owe him half. For Chrissake, the guy thinks he invented panhandling! But I gave him the money, since he told me he'd smash my head open with a lead pipe when I was sleeping. And I know he has a pipe!"

"Geez, Charlie, I thought you guys were friends."

"C'mon, Eddie, would a friend smash your head open with a lead pipe when you were sleeping?"

I thought of John.

"Not a good friend, Charlie, no."

"It's just not right, Eddie, I mean, whaddaya think?"

"You're right, Charlie, it's just not right."

And it wasn't, of course, so I decided to keep Charlie in play as long as I could, and let it go from there. We'd developed other sources in the Four-Six, with problems and promise of their own. First, there was the Fat Kid, a portly teenager who was a manager for the West Hell Cartel, which ran dope out of a huge and mostly empty apartment building on University that was undergoing renovations. On the day that we grabbed him, the Fat Kid was pitching, but none of the hand-to-hands were in the open, so we could only charge him with misdemeanor possession, for the single bag of dope he had when we stopped him. For a Bronx dealer, the charge is like a parking ticket, and so his whispered offer of cooperation was unexpected. So too was his entire presentation, when he sat down with us across a table in an interview room, and had he begun the discussions by saying, "Gentlemen, I propose a merger of our interests," it would have been less remarkable than the initial public offering that he subsequently detailed. You forget sometimes that what dealers do is make deals.

The Fat Kid explained it simply and clearly: he sold heroin, and had done so successfully for several years. He had saved seventy thousand dollars, which he had divided among the bank accounts of relatives. For the next phase of his career, he had a government job in mind, preferably in the post office. It wouldn't do to have a record, so he'd like to work something out. The plan was almost every criminal's—*As soon as I put a little nut together, I'm out of this racket*— and you heard those words in one form or another from three different Al Pacino characters alone: in *Dog Day Afternoon, Carlito's Way,* and *The Godfather Part III.* Whether the idyll of retirement was a honeymoon with a transsexual, a car-rental business in the Caribbean, or control of the Vatican Bank, the plan never quite worked out. But as the Fat Kid negotiated the circumstances in which he found himself, it looked like he was going to make the transition with ease—he had even volunteered as an Auxiliary Police Officer in the Four-O. If his mother had brought him up to be a criminal, she should have been proud.

We had him for a bag of dope, and in return he offered their organization: the time and place of the weekly drop, with the players, the guns, and the thousands of dollars worth of heroin. We were so impressed that we called Mike Donnelly from HIDTA, as it looked like the case might be more than we could handle. When Mike arrived, he was just as taken by the detail and weight of what was offered, as well as the cheapness of the deal. But his next step was not quite what I would have done, and I was as glad of that as I was amazed by what took place later. I thought I had a knack for talking to perps, for interrogations and debriefings, and maybe I do. I was like a little blind kid who could pick out a tune, the first time he bumped into the piano. When Mike took his seat across the table from the Fat Kid, it was as if he straightened his white tie and tails, cracked his knuckles, and played him like a baby grand. And the song that came out of him was one that I'd never heard before.

We had asked about the operational particulars, the code words— *Mojando!*—the apartments, the stash places and re-up times. He'd told us, with no little pride, that they'd found a new connection, whose high-quality dope would permit them to reintroduce the brand Turbo, which was "the best in this neighborhood, for a long time—ask anybody, they'll tell you about Turbo." We had no relationship with the Four-Six Squad, so we didn't know if they were looking at the West Hell Cartel for any robberies, assaults, or homicides. Inexperience was one reason why we didn't press further; another was that what was offered was already at a fire-sale discount, and to ask for more might have queered the deal. Still another was that to be an informant, which was of necessity confidential, was less life-altering than being a witness, which was, by equally firm definition, public in nature. But we knew that Mike worked for a task force that dealt with violent drug gangs, and the West Hell Cartel seemed to fit the bill. Mike introduced himself, and had the kid repeat what he'd told us already, listening patiently as he explained that "'West' is because we work the west side of the street, on University, and 'Hell' is because of the neighborhood, and 'Cartel' because, well, just because it *goes*."

Mike then talked about how smart the Fat Kid was for making this choice, in that he was getting out early from a life that would end badly, and how he could not only escape from the consequences of what he'd done, but also make a little money from it, if his information was good and we all worked well together. "And the way it's gotta work, for us to work together," Mike said, "is for you to tell me what else these guys have done—not just where the dope is, or what money you make. You know you guys are serious, and you know what makes people serious in this business. So let's be straight with each other, and start out right. Tell me what you guys have done."

And the Fat Kid did: he told us how they—he—stabbed another dealer named Chino, over a turf dispute; how they beat down a Rasta weed dealer, with sticks and bats, over an insult to one of their guys' sisters; how they took another man who owed them money down an alley, into a stairwell, and shot him through the chest. That made for a nice trifecta from a teenage auxiliary cop. I wondered if he was such a smart young gangster after all.

Mike thanked him for his honesty, taking careful notes. He was never not genial, or respectful, or firm. "This is good, this is good that we know this, up front. Basically, you have to tell me this stuff for your protection, because we want to work with you, and I think it could work out great for all of us, I hope we work together for a while. The thing is, we have to know everything, for our sake and yours—we can't go after these guys, and have one of them turn around and say, 'Listen, you got me, but what I can give is this . . . ,' and he's gonna give us *you*. He's gonna say that you're the bad one of the bunch, you're the one that has *bodies*. So let's be serious, let's be real with each other. Now, you can tell me everything, but later on, I can't be surprised. Later on, I don't want to hear about you hopping a turnstile, but now, now is the time to come clean. Now, we can deal with anything. We both know you've done shit with your boys, in the West Hell Cartel, but you gotta tell me about whatever else you've done. Neither of us was born yesterday. You know and I know you didn't just walk in and be a big shot—and you are—so now, now's the time to talk."

And the Fat Kid talked some more. He talked about the springtime, when he got a call from a friend who said to go with him, into Manhattan, to help steal a car. They met up and took the subway down to the Upper West Side, near the Museum of Natural History, on Central Park West. They sat on a bench for a while and watched the traffic. His friend would choose the car, when traffic stopped for a light. He picked a late-model Acura, because it was valuable, and a burgundy one, because he liked it, and a white lady driver, because she wouldn't fight. They stepped up together, guns drawn, when she was alone in the car, and she surrendered the vehicle without a struggle. He didn't remember much about the lady, except that she had blond-ish hair and wasn't that old.

"Okay," said Mike. "That's good. You want a soda or something?"

I took his order and left. I brought it back, along with the first dissonant note in the melody. I'd checked his rap sheet, and then I looked up the collar. The Fat Kid had been arrested before: he'd gone into a candy store and picked up a pack of cigarettes, and when he was tired of waiting on line, he walked out. When the owner ran after him, he pushed him aside, telling him he was a cop. The owner then called the cops, who arrested him for shoplifting and impersonation, confiscating his badge. The auxiliary coordinator at the Four-O said that the Fat Kid was not permitted in the precinct.

In the peculiar nature of our profession, past violence presented less of a difficulty than ongoing dishonesty. The fact that he had fibbed about his status was more troubling, or at least differently troubling, than his carjacking. If he was a danger, you evaluated the risk of letting him out; if he was a liar, you questioned the reason. Before Mike Donnelly could confront him with the impersonation issue, the Fat Kid owned up to two more carjackings. One had been the year before, and the details were vague: near Penn Station, in the late fall, he thought it was a red car, and probably a Honda, but definitely a white woman. White people have money, you know. The one before that was still more vague. Calls were made to the Four-Six Squad, the Two-O,

Midtown South, Manhattan Robbery. I thought, No, I was wrong, the Fat Kid's mother would not be proud. Maybe he'll get to pass out the mail for his cell block, but he's not going to work for the post office. He's a dead letter.

Confronted with his arrest, the Fat Kid explained himself, not badly. Like a lot of perps, he didn't really consider it an arrest because he got a Desk Appearance Ticket. He said it was basically a misunderstanding—a dispute with the store owner, who didn't speak English, and then a small oversight on his part. I was more concerned with why he was an auxiliary. Auxiliaries are volunteers from the neighborhood, who patrol in uniform similar to their police counterparts, for which they are often mistaken. Though their service is honorable and useful, I never quite got it, since I looked forward to leaving the uniform behind, and I never understood why someone would go on patrol in the South Bronx without a gun to take with them or a paycheck to take home. The Fat Kid offered a vague answer about being interested in police work, which he certainly should have been. In one sense, he was shifty but also shrewd, playing a chess-game of disclosure and omission; he had also miscalculated badly, confessing to six violent felonies in the hope of escaping a day of community service. What hadn't occurred to any of us was the possibility that the game he was playing was entirely different from that in which we were keeping score, or that he wasn't playing a game at all.

For the shooting, the stabbing, and the beating, the Four-Six Squad had nothing, nothing, and nothing. No complaints, no reports, no open cases or closed ones. Since they were all drug-related, uncooperative victims were par for the course, and in order of likelihood, for a drug-dealing Rasta who had a suffered a beating—perhaps not such a bad one as it first appeared—a refusal to report it was quite reasonable; for an addict who was sliced by men who he feared, it was still possible; but for a man to be shot, under any circumstances, it was highly unlikely. The Fat Kid nonetheless held firm, on the first two, at least: for the shooting, he was there when they took him down the hall to the back of the building, but he was keeping watch on the street when the shot was fired. He didn't know if the victim lived or died because he didn't see him afterward, but it could have been, he admitted, that they shot in the air or beside him, just to frighten him, and the guy got the message and high-tailed it out of the neighborhood. The Fat Kid still had a story, I felt, that stretched but held.

And then the word came back from Manhattan, with three more strikes. If your pocket is picked, you might not report it, thinking your wallet might have been left somewhere; some people might not even report a purse-snatching, chalking it up to the risks of city life. But no one is carjacked and says, *Well, there you go, I guess I'll have to get the bus.* We had next to nothing on the earliest robbery, but just about everything on the latest, and the middle one should have been on file as well. Did a rookie screw up one case, and report it as a stolen car? Did another victim, distraught from the offense, race straight from the crime scene to the river and jump in? Not bloody likely. From then on, Mike Donnelly's interrogation was more like a narrative autopsy, as the story was laid out, cut open, and dissected.

"What time did you meet?"

"What train did you take?"

"How long did it take you?"

"Was it above ground or underground?"

"What stop did you get off at?"

"What street was that?"

"And where did you walk to from there?"

"And where did you wait? What street? What did you see? Was it dark out, cold out, windy? Was there a lot of traffic? How long did you wait?"

"And then what happened?"

"And then what?"

"And then?"

"And?"

At the end, he made him retrace his steps, backward, from the robbery to the street to the train to the Bronx, which is an effective trick for testing the integrity of a story, like reciting the alphabet backward when you've had too much to drink—it's something only the honest and the sober can do, with rare enough exceptions. The Fat Kid passed the test, as far as I saw it: when there were details requested, he supplied them, but he also said he didn't know or remember at various natural junctures, which suggested an ordinary memory, vague at times, with some gaps, rather than the vivid completeness of a fantasy. The earlier carjackings diminished in detail, which was appropriate for their perspective in time, especially if such acts were ordinary for him. He could tell the story backward, without any breaks in the chronology. And yet for the robbery in the spring, on a warm weekend, late in the afternoon, by the museum and beside the park, there was no victim, no witnesses, nothing. It was a lie, or so wrong in the particulars that it amounted to one. Had he slapped his head and said, "Did I say Central Park? I meant Prospect Park, in Brooklyn!"—we could have begun again. But he was firm in his commitment to the story, and we did not, we could not believe him. He had confessed and found a kind of absolution.

I took consolation in considering the little miracle of his half-dozen benighted victims suddenly restored, unrobbed, unstabbed, unshot, but the episode continued to irritate me for a couple of reasons. When we had another caper going, later on, a few bosses would bring it up again, saying that we were the ones who fell for that lunatic's story, which was ignorant and cheap. To have said "Bullshit!" and walked away from the Fat Kid—though PK had by then redubbed him "Mother Goose"—would not have been the reaction of a good cop, but of the opposite. What bothered me was not that he'd told a pack of lies, but that he'd made a series of statements that existed along a continuum from the demonstrably true to the inescapably false. On one side of the scale, we knew that he was a mid-level figure in a small but vigorous heroin operation, and had watched him several hours a day for weeks, during which time he committed perhaps thousands of felonies. That was real criminality, which we could not deny him. And at the far end, which we'd discovered to our dismay, there was complete falsehood, because half-truths—even if you conceded that much—are lies nonetheless. There is no such thing as a half-lie: if I said I was Dr. Conlon it would be as much of a lie as if I said I was Dr. Einstein. But there was no clean break along the scale, from black to white, fact to fiction, and I still don't know where the shift took place.

If an informant is working off a case, there is no need to be friendly, and often there's cause not to be—for certain predatory mind-sets, kindness is not only mistaken for weakness, it is transformed into it. I don't know exactly what motivated Mother Goose, but even had we found sufficient facts to move forward with him, it would have been better to do so without pretense of affection or trust. You run these informants with a short leash and a firm grip. So it was with our next informant, Flaco, with whom I found myself taking the hard line.

Flaco was another grab from the Four-Six, a sale collar that I would have thought weak in any borough, but dead in the Bronx. Late one night, I watched from a rooftop as Flaco hit off a strangely storklike woman in a beat-up old Jaguar with Jersey plates, who in turn hit off a man on the corner. She was a regular customer, but the man was a stranger, and so Flaco wouldn't sell to him. When I gave out the customers, the team was only able to pick up the man, and so when twenty minutes passed without any other buyers, we moved in on Flaco. He was charged with sale, and the man with possession; the stork woman would have been charged with both, but her absence made Flaco's case weak. Nonetheless, he had two prior felony convictions, for burglary and weapons possession, and was eager to cooperate. Stix would handle him, and Tony sat through the debriefing, while I was busy with the paperwork. Afterward, when I talked to Stix and Tony, I was impressed not only with what he had to offer—stash houses, delivery routes from Virginia with young girls bringing up bricks of heroin in cake boxes— but by how taken they were with him. Flaco was a skinny nineteen-year-old whose addict parents had died years before. He'd just found out that his girlfriend was pregnant, and he was desperate to avoid prison.

Tony and Stix looked like they'd just come from a Disney movie, like *Old Yeller,* which ends with the boy having to put his faithful dog down. They weren't dewy-eyed, exactly, but there was a rich lather of sympathy, a feeling that was broken when I said something like, "Dead folks, knocked-up chick, wants to flip. Check." I then sat down with Flaco and had him write out a statement about the sales we had witnessed. He smiled and did so blithely, while Tony and Stix looked on in discomfort. "You know," they said, "with what he's written, if it doesn't work out with us, he's really fucked, he's done for a long time."

"Umm . . . yeah? So?"

Maybe it was because it was late at night, and fatigue had softened them, or maybe because Flaco knew a great deal, and that intrigued them, or maybe they were simply touched, on human terms, because he'd told his sad story with real feeling. Maybe if I had been there, or he was my CI, I would have felt that way, too, but that inch of distance, that slight remove of proprietary interest, was enough to inoculate me against caring about him in any way beyond the utilitarian. He wasn't mine the way Charlie was, which had become something of a team joke—would he come for Thanksgiving dinner with the family, did I give him clothing or just let him borrow my underwear, was I setting up a CI compound like the Callahan Compound, and would we play them in softball? Homeless junkies were part of the landscape, like pigeons, and the people who spent their days feeding them bread crumbs had a hobby that was kindhearted but maybe a little unhealthy. Charlie was a perp, after all, and an especially bad-smelling one at that, and whatever he signified for me, as a cop's son or street spy, was for my own private contemplation. What more was expected of him, when his own family would have nothing to do with him?

I did like Flaco, for what it was worth: he genuinely wanted to be a father to his son, and he was young enough to make a clean start of things. He was reasonably bright and very funny, and spoke in a ghetto slang of almost hieroglyphic purity: *I be, you be, he, she and it be, na 'mean, B? Yo! We be movin' tha D to tha bundle custies, dogg!* But he also talked about his best friend and cousin with expansive and abiding affection, and they were the first names that he gave up, in his bid for probation. At least the boy in *Old Yeller* put the dog down because he had rabies; Flaco would have done it if the dog pissed on the rug.

As it happened, I became a better friend to Flaco than I would ever have thought necessary. When Stix asked an ADA to release him without bail to work for us, he refused. So did the supervising DA for Narcotics: the offer would be three-to-six. For an observation sale, it was severe; for two-thirds of an observation sale, it seemed unreal. Flaco had money and sixteen glassines of heroin on him, but if he hadn't had the two prior felony convictions, he would most likely have been arraigned on a misdemeanor possession charge, which, for once, would have suited us fine. Because we worked in SNEU, especially, the term "repeat offender" was nearly meaningless: almost every dealer we caught was charged with what they did once, twice, or three times, over a matter of seconds, when they did exactly that, hours a day, for months and years. They committed felonies more often than they ate, and if eating had been illegal, our food collars would have been thrown out or pled out because we didn't have the menu, the fork, the tip, the waiter, and the belch, all at once. We could bring in chain gangs of the morbidly obese, sumo wrestlers and opera singers by the groaning busload, and the ADA would say, "Well, according to the record, this was their first meal." But for predicate felons, they are prosecuted in the Bronx as severely as they would be in Staten Island or even upstate; it was a sensible policy—a second chance may be a good thing, a third might not, and a fourth . . . even in the Bronx, that was pushing it. But Flaco had made a serious offer, and it would be a shame to let it go to waste.

My mother had mentioned to me that she worked with a woman named Friedenthal, whose husband was a bureau chief in the Bronx DA's Office. I stopped by Ed Friedenthal's office and explained who I was and what I wanted. He asked for the particulars of Flaco's record, as well as what he knew. "No problem," he said, and after a twenty-second phone call, it was done. Moments like those made me agnostic whenever someone told me "No" after I felt I'd made a good case; clearly, they hadn't listened, or understood, and I just had to ah-tic-ya-late a little louder, or a little better, or to someone else. And, by the way, thanks Mom.

We also had to work out a deal with another Narcotics team, as some of the apartments Flaco gave us were DECSed by them, showing they had active investigations there. A detective named Nick Ferraro was sent down to see us, and his initial mood was cautious. When he talked to Flaco, it became clear that he knew a great deal about Flaco's gang, and even more about their suppliers than Flaco did; when he talked to us, later on, it was just as clear that he didn't like him. "He knows what he's talking about, definitely," said Nick. "But I doubt he's gonna work out. He's too slick, too street, and he's gonna wind up trying to play you off. It's worth a shot, definitely, and we'll help you guys out, but personally, I don't think we'll be using him when you're through."

Whenever we came into contact with Narcotics, whether it was because we had an informant or because we had to get out of the way for a Buy and Bust operation, there was a colonial aspect to our relations. We were the natives who had rich natural resources, while they were the well-armed foreigners who knew how to mine and sell them: at first, they would sit down with us at our tribal feast, offering conspicuous compliments on our colorful costumes and folk-dancing, as they forced themselves to take bites of our barbaric delicacies. If that didn't work, their warships would gather by the shores as they informed us of what would be required. With Nick, there was no feigned heartiness, no announcement of his hope for a long and fruitful partnership as he asked to speak privately with the informant—when that had happened before, CIs had told us that they'd said, "From now on, if you find out anything, you tell us—only us!" Nick also knew about that gang and that neighborhood far better than we did, which was also atypical. Flaco's gang was *his* case, and the possibility that we might have something valuable to add to it was to be pursued, for what it was worth.

Nick gave Flaco a stern lecture about how and whether he was to remain in play: he would step back from selling drugs, telling his partners that he had to be careful while his case was pending. Only if he found that he was arousing suspicion, or was utterly kept out of operational details, could he lend a hand, and whenever he did so, we had to know. We didn't want to see him pitching, or, if he was collared again, for him to try to explain that he was on a secret mission for us. Though Nick got some decent intelligence out of him, and we got a couple of warrants, it worked out as he predicted: Flaco's mood when he dealt with us shifted from the contrite to the increasingly cocky, and Nick would call Stix to say his team had seen him on the block when they did B&B, and it looked like he was working. Flaco grew lax in returning our calls. He was arrested for possession, and then sale, and then we stopped taking his calls. He was sentenced to the original offer of three-to-six, having talked his way back to the exact spot where we first met.

As we continued to work in the Four-Six, we kept in touch with Nick Ferraro. Charlie's next warrant was for a coke spot, in a semi-vacant building, that dealt in weight and had a significant Jersey trade. The apartment itself was vacant, used only for business, and had we the landlord's permission to enter, we wouldn't even have needed a warrant. But Charlie said that he was in on the deal, or at least the superintendent was, and we couldn't approach them. There was no real tenant there, it was only a workplace, and the absence of kids, dogs, or old people was a relief. Since it was a coke spot, Charlie was happy to visit, several times a day—for research, of course—and though that kind of enthusiasm tended to undercut the accuracy of his reports, I made one of my after-hours excursions to the building, and I found everything as he described. Nick confirmed it, through his informants, and PK set it up for us to do the entry together with Narcotics.

It would be my first warrant since Operation Hindenburg in which we would be the first ones through the door. I had practical objections to using ESU, but my real frustration was that taking the door was the most thrilling part of the warrant, and even of the Job, as far as it can be predicted or planned. The preparations for a warrant had grown familiar: the tac plan, with the layout of the apartment, the building, the block, the assignment of roles for entry, search, security; the scribbled marker-board sketches and hazy photocopies that sought to approximate in crude and static clarity a moment that would be a blur of adrenaline and instinct. In the muster room, at the appointed hour, PK led some fifteen cops from two commands through the arrangements, calm and cheerful but never less than precise and well-prepared. Tony and I only had to look at each other in such moments to communicate the mad elation of it, the unspoken circular conversations that asked and did not answer, *If I like my life, why do I like this so much?* Now, I could look at John for the same conversation. It was his job to knock down the door.

There is something in the way the caravan of cars moves from the precinct to the tac point, a few blocks from the target, that seems designed to build suspense. You drive slowly, in single file, and then you stop; the walk-ons and ghosts drift out to the location, to open the lobby or hold the elevators and watch the door; you wait for them for the "go." At the signal, the caravan moves forward, a little faster but still with restrained haste, until you pull out front and break from the cars into a run. The suddenness makes people on the street stop and stare; in the lobby, passersby have no time to ask questions as we pile into the elevator for the sixth floor, the top floor of the building. Others run straight up the stairs. Someone carries the ram for John so he'll be fresh when we arrive. We step out and step forward, I point out the door, John takes the ram and with one shot sends it clean off the hinges. I charge in, gun out, bellowing, "Get down! Get down! Get down!"

Behind me, the cops fan in, and before me, two men sit at the table, shocked. Between them on the table are a large bag of cocaine and a small tinfoil packet of it, cash and a scale. A naked light bulb dangles from a cord above them. The apartment is otherwise bare and empty. We cuff them up, take them out, bag up the drugs. We are sweating like pigs and smiling like beauty queens. One of the guys from Narcotics says, "This one should be in a textbook." We don't disagree.

· · ·

INSPECTOR MULLEN DIDN'T EITHER. HE DIDN'T GUSH OVER it, of course—that was a once-a-week, pat-on-the-back kind of operation for his cops—but he was impressed when I told him about it, about PK and the team, our warrants and CIs, and our beat-Roger month of August. Skills can be taught, experience comes inevitably, and talent was happily abundant, but motivation like ours was a rare thing. Mullen grew more enthusiastic at the prospect of our coming to Narcotics, and it was contagious.

"Whaddaya think, Eddie? Would you like to come up and work for me?"

"All of us, as a team, with PK?"

"It's been done before, and I don't see why we can't do it again."

All of us knew we had something special with the team, a rare combination of intensity and ease, a balance of abilities, and a depth of trust. Maybe we worked all the harder at it, knowing that it was a gift. There must be something inborn in people, a seasonal instinct, that makes them love the heat of Indian summer, knowing that it will be the last basking sunlight of the year. We had from time to time discussed what we wanted next in our careers, whether it was a detective's shield or a sergeant's, but we had resolved more or less explicitly to stick together unless something great came along, for all of us. It was like the end of high school, where all the crepe-paper decorations and cheesy anthems, the TV clichés of "bittersweet parting" and "coming of age," do nothing to diminish the truth that some of you will go and some of you will stay, and much will be better, but the life you have known together is done and gone.

Not all our recent days had been successful—once, when I was away, Alicia and another cop worked in the prisoner van, while the others were either in OPs or on bikes. When they moved in to catch one perp, Alicia stepped out and he started to fight her; the other cop jumped in, and they eventually subdued him, but when they brought him back to the van, they noticed they were light two perps. Technically, the cop made a mistake by leaving the van; morally and in every street cop's view, she did the right thing. Every procedure was followed: PK put the escape over the radio, a search was commenced, and both perps were recovered within a half-hour. My own impulse might have been to handle it unofficially, and other bosses suggested as much aloud. No disposition had been issued for the incident, as yet, for the "failure to safeguard" the prisoners, or for PK's "failure to supervise" the team in the field. But I was relieved when I told Mullen about it, and his response was to shrug and say, "So? It happens."

All the while, we went out for the daily scrimmage, which I liked, and the long, complicated plays, which I loved. The days grew shorter and cooler, but the diversions and wonders did not change. For a few weeks, as we worked in Melrose-Jackson, our sets were blown up hourly by other cops, responding to complaints about a family of raccoons. They threw people into a panic; the raccoons got more calls than gunfights did—they were always "rabid," which was unlikely but possible, and often "attacking children," which was nonsense—and I was amazed by the fear that they inspired in the neighborhood, where robberies and shootings were daily events. Wiseass cops would ask over the radio: *Do you have a scrip, Central, I'm holding three, but they're wearing masks. . . .*

In the Four-Six, we saw Mother Goose at work from time to time, until he was collared for selling to an undercover. In early October, John and I found Charlie and Tommy and gave them some clothes. I shook Charlie's hand, and asked him, "You know what day it is, Charlie?" He didn't. "It's your birthday." Tommy laughed, slapping his back, and said, "Hey, Charlie, how about that! Who knew?" Charlie smiled weakly and thanked me, before looking away. He was touched but also ashamed, because this most elementary fact of his life was news to him. We didn't dwell on it—as soon as we shut down the sixth-floor apartment from the last warrant, the dealers set back up on the third floor. He made his buys for me and put everything else out of his mind.

A few weeks after our talk with Mullen, PK gave us some disappointing news. "I talked to the CO," he said, "and he won't sign off on the transfer. The inspector at the Borough doesn't want him to—he gave him some speech about us being too inexperienced—but he basically doesn't want to give up the team. And the CO's not going to go against him." It was bullshit, we all agreed: hadn't the Inspector thrown us to the Rape Detail without a second thought? All of a sudden we're rookies he has to look after, when it's to our benefit to make a move? For all that, I wasn't devastated—we were still together, doing what we liked—and Inspector Mullen's response was hugely heartening, because he blew up when I told him.

"Of course you hate to give up your workers!" he said. "But if they're doing the job for you, you can't stand in their way. It's bad faith, and it's bad management. What a jackass!"

The CO's refusal made things difficult but not impossible, he said. The "airlift," as we'd come to call the transfer, was still many weeks away, even by the precarious calendar of the NYPD. We might still get on board. And what meant more to me than that remaining hope was the vindication of Mullen's belief in us, that we were ready and deserving to move up—and that we were being treated with cynical disregard.

We closed ranks and went back to work, but something had changed, I think, even then: we had become embroiled in the politics of the Job, and at best, we would leave the PSA amid some ill will. Increasingly, we would have to think about more than collars and warrants, PK and the team, as the larger machinations of the bureaucracy intruded. The good part of the Job took up enough of my life as it was, for fifty and sixty hours a week. I had been living with my cousin Brian, and when he moved out to get married, John moved in full-time. He had become one of my closest friends, and it was a great thing to have him there, but in retrospect I realize how much more of my time was then given over to shop talk. *Remember, you're a cop twenty-four/seven, three hundred sixty-five days a year. You are never off-duty. . . .* I thought back to the Academy, when it seemed laughable for Sgt. Solosky to warn us not to surrender our civilian lives and friends, and here I was—spending five days a week with a bunch of cops, five nights a week with another cop. What else was left to give? I gave my car already—should I sleep in my uniform?

Not long after that, a day or two before Halloween, we went back to the

Four-Six to collar. Somewhere in the distance, there was gunfire, but otherwise it was a little late, and a little slow. We were working at one of our old standbys, 1678 and 1684 Nelson: Brainstorm, Shotgun, Checkmate, crack. I was in an OP, and I gave out a body to John and OV in a catch car, heading north to Macombs, where he made a right. Another one came up to buy, and I asked over the air:

"You ready, guys? You get him? Anyone ninety-eight?"

There was a pause, and I asked again: "John, OV? Is he a hit?"

More silence, and then John called for PK to come over. There was real fear in his voice when he then called for an ambulance, forthwith. PK said for everyone to come around the corner, that it was a wrap for the night. It didn't sound good.

The perp was down on the sidewalk, unconscious and twitching. John didn't look much better. When the ambulance arrived, one of the EMTs lifted his head and said, "I think he's been shot."

I was curious, and leaned in to see the small raised welt. "This looks like a small-caliber round, a twenty-two or a twenty-five, maybe," the EMT continued. "You hear any shots?"

"Yeah," I said. "But they sounded farther off."

As I searched the perp—needles, heroin—I tried to figure out the bizarre scenario the EMT had detailed. Had he been shot just then, as John went for him, or earlier? Could he walk around with a bullet in his head? When Vinnie "the Chin" Gigante shot Frank Costello in the head with a .22, the round went through his scalp and circled his skull like Magellan. What the hell happened here?

The EMTs began to pack him onto the stretcher, and he came to, fighting. It took four of us to hold him down before they could strap him in. The perp's revival lightened John's mood somewhat, and as we followed them down to Lincoln Hospital, he cut me off before I went on any more about what a funny thing it was. "I don't know what the hell that EMT was talking about, but that guy wasn't shot. He ran on me and I knocked him down, Eddie, and I swear, at first I thought I killed him. He ran down that hill, and I chased him, and he started to turn around with something in his hand. . . ." The perp had bounced off a wrought-iron fence before hitting the sidewalk. For a few minutes, John thought it was over, for both of them.

At the hospital, the mood of unease returned when the doctor came out from X-ray: "It's a little weird. He has a skull fracture, but it looks like an old injury."

I turned to John and said, "That's just your luck. Your perp had a pre-broken head."

He laughed, but I wasn't sure if he was kidding when he said, "You want this collar?"

"All yours, big guy."

PK notified the desk at the Four-Six and the PSA of what had happened, and we finished up some paperwork and went home.

Afterward, when we talked about it, I was a little hard on him—John was a strong guy, the junkie was running downhill, and he could have flattened him with a flick of the finger. I grilled him: *How much force was used because you were pissed at him for running? Did you really think he'd stab you with the needle? How well could you see it?* I thought they were questions he should think about, for his own sake, since they were the same ones he'd have to answer—asked less kindly, and not in private—if the perp died. A couple of days before, there'd been a story in the paper about a cop who threw his radio at a junkie he was chasing; it hit him in the head and he died. John said, "I'm not a bad guy, I don't like to hurt people. I became a cop to help people, not to hurt them." He said that he worried now that in the next confrontation, he wouldn't react naturally, he'd second-guess himself, and he'd get hurt. That was a good point: there's a wall at police headquarters full of names, and some are of cops who hesitated.

And the truth of it was brought home a day later, when we set back up again. It was after sunset when I slipped into a tenement on Courtlandt Avenue, went to the roof, and crouched down by the low parapet with my binoculars. I watched for a while and heard a dog bark inside. It sounded big, and then it sounded closer, running up the stairs. There were dealers on the second floor, and I wondered if they'd sicced the dog on me, though a lot of people let their dogs out to shit on the roof. I took out my gun, and I took out my mace, reckoning the distance I'd need for either. We'd been taught that your average opponent can cover twenty-one feet in the time it takes an average cop to sight and shoot a target. I didn't have much more than that from the door to the edge of the roof, where I stood. The mace would be effective only within a dozen feet or so, and there was a light wind. I put the mace away. The dog charged through the door and stopped, barking fiercely, and then advanced again, then stopped. It was as big as it sounded, a pit bull mix, sixty pounds. Twenty-five feet, twenty.

I bellowed: "Get your fucking dog off the roof! Get that fucking dog, now!"